Goodbye,
Little Rock and Roller

Goodbye,
Little Rock and Roller

MARSHALL CHAPMAN

St. Martin's Press
New York

www.stmartins.com

LIBRARY OF CONGRESS CATALOGING-IN-PUBLICATION DATA

Chapman, Marshall.
    Goodbye, little rock and roller / Marshall Chapman.—1st ed.
        p.   cm.
    ISBN 0-312-31568-6
    1. Chapman, Marshall.   2. Rock musicians—United States—Biography.   I. Title.

ML420.C4536A3   2003
782.42166'092—dc21
[B]   2003047030

First Edition: September 2003

10   9   8   7   6   5   4   3   2   1

CONTENTS

FOREWORD

I first met Marshall Chapman in Nashville in the early '70s, "about when the '60s hit the South," as she describes it. She was singing at the Jolly Ox in Green Hills (yes, this is true), wearing a slinky dress with Marilyn Monroe's head printed all over it, and the whole place was going wild. Only a few years out of Vanderbilt, Marshall was then, as she is now, one of the most electric, charismatic performers in the world. I watched her in complete awe. I had never felt so, well, dowdy. And intimidated. Here I was, a little faculty wife with two little kids, trying to write fiction on the side, and here was Marshall, already totally Marshall, already larger than life in every way. At six feet tall, she had a huge talent, huge personality, and great sense of humor.

When I really got to know her through our mutual friends Vereen and Jane Bell, I learned—somewhat to my surprise—that Marshall was also extremely sweet and very vulnerable, with a heart as big as the rest of her. All of her emotions were out of scale, off the charts, like the emotions of the gods and goddesses of the Greek mythology I was teaching my seventh-grade students at the time. It was exciting to be anywhere that Marshall was; you absolutely never knew what she might do next. You couldn't even imagine. (This, of course, is still true.)

I was privileged to be present at some of the famous annual mint julep parties she gave for about two hundred of her most intimate friends at her house on Dudley Avenue. One of my favorite scenes in this book, in fact, is when she describes waking up "around noon facedown in my front yard—which was a vegetable garden—wearing nothing but my underpants. . . . I often found strange bodies in my yard and once even found a man passed out in my bathtub. Only two things were sticking up out of the water and thank *God* one was his nose. . . . Once after a mint julep party, the yard body count was five by sundown." The reason for that vegetable garden? She was trying to overcome her South Carolina blueblood heritage and be *country*.

"For I had rejected marrying the rich boy back home and everything that went with it," she writes, "babies, carpools, Junior League meetings, church on Sunday, cocktail parties at the club . . . you name it. Instead, I was living in a condemned neighborhood in Nashville, Tennessee, where they were paying me money to sing and play my guitar. I was hanging out with Cowboy Jack Clement, Waylon Jennings and Jessi Colter, Willie Nelson, Billy Joe Shaver, and Guy and Susanna Clark, and experiencing all kinds of things I never knew *existed* back in Spartanburg, South Carolina. I thought I'd died and gone to heaven."

Well, I've known Marshall ever since and seen her go through some rough years when that heaven turned to hell for a while.

We've spent a lot of time together recently while collaborating on *Good Ol' Girls*, our musical revue featuring songs by Marshall and Matraca Berg, stories by Jill McCorkle and me, the whole thing adapted and directed by Paul Ferguson. Anyway, in the early stages of this project, Marshall and Matraca had to keep flying over here to North Carolina to teach our musicians their songs. I will never forget all those wonderful hours we spent in my kitchen surrounded by Joe Newberry, Julie Oliver, Andrea and Paul, and various other cast and band members, listening to them sing . . . and *talk*. Lord! Marshall had this habit of going off on a talking jag before each song, a kind of free-form riff about where she was and who she was with, the circumstances in her life that had produced each song. We were spellbound.

"You know," Paul said more than once, "you've got to write that down."

And now, four years later, she has.

It's a strike of genius, a brilliant way to organize a songwriter's memoir—by *song*, not chronology, each one capturing the essence of an important period in her life. "Somewhere South of Macon" is the chapter about her childhood in the mill town of Enoree, South Carolina. Here she captures moments such as her first, child's realization of infinity, and the first time she was drawn to music, dodging roosters as she ran across the yard and into the house of retired mill worker Susie Burnett to hear her play "Down Yonder" on the rickety old upright in her living room.

"Why Can't I Be Like Other Girls?" tells the "full tilt boogie" phase of her life with various "SFBs" (speed-freak boyfriends), including the now-famous iconoclast critic Dave Hickey. I still love the publicity sound bite he wrote for her first album: "Looks like Farrah Fawcett from the back, Peter Frampton from the front, and moves well to her right."

"A Mystery to Me" tells about Marshall's "forty days and forty nights" at a treatment center in the middle of the Arizona desert, then the wonderful event of her falling in love with Chris Fletcher, culminating in the realization that "It's Never Too Late to Have a Happy Childhood."

"Call the Lamas!" movingly recounts the death of her only brother, Jamie, plus the heartbreaking and hilarious family reactions. (Did I mention Marshall's MOTHER yet? Oh my God. Or those two sisters? Her father used to squire them around, calling out, "Y'all better back up! I've got twenty-four feet of women coming through here!")

Marshall's songs take us everywhere, from John T. Flores' country store with Willie Nelson, to a pickup basketball game in Belize, to onstage in San Antonio with Roger Miller, to the Tennessee State Prison for Women where she performed with her band The Love Slaves, to the top of the billboard at Fenway Park in Boston where she was almost arrested during game six of the 1975 World Series, and even to her high school alma mater, Salem Academy, where she sang a rap version of the prologue to Chaucer's *Canterbury Tales*, wearing "not one, but *three* dress code violations from the 1967 Salem Academy rule book."

We meet everybody from Willie Nelson to Will Campbell, with great character sketches and insights along the way. (Jack Clement is described as "sort of a cross between Jerry Lee Lewis and Alfred Hitchcock.") Throughout, Marshall excels at images that perfectly capture a time, place, or a way of life. Here's her mother, coming in from a party to kiss her good night: "I am awakened by her hand gently brushing my hair from my face as she leans down. The cocktail fragrance of her French perfume, the faint scent of cigarette smoke, her warm breath sweetened by the orange-soaked bourbon from an Old-Fashioned . . . And the rustle of her dress as she moves away, followed by the fading click of her high heels . . ." Damn! This woman can really *write*, can't she? (This strikes me as unfair, since I myself am among the singing impaired.)

Marshall's own life story is also a chronicle of the music business and how it has changed over the years, from those "magical" '70s to the '80s when country music "took a turn for the tacky," a phase memorialized by the song she co-wrote with Bobby Braddock, "Hillbillies Ain't Hillbillies Anymore," right up to now.

As she takes on the big question of "Where does a song really come from anyway?" Marshall presents a fascinating, hands-on study of the relationship between art and life. This book is so much fun to read that it's a shock to sit back and realize that secretly it's damn serious, too . . . not to mention irreverent and even subversive. Marshall talks about all those things we're not supposed to talk about: money, sex, class, politics, and even—God forbid!—therapy. She's honest, passionate, brave, and fiercely intelligent. In person, on a stage or a CD, and now on the page, Marshall Chapman is the best company in the world.

—Lee Smith

That's what happens when two worlds collide.
—ROGER MILLER

Was it a vision, or a waking dream?
Fled is that music. Do I wake or sleep?
—JOHN KEATS

I'll never outgrow rock and roll.
. . . and pray I don't outlive it.
—DAVE HICKEY

PROLOGUE

Jerry Lee Lewis once gave me advice on how to live my life. It was New Year's Eve, 1978. My band, Jaded Virgin, and I had just opened a show for him in Atlanta, Georgia.

The Great Southeast Music Hall was hot, packed and ready that night—and so were we. With Marshall amps stacked to the ceiling, we played our usual sizzling and explosive set, working the crowd into a hot and sweaty frenzy before retiring to the small dressing room that'd been reserved for me, my band, *and* Jerry Lee's band. (Jerry Lee had the larger dressing room across the stage all to himself.) I later learned that Jerry Lee's people had not only requested the use of our dressing room, but of our *equipment* as well. When my manager had asked for something in writing—some sort of guarantee that our equipment wouldn't be destroyed—Jerry Lee's manager had replied, "Hell, when I started working for Jerry Lee, I quit guaranteeing anything!"

I also later learned that Jerry Lee had wandered from the safe confines of his dressing room that night and had stood in the wings to check us out while we were rocking away onstage. His road manager JW later told me this was something he had never seen his boss do. He'd never seen ol' Lee-J—that's what JW called him, "Lee-J"—leave his dressing room for *anybody,* much less the opening act.

Speaking of Lee-J, Jerry Lee probably has more nicknames for himself than anybody who's ever been in show business: "The Killer," "JLL," "Ol' Jerry Lee," "The Ol' Killer," . . . the list goes on and on. Anyone who has ever been to a Jerry Lee Lewis show can tell you how Jerry Lee will insert his name into the lyric of a song at the drop of a hat. In fact, once you've seen him do it, you come to expect it. And if he *didn't,* you'd walk away feeling somehow cheated.

There's an expression in show business that says a great singer—a *stylist*—can "take a song and make it his own." And I'm telling you, Jerry Lee Lewis can take a song, make it his own, and stamp his damn *name* on it lest you *ever* forget where it came from. Don't ask me how, but he can insert his name into "Somewhere over the Rainbow" and make you forget all about Judy Garland.

In those days, I had a Polaroid camera that I'd take with me out on the road. It was the perfect accoutrement for '70s rock and roll—instant and disposable. I liked to take pictures of unusual things I'd see out there, so I was taking a *lot* of pictures. Sometimes I'd take them from onstage during our show, sailing the still-developing snapshots like little Frisbees out into the audience. That night at the Music Hall, I was hoping to get a Polaroid taken of me with Jerry Lee for my own personal rock 'n' roll archives.

For my money, when it comes to rock and roll, Jerry Lee is in an upper echelon triumvirate consisting of the father, the prodigal son, and the holy ghost—Elvis being the father and Little Richard the holy ghost. And I always liked that John Lennon quote about "Whole Lotta Shakin' Goin' On" being the only rock 'n' roll song ever recorded: "The rest of us are doing something else," he said.

So after our set, still drenched in sweat, I stepped across the back of the stage, camera in hand, for what I hoped would be an impromptu photo session with The Killer.

The first person I ran into was Phoebe, Jerry Lee's then-fourteen-year-old daughter by his once-thirteen-year-old cousin-wife. Now I wouldn't see Phoebe again for another twenty years. Not until 1998 in Memphis, when I played the Blues City Café, a club she was managing on Beale Street. The gig was a NARAS-sponsored songwriter thing hosted by my friend Keith Sykes. I'd driven over from Nashville that day in time for sound check and, while waiting around (sound checks are notorious for lots of waiting around), I inquired about a dressing room. The bartender told me they didn't have one but I was welcome to use the upstairs office. Trudging up the stairs with my guitar, I heard a booming female voice: "Marshall Chapman! Where have you been? I thought you'd be dead by now!" It didn't take long to figure out who the voice belonged to. There were pictures of Jerry Lee all over the walls. I looked at them, then looked back at her. She was his spitting image, only with long, strawberry blond hair. And *pretty*, if you can imagine that.

"Phoebe?" I said. "Is that you?"

In the ensuing conversation, I asked how she got her name. Turns out "Phoebe" was the name of a character from one of her mother's favorite soap operas. I thought that was cool. Where I come from, you always got named after somebody else in your family, and it didn't matter if they were dead or alive. I'd grown up in Spartanburg, South Carolina, with two other Marshall Chapmans—an uncle and a first cousin. Sometimes I think I went to Nashville for no other reason than to be in a city where I could have my own name. I have friends who've named their children after *things* like an island or a bottle of wine. Names like "Cayman," "Merlot." Names with romantic attachments to the circumstances surrounding conception. My mother once told me that I was conceived on a train going to New York City. She said it wasn't easy either since she and my dad were both real tall and crammed into a sleeping berth. I got the impression that a lot of giggling and maneuvering was involved.

But back to Atlanta and the fourteen-year-old Phoebe. I asked her if she wouldn't mind taking a picture of me with her dad.

"Sure," she said. "Want to meet him first?"

I nodded that yes, I would like that very much. So before taking the now-treasured photo of me and her dad draped over an easy chair looking for all the world like two teenagers at a first prom, introductions were made. "Hi," I said extending my hand, whereupon Jerry Lee withdrew his like a snake'd bit it. He then looked right at me, his eyes burning with a mixture of tongue-in-cheek danger and mock fear, masking what I can now only imagine as disbelief. Then he said—and I've never forgotten it—"Don't you burn out now, hon'."

A year or so later, when I found myself in one of those hospitals for tired people, I began to think about what Jerry Lee had said. I mean it's one thing when your *mother* says "Honey, don't you think you'd better slow down?" But when The Killer voices *his* concern . . . well now, that's a whole nother thing. It might just be time for a little self-reevaluation.

For the past thirty years, I have played in rock and roll bands, written over two hundred songs, recorded eight albums on four different labels, and performed music in so many places it *exhausts* me to think about them: a concert hall in Invercargill, New Zealand, a cave in Matala on the isle of Crete, a maximum security compound at the Tennessee State Prison for Women, Tomorrowland at Disney World, and the Knaughty Knight—a biker club in Morgan City, Louisiana—are just a few of the more exotic venues. Just listing these places makes me wonder how I'm still around.

In 1997, here in Nashville, my boyfriend Chris Fletcher and I bought a house in a Mayberry-for-eccentrics-type neighborhood. For a while, I was perfectly content fixing it up, overseeing little renovations here and there, and working in the yard. That winter, I even bought a twenty-pound log splitter and would go out in the backyard every morning and split wood until the sweat started steaming from my body like those horses in that Alfred Stieglitz photograph. Chris thought I was losing my mind until he started reading some book where the protagonist starts chopping wood to keep from losing *her* mind. After that, he quit worrying. One of the things I love about Chris is that I could go out in the yard and chop wood with nothing on but a pair of men's boxer shorts and it wouldn't phase him in the least. *My* bizarre behavior is not a reflection on *him*. He does, however, draw the line at openly breaking the law. If we're at a museum and I reach over or walk around one of those velvet ropes so I can better see the details of a painting, well, he *will* walk away and pretend like he doesn't know who I am. Anyway, so we bought this house, and right away I started going through the June Cleaver homemaking phase that all my women friends went through in their twenties and thirties while I was out rockin' and rollin'.

It's been over five years now since I've toured with a band, so the phone has pretty much stopped ringing. I may play again, mind you, but I'm starting to dig whatever this is. I still write the occasional song and have a wonderful new collection ready to record, but the chasm separating what I'm interested in and what the mainstream sector of the music industry is interested in has never been wider. Maybe Daniel Lanois will call tomorrow and *beg* to produce my next CD. If that happens, I may drop everything and fly to New Orleans. Just recently, I played a new song for a country-music record-executive friend. The song is about being a particle in space. His comment afterward was "Now is that a boy or a girl?"

Okay, so I do not want to think about writing songs for country radio anymore. I do not want to play smoke-filled clubs anymore. In short, I do not want to leave my one third of an acre *yard* anymore unless it's to go to the local H. G. Hill Food Store. But when the June Cleaver homemaking phase started to lose its luster, I began to write this book.

These are the stories behind twelve of my songs that belong to an exclusive club. I call them my "lifesavers." Each one possessed me at a time in my life when I needed to be possessed or I might have done something fatally rash. I may not have chosen the twelve *best* songs or even the twelve most commercial. Just the ones that have the best stories around them.

In closing, I'll quote an old renegade-writer-ordained-Baptist-preacher friend of mine who years ago closed a conversation of ours with: "Keep it in the yard." And now that I think about it, Will Campbell and ol' Jerry Lee have a *lot* in common.

Songs
(year written)

1. Somewhere South of Macon (1974)
2. Rode Hard and Put Up Wet (1973)
3. Running Out in the Night (1976)
4. Why Can't I Be Like Other Girls? (1977)
5. Don't Leave This Girl Alone (1978)
6. Texas Is Everywhere (1980)
7. The Perfect Partner (1981)
8. Betty's Bein' Bad (1984)
9. Goodbye, Little Rock and Roller (1986)
10. Girl in a Bubble (1986)
11. A Mystery to Me (1994)
12. Call the Lamas! (1996)

1

Somewhere South of Macon

That mill town south of Macon
Still has a hold on me
My folks they feel forsaken, Lord
But me, I'm feelin' free
I'd rather roam and ramble
And live until I die
Than to spend my life as a mill man's wife
Too tired to wonder why

I was born in Spartanburg, South Carolina, on January 7, 1949, the second of four children to James Alfred and Martha Cloud Chapman. In 1902, my great-grandfather, the first James Alfred Chapman, had founded a textile company twelve miles northwest of Spartanburg. It was called Inman Mills. When he died in 1936, his oldest son—also named James Alfred Chapman—took over as president. This James Alfred was called "Mr. Jim" by his employees and "Papoo" by us grandchildren. Papoo ran the mills until 1964, when my father became president. During my father's tenure, mill employment reached an all-time high of a thousand seven hundred and ten employees.

Had I been born a boy, my name would've been James Alfred Chapman IV, and there would have been great pressure for me to continue in the family tradition of running the mills. But I avoided that pressure by being born a girl. I was named Martha Marshall Chapman II after my paternal grandmother. From day one, I was called Marshall.

. . .

During my first five years, we lived in a cotton mill town twenty-five miles south of Spartanburg. The town was called Enoree. About nine hundred people lived in Enoree and most of them worked in the mill. Riverdale, as it was called, was one of the oldest textile mills still in operation in the South. It was built in 1886. For many years, the mill struggled under a succession of different owners and managers. Then in 1928, my great-grandfather was brought in to try and turn things around. He was successful, and by 1934 had gained a controlling interest in the mill. Riverdale would merge with Inman Mills in 1954, the year we moved to Spartanburg.

Riverdale was built on the banks of the Enoree River. In those days, mills were built next to rivers for the water power *and* for the river air, which helped keep the cotton moist and less likely to break while it was being spun into thread and later woven into cloth. Riverdale had four floors and, because it was built on a steep riverbank, each floor opened out onto ground level. This fact was once published in a King Features Syndicate cartoon, along with the fact that Riverdale was the only building in the world to have a road, a creek, *and* a railroad line running underneath it.

Our family lived within a stone's throw of the mill in the "superintendent's house," a big old rambling structure built by mill carpenters in the 1920s. The house sat up on a long, steep hill and had big bay windows that ran from the basement through the second floor. A screened-in porch spanned the front of the house and another, smaller porch ran off the kitchen in the back. That's where Mary and I kept our bicycles. Mary was my older sister by two years. Her bike was a Schwinn and mine was a Rollfast. Our younger sister, Dorothy, was too little to ride a bicycle until after we moved to Spartanburg.

There were four or five bedrooms in our house, but my sisters and I all slept crammed into one because Mother believed in "consolidating the mess." My mother was a very practical woman. She was also tall and good-looking. A man in Spartanburg once confided that as a teenager, he and his buddies used to hide out in the bushes at the entrance to the Spartanburg Country Club, hoping to catch a glimpse of her as she arrived with my father for Friday night dinner dances. "She would walk by, and she was so beautiful, our tongues would catch in our throats and we couldn't talk," he said. Of course, I ended up the spitting image of my father. But I can tell you, he wasn't no slouch.

The only time I ever left Enoree as a child was on Sundays. After church, my sisters and I would pile into the backseat of Daddy's Buick for the drive up to Spartanburg and Sunday dinner with Nannie and Papoo.

Nannie and Papoo lived in the middle house at Three Oaks, a family compound of three almost-connected houses built in 1925 by the first James A. Chapman. The houses were English Tudor with steep slate roofs and beautiful landscaping that included rose gardens, a lily pond, manicured green lawns, and a sweeping front drive bordered by magnolias, evergreens, and huge oak trees. The original property included eighty acres of surrounding wooded hills, but today the houses sit on about five acres.

Great-grandfather Chapman was a sixty-two-year-old widower when he built Three Oaks—the middle and largest house for himself and the two flanking houses for his brother Rob and his personal physician, Dr. Blake. Not a bad move, having your doctor as a next-door neighbor. But then great-grandfather Chapman was a resourceful man. Orphaned at age three after both parents died of typhoid fever, he was raised by aunts and uncles around Spartanburg and Union, then received a degree from Wofford College in Spartanburg before going on to Harvard Law School, where he graduated magna cum laude in 1886. He practiced law for a while in New York City before coming back south to start up the mills. He was tall, good-looking and—according to my Uncle Bob—would sometimes drive his Cadillac coupe with his *knees* while lighting up a big cigar, much to the delight of his grandchildren.

In Enoree, there used to be a small wood-frame cabin behind our house where an old black man named Fesser Smith lived. I say old; he was actually in his late fifties at the time. Fesser stuttered when he talked, but he always had a kind word, and his voice and laughter were like a sweet kind of music.

For as long as anyone could remember, Fesser had been the unofficial yardman for the "superintendent's house" and every spring he would plant a big vegetable garden between his house and ours. I remember summers eating watermelon from that garden and man, oh, man was it evermore sweet. None I've tasted since begins to compare.

Fesser was an institution in Enoree. He'd zip around town on his motor scooter and whenever he saw children playing along the sidewalks, he'd pull over and give each one of us a little piece of candy.

Once, when I was about four, I decided to venture out in search of the source of this candy and it ended up causing quite a stir.

Visions of mounds upon mounds of foil-wrapped chocolate Kisses and sticks of Juicyfruit chewing gum danced in my head as I reached up to open the door to Fesser's cabin that afternoon. Of course, Fesser wasn't home because he was still at work. And the door wasn't locked because nobody locked their doors back then. I can remember standing there in the middle of his cabin like it was yesterday, just taking it all in . . . the sweet smell of pipe tobacco, the cool air, the clean and sparse simplicity . . . everything about it was just so peaceful that it kind of put me in a trance, and I soon forgot all about the candy. And I must have been tired—more tired than hungry—because when I saw Fesser's bed, it looked so inviting that I climbed up on it and fell fast asleep. I can't remember what happened after that, so I e-mailed Mother to see if she had any recollection of the incident.

"Oh, my God," she e-mailed me back. "You 'bout scared us to death! When I realized you were missing, I went all over the neighborhood looking for you . . . the Crockers . . . the Kelletts . . . everywhere. But you were nowhere to be found. So I called James at the mill, and he came home and we were frantic. About that time Fesser came home and came out smiling and said you were in his house. We went in and there you were, on top of a folded quilt on his bed, sound asleep. I don't remember who all was in the house by then because quite a crowd had gathered."

There were a lot of blacks in and around our house in Enoree. Besides Fesser, there was Annie Mae and later, Mary Ethel, live-in maids who looked after us children. I was too young to remember Annie Mae, but Mary Ethel I remember. She would bathe me and dress me, then comb and braid my hair. And I damned well better stay in the yard and not run out onto the highway at the bottom of the hill or she'd give me a good switching. When I was growing up, "Spare the rod and spoil the child" was the axiom by which most parents raised their children. In other words, we got spankings.

But there were no rods in our house. Just a couple of fly swatters hanging by the backdoor. One was labeled FLIES and the other CHILDREN.

Sometimes, when my parents were out of town or out for the evening, Mary Ethel would play a game with us called "Hide the Switch." She'd go hide a switch somewhere in the house, then come back and signal "On your mark, get set, go!" Like idiots, we'd go scurrying off in all directions, darting from room to room, squealing with fear and delight, until someone yelled out, "I found it!" Then Mary Ethel would chase that person down, take the switch out of their hands, and then use it to give them a switching! Of course, it wasn't as hard as the switchings you got for running out on the highway—it was more like a "play switching." But once Mary Ethel got ahold of you, you'd be begging for mercy . . . between shrieks of laughter, of course.

After my first baby tooth fell out, Mary Ethel helped me put it in an envelope to be placed under my pillow at bedtime. Later in the night, I remember seeing a black woman dressed up like a fairy princess standing in the middle of my bedroom. Or was I dreaming? When Mother and Daddy returned from their trip, the first words out of my mouth were "Mama! The tooth fairy is black! I saw her! She was dressed up like a fairy princess and had a magic wand and everything! Look!" I exclaimed, holding up a Mercury head ten-cent piece. "She changed my tooth into a dime!"

Then there was Rosie, who came every day to cook and clean. I remember Rosie teaching me how to tie my shoes on the floor by the kitchen sink.

Sometimes Rosie would bring her son with her to work. His name was Boy. Boy was exactly my age and we usually ended up playing together. He was the youngest of Rosie's many children. Rosie always claimed that by the time she got to Boy, she'd run out of names so she just named him "Boy." Years later, when Boy enlisted in the service, they asked him his name and he said, "Boy." They told him that that was his gender and that they needed a name. So he said, "James Chapman, that's my name." So he was James Chapman in the army and I don't know what became of him after that.

To this day, I have kept a faded one-cent postcard dated Sept. 17, 1950. It was postmarked in Enoree and addressed in pencil to my mother: Mrs. J. A. Chapman / Vanderbilt Hotel / Park Ave. at 34th / New York, NY. I was twenty months old when Annie Mae wrote:

The Childrens and also
my self fine and having a good time
with Mrs. Burnett every day. Oh Mary
just tickle over her. She ask me every
nite when is Sun. Marshall wake up
every morning calling you as usual.

For some reason, I have no Enoree memories of my father . . . and only a few of my mother. In one, my two sisters and I are all upstairs taking our afternoon nap. Every day after lunch, we had to go upstairs and lie down on our beds and stay quiet for one hour. On this day, we were feeling antsy, so the three of us started chanting in unison "Mama! Maah-mah!! How many more minutes?!" Over and over we chanted this, increasing the volume with each chant, until the door burst open and there stood Mama, her six-foot frame filling the doorway. She had a stern look on her face that failed to completely mask her amusement. "If you children don't quiet down, I'm going to add TEN MORE MINUTES TO YOUR NAP!!" and just like that, she was gone.

In another, I am standing in the driveway behind our house and Mother is coming toward me with a switch. I can remember holding my little hand up in front of my eyes and positioning it just so, until she was completely blocked from my field of vision. In my child logic, I figured if I couldn't see her, she couldn't see me. It was a gross miscalculation on my part. I can assure you that the next time somebody came at me with a switch, the old hand-blocking trick was out the window and I ran like the wind.

And I remember one time Mother coming in to kiss me good night as I lay sleeping in my bed. She and my father had just returned from a cocktail party in Greenville or Spartanburg. I am awakened by her hand gently brushing my hair from my face as she leans down. The cocktail fragrance of her French perfume, the faint scent of cigarette smoke, her warm breath sweetened by the orange-soaked bourbon from an Old-Fashioned. She kisses me on my forehead. In the darkness, I can barely make her out, but the exotic smell of her, I remember. And the rustle of her dress as she moves away, followed by the fading click of her high heels as she retreats back down the hallway to my father.

. . .

My first Enoree memory of music happened to coincide with my first spoken words.

I was a late bloomer in the talking department. It got to the point where my parents thought I might be deaf, so they had my hearing checked. When my hearing checked out okay, they thought I might be retarded. I was three years old and had yet to utter anything resembling a word. No *dah-dah*, no *bye-bye*, no *poo-poo* . . . no nothing. It wasn't that I couldn't talk; I just didn't need to. My older sister Mary was such a good talker, she talked for both of us. Mary was my interpreter. I'd grunt something, and Mother would ask, "What is it, honey?" Then Mary would say, "Lalo wants her teddy bear." Mary called me "Lalo" because when she first started talking, "Marshall" was too hard to pronounce. She still calls me Lalo to this day.

Around this time, my Uncle Bob and Aunt Wince came to spend a night. I recently spoke to Bob about this, and he said it was the day after Christmas 1951 and that the next morning they were all downstairs in the dining room, where Mary was playing Tchaikovsky's "Waltz of the Flowers" on her little 78-rpm record player. I was still upstairs asleep and the noise woke me up. Now anyone who knows me well knows I can be grumpy when awakened before I've completely had my rest. So, I padded down the steps in my pajamas-with-feet, walked over to Mary's record player, lifted the needle up off the "Waltz of the Flowers," and announced, "How do you expect anybody to get any sleep around here with all this racket going on!?" I can still see the frozen image of everybody's jaw dropping open. They were speechless. Mother didn't know whether to laugh or cry. Garbo had spoken at last. To this day Mother will tell you, "Marshall never spoke a first word. It was more like a first paragraph."

The first time I can remember "feeling" or being "drawn toward" music was when I first heard Susie Burnett play the piano. Susie Burnett was a retired mill worker who lived just outside Enoree on the old highway going to Woodruff. Sometimes Mother would drive us all out there just so we could hear her play. I can still hear Susie's soft, smoky voice calling out "Why, hey Martha! How y'all doin'?"

Susie was a widow—at least that's what I've always heard. She had a grown son somewhere. Anyway, she lived alone. Her house was built up on red brick pillars so that the underside was open to the outside air, which made an ideal roosting place for the chickens that were always pecking and scratching around in her yard. There were five or six hens and a rooster. The rooster was easy to spot with his colorful plumage and tall stature. I remember one time stepping down from Mother's station wagon and that rooster came charging across the yard at me and it about scared me half to death. He was huge—huge to me anyway, because we were about the same height. He ran right up to me, stopping suddenly to turn his head so he could look at me with one eye like chickens do. Chickens can't look at you with both eyes. They have to use one or the other. Anyway, when he fixed that fierce yellow eye on me with all those red combs around it, I grabbed ahold of Mother's skirt and started shrieking like crazy. Susie came over and shooed him away. "Go on, now! Get!" she said. Then she took me by the hand. "Come on hon', let's go inside where we can have us some fun."

Susie was a natural, self-taught player, and when she sat down and started pounding out a honky-tonk rhythm on that rickety old upright of hers, it was like nothing else in this world. The piano was never in tune, but it didn't matter because Susie was. She'd look right at you and smile while she played. And when she'd tear into "Down Yonder," I would get so happy and excited that my whole body would start pumping in rhythm with the music. "Down Yonder" was my favorite. It was everybody's favorite.

Right before we all moved up to Spartanburg, I remember one summer evening, after supper and before dusk, a bunch of us neighborhood kids were out on our front lawn . . . trying to cut cartwheels, catching lightning bugs, making clover necklaces . . . just doing the typical things that kids in the South used to do in the summertime before there was TV. As it began to get dark, some of the kids started drifting off home. Pretty soon, it was just me and Gene Crocker sitting at the top of the steepest rise in our yard. Gene was thirteen and different from other boys his age. While they were out butting heads playing football, Gene was in his homemade greenhouse raising orchids. Mother once said that Gene was a genius. That was the first time I ever heard the word *genius*. She also said that he had read the entire *World Book Encyclopedia* . . . twice. Gene and his sister Martha—everybody called her Mott—and their parents, Pat and Clyde, were our next-door neighbors.

Gene and I were sitting there watching the stars come out when, out of the blue, he asked if I knew what "infinity" was.

"No," I said. "What is it?"

"Well, it's when things go on forever and never end. See all that black up there around the stars?"

"Uh-huh."

"Well, all that black just goes on forever. There's no end to it. It's infinity."

I thought about that for a while, but my brain didn't want to go there. In fact, it hurt my brain to think like that. So I said, "Well, what if it's a black wall up there? I mean, it could be a wall, couldn't it?"

"Okay, let's say there's a wall," Gene said. "So what's on the other side of the wall?"

Suddenly, I saw it. Infinity. And it hurt my brain so bad that I burst into tears. I should have known right then I was going to be a writer. But it would be another twenty years before I'd see infinity again.

I cut my teeth in a cotton mill town
Somewhere south of Macon
Mama fed me a bottle from a moonshine still
To wash down the beans and bacon
Papa worked the night shift
Mama worked day
Never dreaming one day I'd turn and walk away
Turn and walk away from that cotton mill town
Somewhere south of Macon

Mama told me not to let my petticoat show
North, east, south, west of Macon
Don't ever let my feelings show
'Cause it'd ruin my reputation
I took a walk in the woods one Sunday
The world turned dark and still
I first made love in a cotton mill town
Somewhere south of Macon

That mill town south of Macon
Still has a hold on me
My folks they feel forsaken, Lord

But me, I'm feelin' free
I'd rather roam and ramble
And live until I die
Than to spend my life as a mill man's wife
Too tired to wonder why

I'm gonna slip into my calico dress
And down to the Greyhound station
Gonna lay my hard-earned dollar down
For a one-way destination
I'm gonna tell that late-night driver
Mister, won't you take it slow
While I wave farewell to that cotton mill town
Somewhere south of Macon

Nashville 1974

"Somewhere South of Macon" was the first of eleven songs that I wrote with a songwriter from Lubbock named Jim Rushing. Jim had migrated to Nashville in 1971. This was early on in my career, around 1974. Writing with Jim, I learned a lot about the craft of songwriting. And, of those eleven songs, we've had sixteen cuts over the years.

"Macon" was first recorded in 1975 by a singer on Capitol named Connie Cato. Then, in 1977, I recorded it for my first Epic album, *Me, I'm Feelin' Free*. It was the first single off the album, and it made *Billboard*'s country singles chart. In 1979, a young Scottish singer, Lena Zavaroni, recorded and released it as a single in Europe. Then, in 1987, international troubadour Rattlesnake Annie included it on her Columbia album.

When Jim and I first sat down to write, we decided that since I was from Enoree and Spartanburg, the song would be about a girl leaving a cotton mill town. So right away, I had a lot of empathy going for the main character, and when you're trying to get words to flow, it helps to have that kind of emotional attachment. But since our main goal was to write a hit for a female country singer, the actual *facts* in the song were tailored to that end. As a result, the verses are filled with Southern working-class images like "hard-earned dollar," "moonshine still," "beans and bacon," "calico dress," and "Greyhound bus." One thing we knew for sure—there weren't too many country singers out there from families who owned textile mills. My mother never "fed me a bottle from a moonshine still" and I never wore a "calico dress." And I never called my father "Papa." And Mother never worked the day shift in a cotton mill. Or the night shift either. And though my father once worked a night shift as superintendent, he never worked it as a common laborer. Our family owned the mills, for chrissakes. Daddy knew from day one he was being groomed to be the man.

One of Dad's employees once remarked, "Why Mr. Chapman, you don't just work one shift, you work *all* the shifts!" And there's a lot of truth in that statement. For the mills were never far from my father's mind. When he died in 1983, he was serving as president of the American Textile Manufacturers Institute. During his abbreviated term, he was instrumental in initiating the "Crafted with Pride in the U.S.A." campaign. Sometimes, on a rare shopping excursion, I'll be checking the washing instructions on a shirt or pair of jeans and I'll see it . . . the "Crafted with Pride" logo. I remember one such moment when a salesclerk came up and asked, "May I help you?" and I couldn't find the words to reply.

But back to True Confessions. I didn't "first make love in a cotton mill town" either. The first time I made love was in an apartment in New York City on East 63rd Street between First and York the summer I was twenty-one. But I did, one time, take a baby step toward making love in a cotton mill town. At least, it *started out* in one. In Enoree, South Carolina, to be exact.

I was fifteen and had gone to visit Frances Yarborough, my best friend from childhood. I was staying with my Aunt Susan and Uncle Joe, who lived right across the street from the Yarboroughs. Frances had made arrangements for me to double-date with her and her boyfriend, Stanley Kellett, and I was pretty excited about it. Mainly because my date was Tuck Patterson who happened to be two years older *and* drove a 1964 blue-and-white Ford Galaxie convertible. But more importantly, Tuck was considered a "cute boy" by my older sister, Mary. This would be my first real unchaperoned date in a car.

The four of us took off in Tuck's convertible and didn't stop until we got to the Greer Drive-In, about twenty miles north of Enoree. The evening's feature was *Kissin' Cousins* starring Elvis Presley. As I recall, Elvis played two different characters in the movie, which we ended up sitting through twice. Maybe the title inspired us, I don't know, but by the second showing, there was a lot of kissing going on in that convertible, which by now had its top and windows rolled up—for better acoustics I'm sure.

Now, I was very inexperienced when it came to boys. I had "made out" a few times with my old boyfriend, George Dickerson. We had mostly kissed. But, quite frankly, it all seemed like a big bother to me. I much preferred playing basketball. Hell, I enjoyed *homework* more than making out. I just couldn't understand what the big deal was.

But on this night with Tuck, things were different. When he kissed me, I started feeling things I'd never felt before and it kind of scared me, so I backed off. Besides being real cute, Tuck was a real sweetheart, so he didn't press me or anything. We just talked after that. And with Frances and Stanley still kissing in the backseat, we continued to talk . . . and talk . . . and talk. We ended up talking about everything under the sun, including the Bible, which Tuck said he enjoyed reading from time to time.

Later that night, Aunt Susan asked me how it went. "Oh, it was fine!" I gushed. I'd had three or four Cokes, so I was pretty hopped up. Susan didn't seem like she was ready for bed either, so the two of us ended up talking. I told her all about *Kissin' Cousins*—how Elvis had played the two different characters: one, a moonshiner, and the other, an emissary who'd been sent by the U.S. Army to convince the moonshiner and his hillbilly cronies to let the government use their land for a missile launch site. Aunt Susan sat there listening like she was enthralled. Then the subject turned to Tuck. Now Aunt Susan was the kind of person you could trust with your heart, so maybe that's why I told her that Tuck and I had kissed (and that was *all*!). But in talking about it, I suddenly started crying. Probably puberty kicking in, fueled by the sugar from all those Cokes. Anyway, at one point, I remember blurting out, "Well, he bought me a hamburger and a Coke. . . . I felt like I *had* to kiss him after that!"

When Susan went back up to bed, it turned out Joe had waited up for her. "What was that all about?" he asked. After Susan told him, Joe didn't say anything. He just turned out the light.

But moments later, as they lay there in the dark, Susan was thinking maybe Joe had fallen asleep when she heard: "Damn. It's a good thing he didn't buy her a steak."

.   .   .

"Somewhere South of Macon" never really explains why the girl is leaving. Was she knocked up? Maybe. We're never really sure. But one thing's for sure. This girl has a big and restless spirit. She's not *about* to be hemmed in by anything. She's gonna keep on moving until she finds a place where her spirit can be free. But make no bones about it . . . she is sad about leaving home. And a bit frightened. After all, it's all she's ever known.

So, hillbilly imagery aside, it was easy for me to identify with "Somewhere South of Macon." Especially in the way it addressed the coming-of-age issue and the high price we all pay for freedom. I've always seen it as sort of a *Thunder Road* meets *The Heart Is a Lonely Hunter*.

"This next song is about a little town south of Spartanburg, South Carolina. It's called 'Somewhere South of Macon.'" (pause) "We changed the names to protect the guilty."

That's how I would sometimes introduce "Macon" when I first started performing it. I don't know why I added that last line, other than it always drew a laugh and made everybody want to listen up. Who knows? Maybe I thought the folks back home *were* guilty for wanting everything to stay the same. Or maybe I had some suppressed guilt around the disparity between the life I was living and the life I was raised to live. For I had rejected marrying the rich boy back home and everything that went with it: babies, carpools, Junior League meetings, church on Sunday, cocktail parties at the club . . . you name it. Instead, I was living in a condemned neighborhood in Nashville, Tennessee, where they were paying me money to sing and play my guitar. I was hanging out with Cowboy Jack Clement, Waylon Jennings and Jessi Colter, Willie Nelson, Billy Joe Shaver, and Guy and Susanna Clark, and experiencing all kinds of things I never knew *existed* back in Spartanburg, South Carolina. I thought I'd died and gone to heaven.

Spartanburg 1954–1965

"How does it feel?"

"What do you mean . . . how does it feel?"

"How does it feel being tryouts for a boy?"

"Huh?"

My younger sister, Dorothy, and I are standing at the top of a little ivy-covered hill that separated our yard from the Dargan's next door. We had just heard the news that we had a new baby brother and now the nine-year-old Dick Dargan was asking us how it felt to have been nothing more than tryouts for a boy.

"Your parents *had* to want Mary," he went on, "because she was their firstborn. But you and Dots, y'all were just tryouts for a boy!"

Dorothy looked up at me and neither of us spoke a word. After all, what could we say?

Welcome to Spartanburg, South Carolina, where cotton is king and women have no value other than who they marry. Now, I was too young to think or say anything like that, but that's the way it was. At least, when I lived there. Today, most of the mills have shut down, so cotton is no longer king. As for the rest, I've heard things haven't changed all that much.

In March 1980, I returned to Spartanburg to attend the funeral of Dick's mother, Mary Louise Dargan. Mrs. Dargan had been a popular teacher and counselor at Spartanburg High School and a trusted friend to me growing up. I often referred to her as my "Other Mother."

The First Presbyterian Church was filled to capacity the day of Mrs. Dargan's funeral, with some mourners having to stand in the back. "My goodness!" Mother exclaimed as we entered the sanctuary, "I can't believe there're this many people at a funeral for a woman."

Mother once said, "I had it made in Enoree and didn't know it. Hell, if the toilet broke, someone would come from the mill and fix it. The mill took care of everything." But she was talking about more than the mill. She was talking about the people. For there was no pretense in Enoree. I always thought Mother was more comfortable with the salt-of-the-earth people in Enoree than she was hobnobbing with the rich and powerful. Or maybe *as* comfortable, because Mother would just as soon go to Myrtle Beach and stay in a trailer with her hairdresser, Jewell Keller, as go to The Cloisters at Sea Island, where you had to dress up for dinner every night (black tie on Saturday). But don't get me wrong. When it was "show time," nobody could put it on like my mother. But I never thought she was entirely comfortable playing the role of Mrs. James A. Chapman, Jr. I once heard her say—and this was during cocktail hour, so tongues were running loose: "Hell, I ain't nothing but Jim Chapman's white nigger."

We were fortunate to have lived in Enoree when we did. Mike Becknell, an employee and self-appointed historian at the Riverdale plant, recently wrote me in a letter: "Your family lived in Enoree in what I would consider the best time to have lived here, during the economic boom that followed World War II, just before the breakup of the mill villages."

Enoree was my childhood—that blissful, magical time before the walls go up between black and white, rich and poor, male and female, and your church and my church.

In Spartanburg, I was a tomboy. Most of the kids in our neighborhood were boys, so I ran with them. I used to joke and say that in our neighborhood a girl could either stay indoors and play paper dolls by herself or go outside and play with the boys. There was always a football or softball game going on in the Elmore's field across the street. And the Dargans had a basketball goal where Johnny (Dick's twin) and I would shoot for hours. Johnny taught me how to shoot a jump shot.

At age eleven, I was the quarterback at the Elmore's field, playing with boys three and four years older. I *loved* to throw the football. But with the onset of puberty, I had to give up tackle. The boys were developing hard muscles while I was developing these soft little buds on my chest. *Would somebody please tell me what's going on?* Whatever it was, it didn't seem fair.

By the time I reached junior high, basketball had become my favorite sport. I was the go-to girl on both my church league team (First Pres) and my school team (Spartanburg Day School). But forget school. Those church league games were some of the roughest games I ever played in. I'd sometimes come home looking like I'd been run through a meat grinder.

The girls on the First Pres team were mostly tall, willowy, privileged white girls from Converse Heights, including Ann Cobb (now Ann Cobb Johnson), who I've kept up with over the years. Ann always claimed our team only had one play. It was called *Girls, Cover Your Bosoms and Throw the Ball to Marshall!*

I remember one game against Arch Street Baptist over in the Spartan Mill village. There was this short girl with short frizzy hair guarding me, smacking gum and cursing the whole time. Come to think of it, their whole team was like that. Anyway, this girl had long, pointed fingernails that looked more like talons, only they were painted hot pink. She clawed on me the whole game. I couldn't believe it. It was like trying to play ball with a bunch of yappy little dogs hanging onto your ankles. I think I fouled out on purpose just to get away from her.

All roughness aside, I loved playing basketball for First Pres. We had a good team and ended up winning the YMCA Junior Girls' Sunday School Championship. I still have a faded clipping from the *Spartanburg Herald-Journal* of our team—all smiles in shiny uniforms—raising our trophy for all the world to see. A bright, shining moment. I was in the tenth grade. The next year, I was sent off to a boarding school where they didn't have basketball.

Once, when I was in the sixth or seventh grade, the headmaster at my school tried to recruit me for the boy's team. I was home studying in the living room when the phone rang. My ears perked up as I overheard Mother's end of the conversation.

"Well, what about the locker room, Harry?" (The headmaster's name was Harry Groblewski.)

". . . and what about road games?"

"Uh huh . . ."

"I see . . ."

"Well, I don't know. Let me talk to James. Our main concern is Marshall. Not the boy's basketball team."

"All right . . ."

"Uh huh . . ."

"Well, we'll see . . ."

"Okay, we will."

"All right . . . bye-bye." *Click.*

My father didn't like the idea and I had mixed emotions myself. I can't remember what all happened after that, but I ended up staying on with the girls.

Back then, the girls' game had weird rules. You could only dribble three times and couldn't cross the center line. In Kentucky, the state legislature had banned girl's basketball altogether. I have often referred to this period as the "dark ages of women's basketball." I think the men making the rules back then were afraid we'd ruin our reproductive systems if we played full court. And if a woman can't reproduce, then what good is she?

My first four years in Spartanburg, I went to Pine Street Elementary School, and those were glorious years. The years of learning and absorbing, of running free through the neighborhood, of riding flat out bareback on my horse Delight, of just being a girl, a tomboy, whatever . . . before the chaos of puberty and the yoke of propriety started messing everything up. Puberty was a confusing time, especially for a high-spirited girl like myself. Suddenly, it was *Girls can't do this, Girls can't do that, Always let the boys win, Keep your legs crossed at the ankles, If you're really smart, you won't let* him *know, Don't walk like that, Sh-h-h-h! Be quiet, girls!* Every time I hear that Dar Williams song "When I Was a Boy," I think to myself, *She knows.* That song just kills me!

As a teenager, I never saw myself as a rebel. Hell, I was trying to fit in. Whenever I tell my old friends that today, they laugh and say, "Yeah, right, Marshall!" And to think that all along, I thought I was pulling it off. But something would always give me away.

I remember one time at a high school dance, I abandoned my date to jump up on the bandstand and sing "So Fine" with the band. When I slung that electric guitar on over my pale green and gold brocade dress that Mother had made—I'd already kicked off those horrible dyed pumps to match—I felt just like the song: "So fine . . . so fine / So fi-i-ne, yeah / My baby's so doggone fine / Sends cold chills up and down my spine / Whoa-whoa / Yeah-yeah . . . so fine!"

The band was led by George Woodruff, the school janitor, and featured his cousin Monroe on piano. There was also a drummer and a bass player. But here's the real kicker. We were in a groove because *we had rehearsed.* The week before, Mother had driven me out to the Day School so I could practice with George and the boys. Only they were men. Five black men playing rhythm and blues with a white girl in a big empty auditorium at night with her mother sitting there knitting. Daddy must have been out of town. This was 1964 and all hell was breaking loose all over America, especially in the South. Racial unrest was everywhere. When I think back on this scene now, it seems almost miraculous to me.

There were isolated incidents like the one above. But for the most part, my lights were on dim from the time I was fifteen until I started writing songs at age twenty-five. The high beams didn't really flip on until two years later, when I switched from acoustic to electric guitar. I bought a Fender Telecaster from John Hiatt, put together a kick-ass band, and by the end of the summer, had a recording contract with CBS Records.

I've often wondered why that happened. In the words of Kris Kristofferson, Why me, Lord? Well, I'll tell you why. Because every time I plugged in that electric guitar and began laying down a groove, I'd feel just like I did the first time I heard Susie Burnett playing "Down Yonder" on that rickety old upright in her living room, or the first time I heard Big Joe Turner's voice coming out of Lula's radio in the basement, or that time I saw Elvis from the colored balcony at the Carolina Theater, and later . . . the Marvelettes singing "Too Many Fish in the Sea" at the Beach Club in Myrtle Beach, the Shirelles reminding us of what "Mama Said" at the National Guard Armory in Sumter, South Carolina, Maurice Williams and the Zodiacs begging us to "Stay, Just a Little Bit Longer" at Spartanburg's National Guard Armory, Little Anthony and the Imperials, James Brown and his Famous Flames, Jackie Wilson, Ray Charles and his Orchestra, fourteen-year-old Little Stevie Wonder singing "Fingertips" and blowing harmonica at Spartanburg's Memorial Auditorium. Every time I have ever taken the stage with a band, all I have ever wanted was for everybody within earshot to feel just like I did the first time I heard all those fabulous performers. *Alive, baby . . . electric and alive.*

In grammar school, I had two best friends: Jaime Johnston and Todd Swanson. Jaime and I loved horses together and fancied ourselves as young authoresses. So we wrote a "book." A book about a horse, of course. It was called *The Same Horse.* We wrote the text in pencil on notebook paper and used pencil and colored crayons for the illustrations. For the cover, we used a folded sheet of construction paper, then bound it all together with a stapler.

We tried to make everything look as professional as possible. There was even a "Note from the Author" after the title page.

Our plot was basically a *Black Beauty* rip-off. A beautiful horse gets separated from its kindly owner, then suffers enormous hardships under a succession of cruel, lesser owners, nearly reaching the point of *death*, before miraculously being rescued by the original owner and everybody lives happily ever after. Except for the bad guys, of course, who either disappeared or went to jail.

Todd Swanson was from the other side of the tracks. His dad worked for Southern Railway. But none of that mattered because Todd and I loved Elvis together. Elvis was our bond. We kept Elvis Presley scrapbooks and later became members of the Elvis Presley Fan Club.

The first letter I ever wrote was to Elvis. I was in the second grade and had just learned how to write in cursive. I felt so grown-up using this new technique as I carefully addressed the white business envelope Mother had given me:

Mr. Elvis Presley
Hollywood, Calif.

That's it. Just those two lines. No post office box, no street address, no nothing. Since Elvis was such a big star, I figured *Hollywood, Calif.* would be enough. Those people out there would know what to do.

Mother helped me abbreviate "California": C-a-l-i-f-period. Then she gave me a purple three-cent stamp with George Washington's face on it and showed me how to put it in the upper right-hand corner of the envelope. Later, I added three more stamps on the back, and when Mother saw what I'd done, she got mad.

"Why'd you put those stamps on the back?" she asked.

"So it'll get there *faster!*" I replied.

Mother just shook her head.

"Honey, you just wasted three perfectly good stamps."

I don't think Mother ever thought Elvis, or anybody associated with Elvis, would ever get my letter. Especially with its sparse address. I think she was indulging me, like I was writing a letter to Santa Claus. But Mother didn't know how big Elvis was. Elvis was bigger than Santa Claus because he was *real*. I'd seen him. But I'd never seen Santa Claus and probably never would no matter how late I stayed up waiting for him on Christmas Eve. And forget those fat men in their silly Santa Claus suits. I mean, who would fall for that? I *never* believed in Santa Claus. Not since that Christmas Eve in Enoree we left him a Coke and some cookies on a tray, and the next morning there was lipstick all over the mouth of the Coke bottle. That was it for me and Santa Claus.

As it turned out, the address on the envelope *was* enough. Because about ten days later, a manila envelope arrived in the mail from California containing not one but *two* signed publicity photographs of Elvis, along with an Elvis Presley catalog. The photographs were probably mechanically inscribed, but it didn't matter. I was so excited I couldn't stand it. Mother helped me order an Elvis Presley T-shirt *and* an Elvis Presley sailor cap, which I ended up wearing to school just about every day. I even wore the T-shirt to bed. Mother would have to bribe me to take it off to be washed.

In Spartanburg, we had two black maids and a black yardman. The yardman's name was John Knuckles. Whenever anybody asked John Knuckles his name, he always said, "John Knuckles-with-a-silent-K."

Lula Mae Moore and Cora Jeter were our maids. Lula came every morning weekdays to clean and do laundry. Then Cora would come fix supper and babysit if Mother and Daddy went out.

Lula worked for our family from 1956 until about 1968. My brother was born in 1955. Lula will be the first to tell you, "I raised that boy!" and she's right about that.

I can still see Lula upstairs in Mother and Daddy's bedroom, folding clothes and watching soap operas. Lula *loved* soap operas. Only she called them "her stories." "Y'all go on outside and play!" she'd say. "I got to watch my stories."

Lula was folding clothes and watching *As the World Turns* when the first news flash came on saying that President Kennedy had been shot in Dallas. I was back in my bedroom studying when I heard Lula yell out, "Marshall, Marshall, come quick! The president's been shot!" I immediately jumped up and nearly ran head-on into Lula in the hallway.

"What president?" I asked.

"President *Kennedy*, child. Somebody done shot him in Dallas."

Lula and I raced back to the TV where *As the World Turns* had resumed its normal broadcast.

"Aw, Lula," I said, "If President Kennedy had been shot, it'd be all over the TV. They wouldn't be showing this . . ."

But before I could say another word, a voice came on saying "We interrupt this program to bring you a special news bulletin from CBS." Then the familiar voice of Walter Cronkite announced that President Kennedy had been "seriously wounded" in Dallas . . . with some reports saying he'd been shot in the head.

"Umm, that doesn't sound good," I said.

I didn't know what else to say. But Lula did.

"Sweet Jesus, if you *ever* hear my prayer, hear it now!" she started shouting. "*Please* don't take him, *please* don't take him, *please* don't take our president. Not now! Oh, Lord, with that beautiful wife and those precious children. Please don't take him! We *need* him down here with us!"

While Lula prayed, *As the World Turns* resumed its normal broadcast. I couldn't bear to sit there waiting for more bad news, so I got up and went to the phone. I tried calling Mrs. Dargan next door, but nobody answered. Then I called Aunt Wince.

"Hello."

"Wince, this is Marshall. Have you heard the news?"

"No, what news?"

"President Kennedy's been shot."

"Good!" she said. Just like that.

Now Aunt Wince was a staunch Republican; everybody knew that. Her husband, my uncle Bob, was South Carolina's reigning G.O.P. chairman, having run for the U.S. Senate the year before. So, on some level, I knew her response was just "politics talking." Still, I was taken aback.

"Well, I think it's pretty serious. You might want to turn on your TV."

Lula and I were sitting together on the end of Mother and Daddy's bed, trying not to think the unthinkable, when the final news bulletin came on, the one where Walter Cronkite took off his glasses and cried after telling us our president was dead.

I was fourteen years old and this was my first time to have that sense that the world would never be the same again.

.   .   .

Lula got off work every afternoon at about three. She usually rode the bus home unless it was Friday. On Fridays, Roosevelt would come pick her up in his car. Roosevelt was Lula's husband, only Lula called him "Pappy." Every time Lula or anybody else said the name "Pappy," Lula would always start laughing like somebody was tickling her.

I could always tell when it was Friday, because on Fridays, Lula wore a red petticoat underneath her maid's uniform. I often wondered where she went in that red petticoat. Wherever it was, I wanted to go there too.

No sooner did Lula get off work, than here'd come Cora Jeter, like a shift change at the mill. Sometimes Lula would leave on the same bus that brought Cora.

Cora didn't like for anybody to be in the kitchen while she was cooking. "Child, get out of my kitchen!" she'd say. But if I stayed real quiet, she'd sometimes let me stand there and watch. I loved to watch her make biscuits. She'd roll the dough out on the counter until it was flat and smooth, then cut it up into little circles using the screw top from a Mason jar. If there was any dough left over, she'd roll it up into a little ball and flip it my way. I don't know which tasted better, Cora's fluffy biscuits still warm from the oven or her raw dough balls.

Cora was a character and would tell us the wildest bedtime stories you ever heard. I told one to John Hiatt one time and it ended up being in a song we co-wrote called "Old Habits Are Hard to Break." I say co-wrote. My only contribution was the title and Cora's story.

Cora was always warning us about tree frogs. It got to the point where I was scared to walk under a tree for fear of one jumping down and attaching itself to me. I'd even ride my bicycle down the middle of the street to avoid overhanging branches. "That tree frog'll suck the life right out of you, child!" Cora's eyes always looked like they were getting ready to pop out of her head, especially when she got excited, which was most of the time if she was telling a good story. My all-time favorite was the one about the tree frog.

Cora was originally from down around Union, South Carolina, where she'd picked her share of cotton. I have some Jeter cousins from down there who were slave owners before the Civil War and I've often wondered if Cora Jeter and I weren't somehow related. Come to think of it, she *was* six feet tall.

Yeah, child, we was out there pickin' that cotton.
Me and Pappy and everybody else. And there wadn't a *tree* in sight . . .
'cept for this one little ol' tree. And Pappy, he tells me,
Cora, you stay away from that tree. I mean it now!
And wouldn't you know it, child . . . I walked under that tree
and a *tree frog* jumped down and started wrapping itself around my
waist 'til I turned blue in the face! Um-hum.
That tree frog be cuttin' off my circulation.
Pappy he come running across that field an' says,
Cora, that tree frog ain't gon' let go of you 'til it thunders!
And child, there wadn't a cloud in the sky!

When the snake of love
Starts pullin' you under
And it won't let go
'Til it starts to thunder
And there's not a cloud in the sky
Gonna make him shake
I guess old habits are hard to break

February 9, 1956

The first time I ever heard the name Elvis Presley was the same day I saw him play live.

"They say he white, but sing like he colored," Cora said. Cora had been talking about Elvis all week.

"Elvis . . ." she repeated slowly. "Now what kind of name is that?"

The ad in the *Spartanburg Herald-Journal* proclaimed Elvis "the most talked about new personality in the last ten years of recorded music." It also said he was playing four shows at Spartanburg's very own Carolina Theater. "Today only!" it said, like there might not be a tomorrow. This was Thursday, February 9, 1956—a school day. I was seven years old and halfway through the first grade.

The first two shows were matinees, and patrons were notified that the theater would be cleared before the evening shows to "accommodate the crowds." Sounded like a happening to me. Like the circus that time in Greenville or the Piedmont Interstate Fair.

I remember Cora taking off her apron, saying, "Come on, child, let's go see what all the fuss is about!" I'd just walked in from riding my bike home from school. Next thing I knew, I was upstairs shaking out quarters from the plastic pill bottle I used to stash my weekly allowance.

The paper said the admission price for children was fifty cents. White children, that is. Admission prices for all shows were listed as follows:

ADULTS 85¢   CHILDREN 50¢

Then underneath, in a smaller font size:

Co. Balc.   Adults 60¢   Child 25¢

It's interesting to note, that of the hundred and thirty-five words used in the ad, *colored* and *balcony* are the only two that were abbreviated. Like they were writing in code or something. "They" being the abbreviated minds that would think something like segregation was okay. I once wrote a song with the lines: "But that was then / and this is now / and now is all I know / It might as well have been a hundred million years ago."

Our family lived in Converse Heights, or "seedy Converse Heights" as some have laughingly referred to it ever since a 1964 article appeared on the front page of the *New York Times* calling textile baron Roger Milliken "The Daddy Warbucks of the Republican Party." The article went on to describe Milliken's renowned conservatism, right down to his one-story house in "seedy Converse Heights." Converse Heights was one of Spartanburg's older residential neighborhoods.

There used to be a city bus stop directly across the street from our house on Connecticut Avenue. All the black maids in the neighborhood would use it to get to and from work. No white people I knew ever rode the bus. They all had cars. And it probably goes without saying that none of their *children* ever rode it either. But we Chapman children did. Mother would sometimes put us on the bus in the middle of the afternoon just so she could take a nap.

I remember the first time she did this. She was real pregnant with Jamie, so it must've been toward the end of the summer of 1955. Dorothy was three, I was six, and Mary was eight.

From our house, you could always tell when a bus was coming. As soon as one turned off Woodburn Road, you could hear its engine rev as the driver downshifted for the gradual climb up Connecticut Avenue. From a distance, it sounded like a blender being turned up from a real low setting.

I think Mother's decision to put us on the bus that first time was purely a spur-of-the-moment thing. I don't think there was any premeditation at all. I mean, there she was, eight and a half months pregnant, with the three of us probably driving her crazy. Suddenly she hears the distant sound of a city bus making the turn off Woodburn Road and . . . bam! A light bulb switches on in the thought balloon above her head.

"Hey y'all, come on!" she says, hurrying us out into the yard. No sooner had we crossed the street than here comes the bus. We could see it chugging its way up Connecticut Avenue.

Mother was standing on the curb waving at the driver like somebody drowning trying to flag down an oncoming ship. I was standing right beside her and all I could think was *Gee, I hope that bus doesn't hit Mama's stomach.* But she moved back just in time.

As the bus doors opened, Mother stepped up inside with the three of us scrambling along behind her. Then she said something to the driver and handed him a dollar bill. I couldn't hear what all she said, but whatever it was, it made him laugh as he pressed the little lever on the coin changer hanging from his belt.

"Here you go," he said cheerfully, handing Mother her change.

Mother dropped the coins in the fare box.

"See you later!" she waved.

As the bus pulled away, I turned and watched her walk back toward the house.

Of course, we thought we were on some grand adventure. We didn't feel abandoned or anything like that. Mother had made the whole thing sound like a ride at Disneyland. And what a ride it was. We got to see parts of

Spartanburg no privileged white child from Converse Heights had ever seen. At one point, the three of us and the driver were the only white people on the bus, and it was packed.

Our ride lasted a little over an hour. That's how long it took the bus to run its route and end up back in front of our house. By then, we were ready to be home. I think some of us were beginning to feel like maybe we'd been "had" and Dorothy was starting to fuss.

After that maiden voyage, getting us back on the bus just so she could take a nap became more of a hard sell for our mother. This was no ride at Disneyland and now everybody knew it. Any future rides would have to involve something a little more tangible. Like ice cream. Or a trip to Cleveland Park or a movie. Or . . . cash. Nobody in my family has ever been above offering or taking a bribe from another family member. Especially when money or heirlooms were involved.

Now, I've told people this story and could tell they were . . . well, taken aback. I could see them thinking *How could a mother turn her children loose on a city bus like that?* But it was a different world back then.

Once, when Mary was six and I was four, Mother put us on a passenger train by ourselves to go visit Mama Cloud and Papa Cloud (our maternal grandparents). Mother simply asked the black porter to keep an eye on us, then gave him a tip and that was that. Mary and I rode the Seaboard Line from Clinton, South Carolina, to Rockingham, North Carolina—a distance of about a hundred and twenty miles. Mother had put us on in Clinton so we wouldn't have to change trains.

I loved riding the train. The *clack clack clack* of the wheels on the track and everything whizzing by outside. I was transfixed. Then every fifteen minutes or so, the porter would stroll down the aisle with a big smile and ask, "How you girls doin'?"

"Fine," we chimed in unison.

For the ride home, Papa Cloud wired shipping tags to the straps of our sundresses. "Real, heavy-duty shipping tags," Mother said. "You could have cared less, but Mary was mortified and tried to take hers off."

The way I see it, if other mothers in Converse Heights never put their children on a Spartanburg city bus, it's only because they weren't as ingenious as my mother. The woman was exhausted and needed a nap, for chrissakes. I'm *glad* she put us on the bus. Hell, she could have gone postal on us.

.   .   .

I remember one time getting on the bus with Cora, and the driver wouldn't pull away because Cora was sitting in the front instead of in the back, where blacks were supposed to sit. I had taken a seat just across the aisle and could see the driver glaring at her in his rearview mirror. When Cora looked up and saw the way he was looking at her, she frowned and said, "Drive your bus, man. My feets is tired!"

Cora was six feet tall and strong as an ox, but she had real bad feet and her walk was more like a shuffle. She wore men's wingtip shoes with holes cut in them so her toes and bunions would have a place to go. But bad feet aside, any showdown between Cora and this mealy-mouthed bus driver, and my money's on Cora every time. But strong as she was, she wasn't as strong as the whole system of segregation, and that's probably why I instinctively moved back across the aisle and snuggled up next to her. I wanted to protect her from whatever this was. I didn't know it had a name. *Segregation?* I'd never heard of the word. Sometimes you don't have to know the name of something to be living right smack dab in the middle of it.

When Cora and I arrived at the Carolina Theater that afternoon, there were people milling around all over the place, wide-eyed with excitement. The first matinee had yet to begin and already folks were being turned away. Had I not been with Cora, I probably would have been turned away too, because the main floor was sold out. The only remaining seats were in the "colored balcony." My guess is, the balcony seats didn't sell as fast because the show was basically a "hillbilly package" show. Besides Elvis, there was Justin Tubb, the Louvin Brothers, the Carter Sisters, and Benny Martin.

Once the show began, the blacks in the "colored balcony" didn't pay much attention to the other acts. There was some scattered, polite applause, but most of the people around Cora and me were talking and laughing and visiting with each other like nothing else was going on.

But all that changed the minute Elvis hit the stage. When he came on, it was like a big bolt of lightning had struck the Carolina Theater. Cora started screaming and laughing at the same time. I couldn't believe how everybody just went berserk. The white girls downstairs were screaming so loud you could barely hear the music. The whole thing was like a big explosion.

Elvis didn't play that long, probably no more than about thirty minutes. But it didn't matter. I was completely blown away. Susie Burnett was one thing, but Elvis Presley was something else.

You know how babies bond with their mothers at birth? Well, I'm thinking I must've held out so I could bond with Elvis that afternoon. Because that's exactly what happened.

Twenty-two years after "Somewhere South of Macon," I wrote another song about leaving home called "Leaving Loachapoka." This time, there was no sadness, no conflict, no guilt, and no apologies. Just pure desire and confidence and white-light energy.

Again, I changed "Spartanburg" to the name of another town in another state. Only this time, it wasn't to protect the guilty, the innocent, or anybody else. I just simply loved the *sound* of *Loachapoka, Alabama.* It was like a two-word poem.

Loachapoka is a little town just outside Auburn, Alabama. I've never been there, but in 1980 there was a red-haired drummer in my band from there named Ricky Rowell. I used to introduce Ricky three or four times a night just so I could say "Loachapoka, Alabama." It just felt good on the tongue, like a Roger Miller lyric. I always knew that one day, it would be in a song.

> *Going ninety miles an hour*
> *With her hair on fire*
> *Running on a tank*
> *Full of burning desire*
> *She's heading out old highway*
> *Number fifty-nine*
> *Leaving Loachapoka, Alabama, behind*
> *Leaving Loachapoka*
>
> *She got great big dreams*
> *Too big for a small town*
> *She got songs in her head*

Just swirling all around
Now she's singing 'em out loud
And it feels so fine
Leaving Loachapoka, Alabama, behind
Leaving Loachapoka

Hello Nashville
Music City
You better look out
'Cause she's the real nitty gritty
Got a light inside
She's gonna let it shine . . .
She's gonna let it shine

And as the sun goes down
In all the little towns
And as the people in the houses
Begin to settle down
There's a flash of life
Across the Tennessee state line
She's leaving Loachapoka, Alabama, behind
Leaving Loachapoka
Leaving Loachapoka, Alabama, behind
Leaving Loachapoka

2

Rode Hard and Put Up Wet

"Rode Hard and Put Up Wet" was the first song I wrote by myself that felt like I wasn't trying. It just poured out one hungover afternoon in late summer of 1973. I'd woken up around noon facedown in my front yard—which was a vegetable garden—wearing nothing but my underpants.

Now this was not an unusual occurrence in 1973 Nashville, Tennessee, because that's about when the '60s hit the South. I often found strange bodies in the morning in my yard, and once even found a man passed out in my bathtub. Only two things were sticking up out of the water and thank *God* one was his nose, or I'd've had a corpse on my hands. Once, after a noon mint julep party, the yard body count was five by sundown.

So I'm lying facedown between the corn and the pole beans and would have stayed there god-only-knows how long, if not for this sound . . . like someone beating a gong right next to my ear, jarring me into a reluctant consciousness. Turning my head, squinting up into the midday sun, I spied my tormentor. At the top of a fifteen-foot stalk of corn was a damn bluebird just singing its little heart out.

But let me expound on this vegetable garden for a minute. You see, I had all kinds of stars in my eyes back then, waiting on tables by day and playing music in bars at night. I was just dying to break into the country music scene. With my South Carolina blueblood background, I figured if I plowed up my entire front yard and planted *crops*, people would think I was from the country. Of course the reason that corn stalk was fifteen feet tall was because I'd planted *horse* corn, not knowing the difference between that variety and the ones fit for human consumption.

But let me tell you, I was *into* it! Why Mrs. Chrisman, the mother of a former Vanderbilt classmate (Woody Chrisman, aka Woody Paul, who went on to become a member of the Grand Ol' Opry with the musical group Riders in the Sky), would come over and teach me how to can tomatoes, for chrissakes. (Mrs. Chrisman had grown up a dirt farmer's daughter in Triune, Tennessee, just south of Nashville.) But no matter how hard I tried earning my country diploma, something would always give me away. For example, one day a friend and I were surveying the garden, trying to decide what to harvest for lunch.

"Let's make some coleslaw!" my friend exclaimed.

"I didn't *plant* any coleslaw," I replied, as we both stood there looking at the prettiest row of cabbage you ever saw.

As for my hangover that summer day, it was well earned. The night before, I'd gone out with my next-door neighbors, Matt, Ellie, and Bubba. (Bubba was from Greenville, South Carolina. His real name was Marion Bothwell Crigler III. Only in South Carolina do people have names like that.) Anyway, we'd gone out to a club called the Exit/In to hear a terrific new songwriter named John Prine. John's first album had just been released on Atlantic, and it seemed like the whole town was abuzz with anticipation about hearing this great new talent.

For music lovers and creators, the early '70s in Nashville was a magical time. Comparisons have been made to Hemingway's Paris in the '20s as described in his book *A Moveable Feast.* If you were young and talented, it didn't matter if you'd had commercial success or not. You could waltz into the Ritz Café (where the Gold Rush is today) and co-owners Tupper Saussy and Mary Walton Caldwell would greet you with a smile and a stemmed glass of properly aged French wine, and perhaps, a plate of *rosbif à la béarnaise* with some *haricots verts* and *pommes de terre soufflé* on the side. Mary Walton died in 1997, and last I heard, Tupper was languishing in the slammer for refusing to pay his income taxes. But in 1973 they were the most glamorous twosome I'd ever seen. Tupper, well-educated and articulate, looked like then–Canadian Prime Minister Pierre Trudeau. He'd written plays and books and recently'd had a pop hit "Morning Girl" with his group the Neon Philharmonic. I had the wildest crush on him for about a month or so.

One night after closing down the Ritz, Tupper escorted a bunch of us out to his house on Belle Meade Boulevard. Tupper was married to Lola Haun at the time. The Hauns were one of Nashville's most socially prominent families. I don't remember Lola being there that night. I just remember playing in a spirited game of basketball by the light of a moon so full and beautiful that afterward I was inspired to take a moonbath right there in the middle of their driveway.

As for Mary Walton, she was tall, striking, in her late forties, early fifties—handsome in a Katharine Hepburn kind of way. One night—or early morning—after Mason Williams ("Classical Gas") had played the Exit/In, a bunch of us ended up in Mason's room at the old Anchor Motel. I remember Rick Cunha from Mason's band being there, singer Marie Cain, Diane South (Joe's wife), and, sitting on the desk smiling down on us all, was Mary Walton. I don't know why we were all there, but back in those days, going to sleep was always the last thing on anybody's mind. At one point, Mason began to cut a fully clothed Marie out of the feet of her panty hose with a pair of scissors. The way he did it—taking his time, concentrating like a surgeon performing a delicate operation—was one of the most amazing things I'd ever seen in my life. (Nobody *ever* did things like that at Vanderbilt where I'd been a student only two years before.)

When the sun came up, the party didn't break up. It moved. We all spilled out onto the street, then got in formation, with Mary Walton leading the pack like some grande-dame version of the Pied Piper. We must have been a sight for the early morning commuters as we shuffled along West End Avenue, as my father would say . . . "on the wrong end of the evening."

We continued along in this fashion until finally we arrived at the Ritz Café, where Mary Walton unlocked the front door and ushered us all in.

A chilled flute of French champagne materialized in my right hand as I joined the others at a long table elegantly set on white linen. I can still see Mary Walton standing in the kitchen doorway, smiling her brilliant smile, as she whisked up some eggs for omelettes which she served with the Béarnaise sauce and steaming cups of strong French coffee. Talk about a moveable feast . . . *quel bon repas*!

The music scene has changed a lot since those days. Now it's all business. Nobody hangs out anymore. Everything goes through the proper channels. Hell, back then, if you were a songwriter, there were as many different ways to pitch a song as skin a cat. When Kris Kristofferson wrote "Sunday Morning Coming Down," he rented a damn helicopter and landed it on Johnny Cash's front lawn out by Old Hickory Lake. When Cash emerged from his house, Kris just handed him a tape and then *lifted off,* leaving the surprised superstar blowing in the wind. Stuff like that happened all the time. Everything was bigger-than-life.

The Exit/In, in particular, contributed to the magic. You'd walk through a friendly bar area where booths lined the walls, to a curtain where the person "doing the door" would collect a cover charge. Beyond the curtain was where the music happened: a split-leveled room of tables and chairs, with a raised stage in the far corner by an exit door where the bands would load in and out. I always liked to sit behind the rail in the middle of the room where the PA sounded best.

If a show was in progress, you kept quiet unless the performance dictated otherwise. There were two shows a night, and on big nights, the room was cleared between shows. Steve Martin, Fats Domino, Tom Waits, Roger Miller, Bobby Blue Bland, The Amazing Rhythm Aces, Martin Mull, Jimmy Buffett, Dizzy Gillespie, Willie Nelson, B.B. King, Linda Ronstadt, Wayne Cochran, J.J. Cale, Buddy Rich, The Nitty Gritty Dirt Band—all played the Exit. It was a good mix of veterans and newcomers and of *every* kind of music and entertainment. One night, Steve Martin led the entire audience out into the street and marched them all the way to McDonald's, where he jumped behind the counter and began taking orders. Yet another moveable feast.

In those days I was living in a fifty-dollar-a-month apartment—a couple of rooms on the side of an old house in a condemned neighborhood just west of Vanderbilt University. You could say I was the beneficiary of some rather shady dealings between Vanderbilt and Metropolitan Nashville. Vanderbilt had been trying to flush out the surrounding homeowners for years so they could tear down the houses and build more parking lots. As soon as an old-timer would die, they'd somehow acquire the property, then divide the house into renting spaces for ridiculously low prices, the philosophy being that if enough low-rent tenants moved in, the rest of the homeowners would move out voluntarily. I lived at 3008-A Dudley Avenue for nearly four years. With the low rent, I was able to save up my waitress tips and door money from gigs and travel to far away places like Ketchum, Idaho, and London, England, where I'd stay for a season.

If you've never lived in a condemned neighborhood, consider yourself deprived. Our neighborhood was an eclectic mix of students, hippies, and young professionals with small children, musicians, bemused older couples, and even some Hell's Angels. Because we knew our time together was limited—the spectre of the wrecking ball hanging over us all—there was this neighborhood spirit that was unlike anything I've experienced before or since. We all got along and nobody cared what anybody else did. Besides the crops in *my* front yard, there was a twisted-chrome car fender exhibit in the yard two doors down.

The day the Hell's Angels moved in, Bubba and I dyed all our T-shirts black in honor of the occasion. I never will forget stirring those T-shirts in a big pot of boiling black Ritt dye on my little gas stove. You know, when you think about it, if everybody would look at the world as one big condemned neighborhood—a concept that astronomy would, in fact, support—then things like lethal injections, terrorism, and war would seem like really dumb things to do. Or *tacky,* as Will Campbell would say. And as for the whole theory, Jerry Lee would simply say: "Think about it, darlin'!"

But back to John Prine at the Exit/In. Of course, going out on the town back in those days was considered a major maneuver and preparations had to be made. You had to get primed, and that could be tricky. I remember one time being at a Rolling Stones concert in Louisville, Kentucky (Steel Wheels, 1989). After the opening act and just seconds before the lights were cut and the Stones hit the stage with "Start Me Up" behind a loud string of fireworks, a guy sitting in front of me passed completely out of his seat. As he fell to the tarpaulin-covered stadium floor, his buddy shook his head and said: "Oops! Peaked too soon!"

In our preparation to hear John Prine, the feeling that this was going to be "one of those nights" kicked us all into high gear. We were flying by the time we got to the club, where the line of people waiting to get in stretched all the way around the block. What transpired for the next few hours was nothing short of miraculous. Hearing John Prine sing songs like "Sam Stone,"

"Hello in There," "Angel from Montgomery," and "Paradise" was enough to make me think I'd died and gone to heaven. But then all these *other* song-writers who'd come to pay their respects started materializing from the audience and, one by one, got up and sang *their* songs. Kristofferson did "Me and Bobby McGee"; Steve Goodman, "You Never Even Call Me by My Name"; Waylon Jennings, "Good-Hearted Woman in Love with a Good-Timing Man"; and David Allen Coe delivered "Would You Lay with Me (in a Field of Stone)." It was a song feast that lasted deep into the night. When it finally ended, I was so exhilarated, I don't remember how I got home. But once there, Matt, Ellie, Bubba, and I sat on their concrete front porch trying to articulate, between long silences, some of what we had just witnessed. We didn't want it to end.

But somebody had to throw water on the campfire, so Bubba disappeared momentarily, then returned with a Mason jar full of moonshine whiskey. The last thing I remember was Bubba saying he'd bought it from a bootleg-ger back in South Carolina.

Now a case could be made that I had felt obligated to imbibe, based on the cocktail-circuit heritage that Bubba and I shared as fellow South Carolinians. My parents and Bubba's parents were good friends. Even our grandparents had been good friends. I'd heard all the stories about how they used to climb this hill outside of Greenville to get corn whiskey during pro-hibition, and how they'd all be in such a good mood when they came back down. Also, I was raised a good Presbyterian, so the concept of predestina-tion had been presented to me at an early age. So an even stronger case could be made using the "predestination defense": *Your honor, we have facts here that will prove to this jury without a doubt that my client was* predestined *to drink the moonshine from that Mason jar.*

Anyway, that's all I remember until the notes from that bluebird's cheer-ful song started knocking against my skull like a jackhammer. Then it was all I could do to crawl across the garden and up onto my porch, where I promptly laid back down again. That cool concrete felt so good against my face that I just laid there for a while. Then Ellie came by with cups of coffee and a cigarette, and together we sat there smoking and sipping and remi-niscing about the night before. After she left, I went on back inside and picked up my old Martin D-28 and started playing a Chuck Berryesque-type rhythm, stopping occasionally to write down lyrics with a #2 pencil on a yellow legal pad. As has been the case with most of my songs, the words and music came together, beginning with the very first line.

Well I feel like I been rode hard and put up wet
Lord knows last night was a night I will never forget
I can't remember what happened
But it must've been the best one yet
'Cause I feel like I been rode hard and put up wet

Honky tonkin' in Nashville
All night long
I heard John Prine, Kris and Waylon
They were smokin' a song
There was Johnny Rodriguez,
David Allen Coe, whoa-whoa
It was a swarm herd of songbirds
Doin' time on Music Row

Now I feel like I been rode hard and put up wet
Lord knows last night was a night I will never forget
I can't remember what happened
But it must've been the best one yet
'Cause I feel like I been rode hard and put up wet

Later on that night
I had to fight my way back home
Then safe and sound
I heard the ringin' of the telephone
Any sense at all
And I'd've left that damn thing alone
But a fool loves company even more
As the night moves on

Now I feel like I been rode hard and put up wet
Lord knows last night was a night I will never forget
I can't remember what happened

But it must've been the best one yet
'Cause I feel like I been rode hard and put up wet

Well then I went next door
Wearing nothin' but my underwear
There was Matthew, Ellie and Josh
Yep, the gang was all there
Bubba had a jug o' moonshine
From South Caroline
Well, I thought I was dead
But they said I sang one last line . . .

Nothin' could be finer
Than to be in Carolina
In the morning

"Rode Hard and Put Up Wet" ended up on my first album *Me, I'm Feelin' Free* (Epic 1977), but not without a struggle. The record company had wanted an album of mostly ballads—safe love songs, sweetened with strings—hoping one would slip through to country radio. "Rode Hard and Put Up Wet" ended up the lone wolf in countrypolitan clothing.

Epic, of course, wanted *Me, I'm Feelin' Free* to sell so they could recoup their investment in recording costs. And I wanted it to sell so people could hear my songs. Unfortunately, most record company marketing plans are based on what is currently hot, which can sometimes make it difficult for anything new and original to break through. The larger corporate labels don't know *why* something hits, but they can read their weekly sales reports and know *when* something hits. Then they scramble to sign acts like that act until the music all starts to sound alike and the record-buying public no longer wants to buy records. Only then do they start looking around for something new. And if that "something new" sells a lot of records, it's usually because they have smart, aggressive management and/or a strong fan base from relentless touring.

That's how Willie Nelson broke through. Willie made it in spite of CBS records. Many of the powers that be were initially put off by *Red Headed Stranger.* "Sounds like a damn demo tape!" "Hell, Roy, that bass ain't even in tune!" Willie was an original and so different from what they were used to hearing that many of them didn't get it. I have heard from usually reliable sources that only 25,000 copies of *Red Headed Stranger* were initially pressed. Hell, Willie had already become a folk hero in Texas starting with his first Fourth of July Picnic in 1973. A crowd of 70,000 old-time country music fans, hippies, members of the New York press, and assorted movie stars had showed up in the middle of a sun-baked field in Dripping Springs, Texas, to hear Willie and his family and friends play music. By 1975, the year *Red Headed Stranger* was released, 100,000 more would show up in Liberty Hill for his third annual picnic. Meanwhile, word was spreading all over the country.

I have heard that CBS so underestimated how many souls were out there waiting to buy *Red Headed Stranger* that they damned near killed the record. Only after running all four pressing plants twenty-four hours a day, putting all other releases on hold, were they able to meet the demand.

I doubt an artist as original and talented as Willie could even get signed the way things are today. The country music business has become white-bread-with-the-edges-cut-off . . . homogenized . . . and hell, back then, Willie didn't even *bathe* on a regular basis.

One song from *Me, I'm Feelin' Free* that managed to make *Billboard*'s country singles chart was "Somewhere South of Macon." It debuted at #100, then disappeared the next week. I was told that the line "I first made love in a cotton mill town" was deemed too sexually explicit for country radio. Meanwhile, Charly McClain, another singer on Epic and former candidate for Miss Tennessee, had a song on the charts that fared a lot better. It was called "Lay Something on My Bed Besides a Blanket." My take is that country music, with its snickering-behind-the-barn mentality about sex, and country radio, in particular, with its predominantly male programmers and DJs, just weren't ready for a young woman singing openly and directly about her own sexuality. It was far easier for them to relate to a song like "Blanket" which presented the male fantasy of a woman's feelings.

That's why Loretta Lynn has always been one of my heroes. Loretta was, perhaps, the only female country singer in the '60s and '70s writing about the male/female thing from a woman's point of view. You need go no further than "Don't Come Home a-Drinkin' with Lovin' on Your Mind" (1966) to know what I'm talking about.

. . .

In 1980 "Rode Hard and Put Up Wet" was recorded by singer Johnny Lee for the soundtrack of the movie *Urban Cowboy*. Next time you're surfing the cable and come across *Urban Cowboy*, check out the scene about fifteen minutes in, when John Travolta has just walked into Gilley's. While the camera slowly pans from his cowboy boots up to his face, Johnny Lee is singing "Rode Hard and Put Up Wet" in the background. When I first saw the movie, I couldn't believe they had changed the words to the "Nothin' could be finer than to be in Carolina" coda to "Nothing could be keener than to be in Pasadena." I got this sick feeling in my stomach that I'd never felt before and promptly got up and ran out of the theater. But no matter how fast I ran, there was no going back. I couldn't undo what had been done no matter how many times I laid facedown in my vegetable garden with nothing on but my underpants. It's a long way from Dudley Avenue to Hollywood and Vine.

3

Running Out in the Night

I wrote "Running Out in the Night" on a late summer evening in 1976 at my friend Joy Wahl's house. I'd been living at Joy's off and on for about eight months, ever since that freezing January morning I showed up at her doorstep with nothing but a toothbrush and a batch of unfinished songs.

I'd met Joy years before at a popular Nashville watering hole, the lounge at the Jolly Ox in Green Hills. I played a solo gig there for a couple of years after my Vanderbilt days. I was the "lounge entertainment." My job was to sing songs for hungry customers while they waited to be seated in the dining rooms where they could order up a steak. I also worked there as a waitress during lunch. After lunch, I'd settle up, grab a bite, then go home and nap until it was time to come back with my guitar. I'd play eight, sometimes nine sets a night, from "happy hour" until one or two in the morning. Forty-five-minute sets with fifteen-minute breaks. I did this six nights a week. It was steady work, and I was grateful to have it.

The only drawback occurred during my night shift. The Jolly Ox sound system was set up so that the person calling customers to the dining area and the person doing the lounge entertainment shared the same speakers. I'd be up there singing "Take the ribbon from my hair / Shake it loose and let it fall" when suddenly there'd be a loud click, followed by static and feedback and a voice would come booming out of the speakers: "Jones—party of two—your table is ready!—Jones—party of two—your table is ready!" I'd freeze like a mannequin during these abrasive interruptions, moving only my lips as I mouthed along with the announcement. Then I'd pick right back up where I'd left off—"Layin' soft against your skin / like the shadows on the wall"—like nothing had ever happened. The crowd loved it.

After a few months of this, I decided to talk to the manager, Dick

49

Rivera—a mustachioed, amiable sort—and propose that they enlarge the stage so I could bring a band in there with my *own* PA: two Shure columns with a six-channel Vocal Master that I'd recently bought from songwriter Alex Harvey ("Delta Dawn," "Reuben James") for five hundred dollars. I would later sell the system to a traveling evangelist for six hundred. My mama didn't raise no fool. At least not when it comes to money.

The Jolly Ox was a chain of steak houses out of Dallas, Texas. Everything about it was done according to a corporate manual. There were even guidelines as to what *sort* of entertainment should be in the lounge. Basically it called for a human jukebox singing the top-40 songs of the day. If you were male, your hair couldn't go over your collar. If you were female, you had to wear a dress. The Jolly Ox wanted their entertainment safe . . . you know, homogenized. So I promptly went out and bought a cheap formal-length dress with a halter-type top, made out of this *slinky* material that had Marilyn Monroe's head printed all over it. Our bass player loved that dress. He once confided that from his vantage point, one of Marilyn's heads would occasionally come into contact with a certain half of my anatomy, causing Ms. Monroe to wink at him during some of our more up-tempo numbers. This guy also smoked a lot of reefer. Said it improved his concentration.

Knowing what I know now about how the world works, I'm amazed that Dick Rivera ever considered my proposal, much less accepted it. Then again, I can be very persuasive and charming, not to mention manipulative, whenever I want something *real bad.* This has occasionally gotten me into trouble, but in this case, things worked out . . . at least for a while. Word quickly spread about me and my band, and before long, the lounge at the Jolly Ox was packed every night with some souls not necessarily there for the steaks. Soon the seater/greeter was announcing the tables *between* my songs. Sometimes they'd hand me the list and *I'd* announce the damn names for the tables, making it part of the act, and everybody had a good time. One day, some corporate types showed up from Dallas to check up on things, which included hearing me and the band. I could see them sitting out in the audience. They were hard to miss in their matching red jackets with the Jolly Ox logo emblazoned on the pockets, tapping their pencils out of rhythm as they tried to figure out just how we fit into their scheme of things. Later, one of them suggested to Dick Rivera that I sing something popular like "Tie a Yellow Ribbon 'round the Old Oak Tree."

band. For a while, Jack Clement—or "Cowboy" as his friends liked to call him—was coming in almost every night.

Jack Clement was not only a songwriter ("Ballad of a Teenage Queen") but a record producer (Jerry Lee Lewis, Charley Pride, Waylon Jennings, Johnny Cash) and filmmaker as well. He was also one of the most unusual people I had ever met. I never could figure out why he was called "Cowboy." He didn't wear the boots or the hat. In fact, he was the most un-cowboy looking-like person you could imagine. Sort of a cross between Jerry Lee Lewis and Alfred Hitchcock.

Jack had started out in Memphis working as a producer and engineer for the legendary Sam Phillips at Sun Records. He eventually ended up in Nashville, where he started building recording studios. He was the first independent record producer to work for a major label (RCA) and the first independent producer of a major motion picture. *Dear Dead Delilah,* a Southern gothic thriller starring Agnes Morehead and Will Geer, was filmed entirely on location in Nashville.

Jack and his publishing partner, Bill Hall, were the first people I met in the music business. I was but a sophomore at Vanderbilt at the time. Jack's hair was dyed blond, and I mistook him for a professional wrestler. Four years later, I was following him around like a puppy dog. Jack was an iconoclast, a visionary . . . a pied piper for songwriters and dreamers everywhere. I was crazy about him.

One time my parents drove over from South Carolina to attend my second annual mint julep party. Mother and I were standing on my front porch watching the guests arrive when suddenly she noticed a man waltzing around in my vegetable garden. Now there were speakers out in the yard playing everything from Glenn Miller to Simon and Garfunkel, but this man was obviously dancing to his *own* music.

Whenever my mother doesn't approve of something, the hairline above her forehead shoots back about an inch and a half. Just like it was doing right then.

"Who's that man?" she asked.

"What man?" I replied.

"That man right there," she said, trying not to point. "You know the one I'm talking about. The one that looks like he's *on* something."

"Oh, *him* . . ." I said. "That's Jack Clement. He's always on something."

"Is he stoned?"

"Probably."

"Well, I'll give him three years to live."

Naturally, first chance I got, I told Jack what Mother had said.

His immediate response was "Oh, Yeahhh . . . ?"

About thirty minutes later I looked out in the yard and couldn't believe my eyes. Jack and my mother were dancing together. And even more shocking . . . Mother seemed to be enjoying herself.

"That man is a remarkable dancer!" she later exclaimed as she stepped back up on the porch.

"But he's only got three years to live," I reminded her.

"I don't care. He's *still* a marvelous dancer."

Mother didn't know it, but Jack had once been a dance instructor at Arthur Murray studios. Probably the only ex-marine to hold that distinction. Kristofferson may have had Jack in mind when he wrote, "He's a walking contradiction, partly truth and partly fiction."

One night, while I was on break at the Jolly Ox, Jack invited me to drop by his "Cowboy Arms Hotel and Recording Spa" after the gig to take some acid. Since I'd never done *that* before, I, of course, accepted. We ended up laughing ourselves silly until dawn. First, we watched *Dr. Strangelove* and *Deep Throat* as they ran *backward* through Jack's video machine. Now I'd never seen an adult film run *forward* through a video machine so I really had no reference point. But I can tell you it was beyond bizarre and extremely funny. Things were coming out of things when they should've been going in, and going into things when they should have been coming out . . . and . . . well . . . anyway, we spent the rest of the night composing a letter to President Nixon explaining why Jack should produce an album of him playing the piano since he'd had so much success with that *other* piano player, Jerry Lee Lewis.

Now, where was I? Okay. So I met Joy Wahl one night at the Jolly Ox lounge. She was a writer for one of the big ad agencies in town and I used to enjoy talking with her between sets. She had a big, friendly smile and was one of the brightest and funniest women I'd ever been around. Three years later, when I showed up at her doorstep with my toothbrush and batch of unfinished songs, Joy had quit the agency and was working freelance. I had just blown back into town after breaking up with a guy in Boston, so we were both at loose ends with a lot of free time on our hands, which can be a dangerous thing.

Joy wasn't musical. In fact, she was tone-deaf. But after she showed me a poem she'd written called "The Thunderbird Man," I knew she was for real. So we started writing together. At first, Joy helped me finish and fine-tune some of my songs, then we started writing from scratch. We kept on writing—both together and separately—until one day we decided we had enough songs to start our own publishing company. So we called BMI to find out what to do.

BMI sent us a form. On it, we had to list five possible names for our company. We were surprised when only one cleared—Enoree. I later learned that each submitted name has to clear a global file containing over a million registered company names. Anyway, that's how our company became known as Enoree Music.

Enoree, as you may recall, is the name of the cotton mill town where I lived as a child. It is also the name of the river that runs through the town. I once fell into Two Mile Creek near where it joins the Enoree River. My sister Mary saw me floating by and managed to pull me out. We both had on our winter coats and trudged home shivering and scared, only to get a spanking for leaving the yard.

Enoree is a Cherokee word meaning "land of the muscadine." I don't know why Joy and I ever considered it for the name of our publishing company. Maybe it represented the place where you come from, and the river that hopefully might carry you some place else. Some place big as the ocean. And if you could get there without drowning, so much the better.

The day the BMI forms came in the mail, I went out and bought some ribbon for Joy's typewriter. After that, we decided to call it a day. At least as far as *business* was concerned. We aimed to set a precedent that day. We didn't want the business part to overtake the writing. By the way, I recently called Joy to verify some facts I thought I might want to use in this chapter, and she happened to mention that I never paid her, nor offered to pay her, any rent for the nine months I crashed at her house. I was appalled to learn this and know that it was true. In all fairness, she said that in those days, she never once thought to ask me to pay any rent, and my mind-set was that it

was only a matter of time before I'd be as big as Elvis and would then reno-
vate Joy's twelve hundred square feet into Graceland. Anyway, we came up
with a figure and I mailed her a check. I may not call anybody else. Billy Joe
Shaver once wrote, "I'll die 'fore I live it all down." Hell, I could go *broke* trying to live all my shit down. Cleaning up your past can be expensive.

"Running Out in the Night" was inspired by two running-out-in-the-
night experiences. One happened leaving Boston on Christmas Eve 1975;
the other, leaving a cabin somewhere in the middle of West Tennessee in
late summer 1976.

After the wrecking ball came to my beloved condemned Nashville neighborhood in the spring of 1975, I was lost for a while. The apartment I
moved into after Dudley Avenue felt cold. On top of that I was involved in
an affair that was fast going nowhere. I was just beginning to write songs
and to pick up some out-of-town bookings in places like The Last Resort in
Athens, Georgia, and The Hub Pub Club in Banner Elk, North Carolina.
But I didn't like being on the road by myself and, without a record deal,
there really wasn't a reason to be out there. It was a confusing time. I even
got a letter from a family friend who said I should move back to Spartanburg and help my father run the mills. Once during a brief visit to Spartanburg, my father sat me down and told me I should come on back home. We
were sitting at the kitchen table with the dishwasher running its cycles in
the background. After a long silence, he looked right at me and said,
"Honey, you told me you were going to give this Nashville thing two years.
Well, it's been over two years now and it's time you came on back home." It
broke my heart to hear him say that. I may have been at loose ends, but one
thing I knew for sure: Better to be lost in Nashville not knowing what would
happen next, than to be lost in Spartanburg knowing *nothing* would happen
next.

By the end of that summer, I decided I was having a nervous breakdown.
So I scooped up my puppy, Victrola Irene, and together we fled Nashville for
the beach.

Victrola Irene was a short-haired mutt—white with black spots—that I'd found one morning out by my garbage can. She was sitting there looking at me with her head cocked to one side just like Nipper—the dog on the RCA Records logo. She was a cute little puppy and I was crazy about her, but the first time she went into heat, she ran away and I never saw her again. Anyway, we took off in "Whitetrash," a 1961 white Ford Galaxie that I'd bought from a Church of Christ friend of Mrs. Chrisman's for two hundred dollars. I drove that car for five years.

Remembering something a friend of my mother's had said years before ("Marsh, it's *impossible* to have a nervous breakdown at Pawley's Island."), I pushed Whitetrash to the limit, hoping to reach Pawley's Island before one of us broke down. I remember growing up, how my mother and her friends were always on the verge of having nervous breakdowns: *If you children don't stop making that noise, I'm gonna have a nervous breakdown!* I have often wondered and still do: exactly how does one *diagnose* a nervous breakdown? Does the doctor take a smear of your nerves, view them under a microscope, then say, "Yep, they're broken all right. Why, in all my twenty-some odd years of practice, I have *never* seen such shot nerves!"

Pawley's Island is a barrier island along the South Carolina coast between Georgetown and Myrtle Beach. It's also one of the oldest summer resorts on the Eastern seaboard. Nearby rice planters built the first beach cottages there in the early 1700s. Families of plantation owners used to stay there from spring until early fall to escape mosquitoes and the threat of malaria. The island is about four miles long and completely surrounded by saltwater. The south end is so narrow that at high tide, you can fish from either end of your house, from the Atlantic out front or from the marsh creek out back that separates the island from the mainland. At low tide, an aroma arises from the salt marsh that smells like good sex in the tropics. Sometimes, when the wind blows up from Georgetown, you can smell the paper mill. Most people find this smell offensive, but I love it. My brain has associated that smell with the pleasures of Pawley's for so long that it no longer acknowledges any negative signals from my olfactory nerves regarding the stench that arises during the sulfate process whereby wood is turned into pulp before being made into paper.

Once, in 1982, I was riding with my band, The Road Scholars, along the

King's Highway between gigs in Charleston and Myrtle Beach. As we crossed the big bridge that spans the Intracoastal Waterway outside George-town, one of the guys rolled down a window so he could catch a breath of fresh salt air. But there was no breeze off the ocean that day. The wind was coming from the mainland, which included the nearby paper mill. Immedi-ately, there were sputters of protest from the guys. The sulfurous stench was so bad that our sax player, Rock Williams, was awakened from a deep sleep in the back of the van. "What in the hell is that funky smell?" he called out in his soft, deep, Barry White voice.

"It's God breathing," I replied.

Rock rolled his eyes at me like he was questioning my sanity. It was a look I had seen many times.

Pawley's Island has managed to resist the commercialization that's crept into just about every other vacation spot along the East Coast. In fact, Pawley's prides itself on resisting change at every turn. Many houses still have no air-conditioning or carpeting. Instead, they have screened-in porches and gabled windows designed to catch the ocean breeze. A popu-lar bumper sticker reads: ARROGANTLY SHABBY. That pretty much sums up Pawley's.

Snug Harbor is one of the older houses on the island. It has large screened-in porches across the front and back with connecting walkways along both sides. The front porch is for sitting and the back for eating. The house belongs to the Harrelsons from Sumter, South Carolina. It's been in their family since it was built in the late 1800s. Hurricanes have loosened a few of its joints, but Snug Harbor still stands proud. I first visited there as a child in the 1950s. Since 1991, I've gone there for a reunion week with my summer camp buddies Monte Parsons and Lucy Harrelson DuPre along with Lucy's sister-in-law, Kim Harrelson. We call ourselves "The Lost Wives" and vacation under assumed names. I am "Lantana"; Lucy is "Garde-nia"; Monte, "Magnolia"; and Kim, "Alamanda." Basically, we sit around and tell stories and giggle a lot. Other than that, we cook, eat, read, take naps, and walk on the beach. One of our favorite activities is reading the police blotter from the weekly *Coastal Observer*. I read the following excerpt aloud to Kim over sandwiches in a local food store/eatery, causing an eavesdropping employee to fall into a pyramid of canned goods he'd been carefully stacking:

A South Waccamaw Drive man said he was threatened by a man with a large pot belly who was fishing from his private dock. When the resident's wife asked the man to leave, he told her to "get her rich ass back in the house and shut up," according to the report. The husband then told the man to leave. "You aren't man enough to make me and if you try I'll kick your ass," the angler replied.

Journalism at its finest.

But back to 1975. Though my psyche was shattered, Whitetrash, Victrola Irene, and I managed to arrive all in one piece as we pulled into the oyster-shell drive behind Snug Harbor. To this day, Mrs. Harrelson gives me a lot of flack for showing up at their house with a dog.

"That's just not done, Maah-shul. I know your mama raised you better than that."

And she loves to tease me about my so-called "nervous breakdown." But after a week of rest and relaxation and home-cooked meals prepared by Mamie, the Harrelson's longtime cook, I was restored enough to feel restless again. So I telephoned a musician friend from my Vanderbilt days.

CW—not his real name—had married and had two babies while we were still students. After graduation, he'd moved his family to Boston so he could work on getting his doctorate at M.I.T. Anyway, as we talked, I could tell CW was upset. Turns out, his wife had recently left him, taking their two children back to Nashville, where she was now filing for divorce. I can't remember what all was said, but by the end of the conversation, it was somehow decided that I would go to Boston.

Once there, I moved into CW's tenement apartment which looked like something right out of *West Side Story*. There were clothes hanging out on the fire escapes, people sitting in open windows, children throwing bottles in the alley, the late-night sounds of couples arguing or making love. It was all exotic to me. I'll have to hand it to CW. He could live off practically nothing better than anyone I've ever known. Soon I was introduced to some new grocery items like powdered milk and powdered eggs. Neither one of us had a dime. The only thing I had besides my suitcase and guitar was an LP of Big Joe Turner's greatest hits. While CW was working on his doctorate at M.I.T., I'd be dancing around the apartment to "TV Mama," "Flip Flop and Fly," and "Boogie Woogie Country Girl." Once, a man from CW's church came by to talk to me. He had creepy eyes that never blinked. I felt like I would suffocate if I looked directly at them. When he asked me if I knew how much Jesus loved me, I told him that that was none of his business and I would appreciate it very much if he'd get his Jesus-loving ass out of my kitchen. I didn't know much then, but I knew I didn't need no middleman with creepy eyes getting between me and my Jesus!

I loved that tenement apartment, but CW thought we should live somewhere "nicer," so we moved across the Charles River into a downstairs apartment at 77 Prentiss Street in Cambridge, near Somerville. We could afford the higher rent, thanks to extra income earned playing music on the sidewalks of Harvard Square.

CW was a gifted musician. He could play guitar, harmonica, fiddle . . . just anything he set his mind to play. We had played a lot together while students at Vanderbilt. Sometimes on a weekend night, I'd call CW from some fraternity party—usually after my date had passed out—and we'd hitchhike, with our instruments, down West End Avenue to lower Broadway and the backdoor of the Ryman. CW had grown up knowing a lot of the Opry regulars, so we often ended up in Roy Acuff's dressing room, where CW and Mr. Acuff would swap out on old-time fiddle tunes while Charlie Collins and I played along.

By the time CW and I arrived at Harvard Square, we had us a good little repertoire going. I'd back him on my old Martin guitar while he fiddled "Devil's Dream" and "Sally Goodin," then he'd back me while I sang "Your Cheatin' Heart" and "I'm So Lonesome I Could Cry." We were a big hit on the street. Everybody else was singing Tom Paxton and Arlo Guthrie. We were the only ones singing country. They didn't know what to make of these two exotic bumpkins from Tennessee.

Every Friday and Saturday night, we'd find us a good spot on the sidewalk near the Harvard Co-op, then take out our instruments and start playing. People would stop and listen, pitching quarters, sometimes dollar bills into our open cases before moving on. As soon as we had fifty dollars or so, we'd close shop and walk to a nearby restaurant where we'd order up a nice dinner with a bottle of wine. Yes, there were a few happy moments during my stay in Boston, but my two most *vivid* memories stem from two horrible fights. One occurred the night CW and I crashed the gate at Fenway Park to see the sixth game of the World Series. The other happened two months later on Christmas Eve—the night I left CW and Boston for good.

Looking back on my Boston experience, I can see now that I went there to hide from myself. I was in the last throes of being torn between what I thought my family expected of me—i.e., settle down and get married—and my own particular destiny. Another factor was my father's deteriorating health. In late September, he'd had a quadruple bypass operation at New York's Presbyterian Hospital. CW and I had taken the train down from Boston to be there with my family. But as soon as they carted my father away for the surgery, we bolted the hospital vigil for the nearest subway station. We'd brought along our musical instruments in case we needed some quick cash to cover travel expenses. I thought we were going to Washington Square, but CW laughed and said, "Let's go where the money is!" So we rode the A-train all the way down to Wall Street. There we set up shop just below the statue of George Washington in front of the New York Stock Exchange.

Most New York street musicians play music in parks or along broad sidewalks where there are lots of tourists. Check me if I'm wrong, but I believe we may have been the first street musicians to ever play Wall Street. Needless to say, the cops didn't know what to make of us. Maybe our audacity took them by surprise. For whatever reason, they left us alone. After a few songs, all I had to do was look over at my open guitar case to know I was no longer in Boston. No quarters here. Only bills. Lotsa bills. Big bills. One older, pin-striped gentleman stopped to listen while I played "A Woman's Heart (Is a Handy Place to Be)." As I sang the last line "I just wish the heart that's broken now was not a part of me" (not missing the irony of my father's current situation), the pin-striped gentleman pulled a folded handkerchief from his pocket and started dabbing at his eyes.

"I've been coming down here for over forty years," he said. "And this is the most beautiful thing that has ever happened." With that, he pulled out a twenty and dropped it in the kitty.

. . .

Don't ask me why, but shortly after my father's open-heart surgery CW and I decided to tell our families that we were getting married. Hell, we weren't even in *love* with each other. I was thinking it was a good compromise between what I thought my family wanted for me and what I thought I wanted for myself. They would like the fact that CW was well educated, and I'd have a friend to play music with. For some reason, this "engagement" put a lot of pressure on a once easy friendship and we started having these little quarrels. Nothing serious really. At least for a while.

By mid-October, it was getting too cold to play music on the street. But looming on the horizon was something that, for the next couple of weeks, would distract us from seeing just how unsuited we were for each other. As fiancées, anyway. The Boston Red Sox were making a run for the 1975 World Series.

CW spent most of his days at M.I.T. working on his dissertation. Other than typing it, my sole contribution was to insert a line from a Waylon Jennings song for the quote after the title page: "I don't think Hank done it this a-way." I spent most days just walking around our neighborhood before busying myself with dinner preparations, totally unaware of how depressed I was becoming. Pretty soon, the only thing I looked forward to was World Series game days. I was alive with anticipation on those days. We'd sit down for dinner at a little table in our little kitchen with a little black-and-white TV sitting there like a fascinating dinner guest. All our attention was focused on the screen. The Red Sox players—Fred Lynn, Denny Doyle, Yaz, Luis Tiant, Dwight Evans—became the most important people on the planet to us. We watched them sweep Oakland for the American League title, then play the first five games of the World Series against Cincinnati's Big Red Machine. And by the end of each game, we usually had finished off a big green bottle of Gallo wine.

Then came game six: October 21, 1975. It was supposed to have been played on October 18, but there'd been a three-day rain delay. I'd been cooped up in our little apartment during this New England drenching, so by game day, I had me a high-running cabin fever to go along with the pennant fever that was sweeping the city.

That evening, as CW and I sat down in front of the TV, the feeling that this would be no "as usual" World Series game began to fill the air. As the game progressed and got more exciting, and as the Gallo continued to flow, somebody—I can't remember who—suddenly blurted, "Let's go over there.

Let's go to Fenway Park right now. Maybe somebody'll let us in!" We stared at each other for a second, then jumped up and started throwing on our jackets. I turned off the TV, grabbed the half-gallon of Gallo, and just like that, we were out the door. We roared off into the night in CW's truck, the play-by-play blaring from the radio. As we drove across the Charles River, it seemed like we were breaking a curfew. There wasn't another moving car in sight. Every soul with a heartbeat was watching the game that night in Boston.

As soon as we saw the lights above Fenway, we pulled over to park. Then we half-walked, half-ran the rest of the way. There were people milling around everywhere. The air was so charged it felt like we'd all blow up if anybody struck a match. We kept walking around just outside the gates, asking people left and right "How do we get in?" "How do we get in?" Then this guy comes up and says, "Quick, follow me! Through the laundry!" So we follow this guy. He must've worked there and had a key or something. Next thing I know, we are walking fast through a big warehouse-type laundry room to a ladder going up through a manhole-sized opening in the ceiling. As we climbed up the ladder we heard "Look out! . . . on the roof . . . there's acid!" Evidently, the flat roof of the laundry had been sprayed with some kind of acid to keep out gate-crashers. I was wearing a brand-new goose down vest and as soon as I crawled out, I looked down and noticed the nylon fabric disintegrating. There were goose down feathers flying everywhere. But I didn't care. We were okay so far and so was our jug of wine. I still had it hooked in my right index finger. Carrying it while climbing that ladder had been no mean feat.

Next, we scurried across the roof to a telephone-like pole with an attached metal ladder running up the side. A few guys were already making their way up, but it was slow going. The entire pole and ladder had been wrapped in strands of barbed wire. I glanced up and saw what looked like the back of a huge billboard. A guy pointed to the pole saying "Up there!" With no idea what might be "up there," CW and I started making our way up through this barrier, lifting strands of barbed wire as we went. CW had chivalrously insisted that I go first. That way, he said, he could catch me if I fell. I had no intention of falling, but I went ahead anyway. I climbed the first couple of rungs, then held the barbed wire out for CW to pass up the Gallo. It was slow going. Occasionally, we'd hear the sharp crack of a bat hitting the ball, followed by the deafening roar of the crowd. But the buzz of excitement was constant. It all sounded so close, but we couldn't see anything. I felt like Jonah in the whale.

Finally, I reached the last rung and the end of the barbed wire. I then crawled out onto a narrow, fire escape–type platform. I was groping around in the dark, trying to figure out how to stand without falling back down to the roof. Finally, a hand grabbed my hand and helped me up to where I could grasp the top of the billboard and pull myself up the rest of the way. As my head rose above my hands, I was immediately blinded by brightness. Too much light and too much beauty. As my eyes adjusted . . . to the lights, to the manicured green grass, to more lights, to the crowd, to the pitcher's mound rising from the perfect diamond of baselines, to the graceful athletes in their uniforms . . . the excitement, the Green Monster to my right . . . it was all there. Tears began to well up in my eyes. Then I became calm. Maybe it was predestination, but I was *there,* by God.

Boston had been ahead 3–0 when we'd left our TV set. Now it was 3–3. Tiant was still on the mound, but Cincinnati was starting to rough him up. Now, I'd like to tell you, like millions of baseball fans have since, that I saw Carlton Fisk hit his now infamous home run to win the game for Boston in the bottom of the twelfth, but I'd be lying. I did see Cincinnati score two in the seventh and one in the eighth to go ahead 6–3. And I saw Bernie Carbo pinch-hit a home run into the center-field bleachers with two on and two out in the bottom of the eighth to tie the game at 6–6. The last great play I saw happened right under us. In the top of the eleventh, Dwight Evans made a leaping one-handed catch of a Joe Morgan drive, leaning back into the crowd just below our perch. He was so close I could see the whites of his eyes. Then I felt something tapping on my leg. I ignored it for a while until the tapping started feeling like somebody trying to *hit* my leg. When I looked down, I looked right into the eyes of a Boston policeman holding a billy club. Beyond him, gathered on the roof of the laundry, stood about twenty more policemen, looking like a lynch mob. Their necks were craned back as they all looked up at us and, oh god, were they mad. There were no whites in their eyes. Just squinted rage.

The strange thing is I wasn't nearly as scared as I should have been. I was too busy checking out the whole scenario, which reeked of racism. A nasty, big-city kind of racism. Up until that moment, I had only been exposed to the genteel type back in the South I grew up in. Oh, we had our share of the nasty, violent kind, but I'd only heard about it. This was right in my face.

What was interesting was that the only policeman who didn't look like he wanted to kill me was the one who'd been made to climb the barbed wire–wrapped pole and was now tapping me on the leg. He was also the only policeman with black skin. When I looked down into his eyes, I didn't see hate. I saw embarrassment. I could hear the white mob below yelling "Hit him! Damn it, nigger, hit him!" It was obvious they thought I was a man . . . and this rookie policeman was something less than that. The strangeness of the situation caused an immediate feeling of kinship between me and this black man. On some level, we both knew that he was my brother and I was his sister. "You don't have to hit me anymore," I said. "I'm coming down."

Now there had been about twelve of us up there. I was the only woman and the last to come down. As I made my descent, I could hear the cops cursing and beating on the others. Man, it sounded like they were cracking some skulls with those nightsticks. The minute my feet touched the roof, one of them grabbed me and started getting rough. I immediately ripped open what was left of my goose down vest, stuck out my chest as far as I could, then, cupping my breasts in my two hands, lifting them, I began to yell at the top of my lungs "I AM A WOMAN! THESE ARE MY BOS-OMS! DO, NOT, HIT, ME!!" It worked. They backed off. But the cursing continued: "You fucking bitch! What were you doing up there? Why aren't you home doing the dishes?"

The funny thing is: I don't remember CW at all coming down off that platform. I don't remember him during the confrontation with the police. I don't remember him going back down through the laundry. He may have been there trying to help me, I don't know. I was so focused in on my own survival that there was no peripheral vision left to include him. But I remember him once we were back on the street.

I don't know how long the pain had been there before I became aware of it, but as soon as I was aware of it, I tried jerking away. But that only made things worse. It was my arm. Something was clamped down on my arm like a vise. Finally, I looked over and there was CW with the craziest look in his eyes I'd ever seen on a human in real life. He had me by the arm so tightly I thought it would break. He was half-pulling, half-dragging me along like a caveman dragging his woman back to the cave.

Now I have *never* liked for *anybody* to hold on to me in a moving crowd. It messes with my stride. When I was a little girl, my great uncle T.B. used to take me to basketball games at Wofford College in Spartanburg. After the game, we'd be exiting the field house with the crowd, and Uncle T.B. would be holding on to my upper arm. I'd try to jerk away, but he'd just hold on tighter. It used to piss me off. When Mother later asked "How was the ballgame, honey?" I said it was okay . . . but I sure wish Uncle T.B. wouldn't hold on to my arm so much walking back to the car. "Oh, but honey, that's what gentlemen are *supposed* to do with ladies in a crowd." I made a mental note right then to add "Can't walk good" to a list that was fast growing in my mind under Reasons I Will Never Be a Lady.

"Stop it! You're hurting me!" I yelled and started striking at CW with my free arm. Then suddenly, both arms were free and I blindly started running. I stopped only once to look back and saw that four or five street thugs had CW down on the sidewalk. A couple of them were beating and kicking him, but I didn't care and turned away. I was free and nothing else mattered. It felt so good to be walking and breathing again in my natural stride with both arms swinging. I could feel the pain and swelling in my right arm, but so what? *Just keep walking, girl!* About that time I became aware of a jingling in my pockets. *Oh my God, the keys. Oh shit! I've got the keys to CW's truck. Now all I have to do is find it.* I vaguely remembered us parking on an embankment beyond the big red blinking Cisco sign. Within a few minutes, I walked straight to it. Now *where are you gonna go? The apartment? No way! South Carolina? Been there. Nashville? Nothing to go back to.* As I turned the key to start the truck, the radio came on full blast with the game still going. It was the bottom of the twelfth with the score still tied. I started driving. Just driving down streets with no names. Carlton Fisk was stepping into the batter's box. *Come on, Pudge! Hit one outta the damn ballpark!* And that's exactly what he did in one of the most dramatic moments in baseball history.

After that, I drove around for a while watching the city celebrate the amazing victory. People were screaming and honking their horns. There was unbridled joy in Beantown that night. But not for me. For I knew there was music I would have to face before the night was through. And it was playing in a minor key.

. . .

When I got back to our apartment, there was a trail of blood across the porch leading to the front door. Then I noticed the window next to the door broken with more blood on the remaining shards of glass. Reluctantly, I opened the door and went in. CW was lying facedown on the bed moaning in pain. He wanted to kill me but he didn't. I should have packed up my things and left but I didn't. I stayed for two more months, trying to act like the perfect wife. But things would never again be the same.

That Christmas Eve we started quarreling about something, I can't remember what. I just remember that it was snowing like crazy outside. As the tension mounted, I decided to walk around the block so I could get a breath of fresh air. But as soon as I stepped outside, CW started following me. So I started running. Then he started running. I was running for my life right down the middle of Massachusetts Avenue. I'd never seen so much snow.

I'd gotten off to a pretty good start but CW was beginning to close the gap. Then I saw a police car up ahead and I started waving my arms. "Stop! Don't let him get me! He's crazy!" I yelled. By the time I got to the car, CW was close enough to reach out and grab me. But not before I jumped into the backseat, where I found myself seated next to a German shepherd police dog. The dog just looked at me like "Who are you?" Then the policeman ordered me out.

"Okay, but do not let him touch me!" I yelled, referring to CW, not the dog.

"Fine, lady, but ya gotta get outta there! The dog's trained to kill."

The dog seemed fine to me. Probably the sanest one in the bunch.

It didn't take long for the policeman to suss out the situation. CW was in a foaming-at-the-mouth rage, so the policeman let me slip safely into the passenger side of his car. I could see CW ranting and raving just outside the driver's side window. But he might as well have been standing on the moon. I knew I was out of there.

"Could you take me to Logan Airport?" I asked.

"Nah, it's outta my jurisdiction. I'll take you to the nearest hospital."

I didn't have a dime on me. But luckily I had my checkbook. At the hospital, one of the intake personnel agreed to call me a cab.

. . .

"Where to?" asked the driver.

"Logan International Airport," I replied. I waited until we got there to let him know I was paying with a personal check.

"It's good," I said, looking him straight in the eye.

He shrugged. "Merry Christmas, lady. I hope you get wherever you're going."

I stepped into the terminal and it was a mess. People were everywhere, some sleeping on the floor. Flights were being cancelled left and right. The snowstorm had been upgraded to a full-blown blizzard, which meant no more planes coming in. Finally, I found a flight to Charlotte, North Carolina, and got on standby. I wrote my last check.

As soon as we were airborne, the pilot came on announcing that the airport was now completely shut down. We were the last flight to take off. I settled back in my seat and began to relax. I was going home for Christmas, by god. The only place I knew where they'd have to take me in: Spartanburg, South Carolina.

Spartanburg is about an hour's drive from the Charlotte airport. As it turned out, the man seated next to me was going there too and ended up giving me a ride. At one point he asked, "What's your name?"

"Eudora Welty," I replied.

"That's a pretty unusual name," he said.

Once in Spartanburg, I had him drop me off about five blocks from my parents' house. Besides not wanting him to know who I was, I just plain wanted to walk. It was probably forty degrees out, but it felt downright balmy compared to what I'd just left behind.

When I got to 847 Glendalyn, I stood in the front yard for a while looking in the living room window. I could see my father sitting in a chair by a crackling fire in the fireplace. Nobody in the world knew where I was in that moment and it felt good. Then I stepped up to the door, opened it, and walked on in the house. Mother was the first person I saw. She took one look at me and said, "You look like you could use a drink."

The other "Running Out in the Night" episode happened the following summer in Nashville. I was waiting tables at a club called Mississippi Whiskers that served great Mexican food. One day they fired me for playing pinball when I should have been paying attention to the customers. "You can come back if you bring your guitar," they said. "We could use some good entertainment. What we don't need is a bad waitress." That was my last waitress gig. After that, it was always music.

I put together a group called The Lost Love Band. We even had background singers. Marcia Routh and Pebble Daniel sang with me when they weren't on the road with Delbert McClinton and Jimmy Buffett. With this band, I was mostly performing songs I had written. Pretty soon we were drawing the songwriter crowd: Waylon and Jessi, Guy and Susanna Clark, "Cowboy" Jack Clement, Bobby and Jeanie Bare, Captain Midnight, and Tompall Glaser were among the regulars. By the end of the summer, some folks from CBS Records started showing up. Next thing I know, I'm doing a photo shoot and interview for the cover story in *Hank,* Nashville's first underground music magazine.

I was starting to attract a lot of attention. It was pretty heady stuff and I was not prepared. It got so I couldn't eat breakfast in the morning without having these gagging spells. So I went to a Nashville psychiatrist who wouldn't talk to me but gave me a prescription for Thorazine. That night, Joy Wahl and I each took one just to see what would happen, and the answer is . . . nothing! We just sat on either end of the sofa in her living room staring at each other like idiots for twenty-four hours. Granted, I didn't *gag* in those twenty-four hours, but that's only because I would have been *doing* something. The only thing you can do on Thorazine is sit and stare. I only took Thorazine one other time and that was the night Billy Sherrill came to hear me at Mississippi Whiskers.

Everybody knew who Billy Sherrill was because he had pretty much single-handedly invented the "Nashville Sound," producing hit after hit for artists like George Jones, Tammy Wynette, and Charlie Rich. He was "the man" at CBS Records in Nashville. There were others there like Bonnie Garner and Ron Bledsoe, whose musical tastes included some of the newer acts like David Allan Coe and Willie Nelson. This new music was labeled "outlaw" by some, "progressive" by others. Bonnie and Ron wanted to sign me to the label, but Sherrill had to okay it.

Since I'd never auditioned for a major record label before, I was extremely nervous. Therefore, taking a Thorazine seemed like the natural thing to do. So I did. Then about thirty minutes before I was supposed to be on stage, I began to have a *strong urge* to go take a nap in the backseat of Whitetrash. All I remember after that is someone trying to: (1) make me drink coffee and (2) walk. I found both of these things very hard to do. No, I don't remember being on stage that night, but it didn't matter. I was offered a five-album deal with CBS Records. Gidget goes to Nashville and gets a record deal. I didn't even know what headphones were.

That same summer, I'd started running with this wild songwriter who'd had a few songs cut by Johnny Cash among others. He was exotic-looking, with long, black, shiny hair and high cheekbones. He looked like an Indian prince to me. I never knew what he was gonna do or say next, so I started hanging out with him. One night he told me he wanted to introduce me to his mother. Turns out Mom lived in a cabin out in the middle of some woods off Highway 70 about a hundred and ten miles west of Nashville. She couldn't have been all that thrilled to see us pulling into her drive at one o'clock in the morning either.

Back then, there was a well-known physician in Nashville named Dr. Rippy who prescribed these little white pills for truckers and road musicians so they could stay alert driving those long distances. "White Crosses" they were called. They'd keep you awake, all right. And you didn't have to be a trucker or a road musician either. It wasn't long before writers were flying in from New York to get them. And any songwriter worth a grain of salt stayed high on them most of the time. As Billy Joe Shaver said recently, "Hell, come to think of it, we *were* writing a lot of up-tempo songs back then." Dr. Rippy wasn't seen as a criminal. "Savior" would be more like it. And he probably fell asleep every night with a smile on his face just thinking about all the lives he was saving keeping those hard-working truckers and musicians from falling asleep behind the wheel. Soon the songwriters started getting the pills from the road musicians and, well, the songwriters didn't *have* to drive anywhere, so they'd just stay up for four or five days, driving the alleys of Nashville, grinding their teeth and churning out those up-tempo songs.

I never did like taking speed. And I sure as hell didn't need anything revving me up. Once at Vanderbilt, I took a Dexedrine to keep me awake so I could study for a French exam. I was supposed to have read an entire anthology of French poetry but hadn't looked at a page until the night before. I figured it'd take all night to read all those poems, so I took the pill, a gift from one of my classmates. The first poem I read was by a guy named Alphonse de Lamartine. It was all about these swans taking off from the surface of a lake, the reflection of the sun on their wings, and so on. It was by far the most beautiful poem I had ever read in my entire life, including the ones in English. It was so magnificent, I couldn't stop reading it. It was like I had found the key that unlocked all the secrets of the universe. It wasn't a long poem, but it was so profound that I felt compelled to read it . . . over and over again. And each time I read it, more was revealed until . . . until I realized the sun had been up for hours and I had fifteen minutes to make it to class.

The test had ten questions. To my great relief, one of them had to do with Lamartine. So I opened my bluebook and began to write. Oh, I wrote about the swans and how they symbolized humanity's struggle to reach God, stuff like that. All the revelations from the night before poured out onto the paper. I was still writing when Monsieur Poggenberg said, "Time's up!" A week later, we got our test papers back. My grade was A+/F with the inscription "See me after class."

About ten years later, I took my only other hit of speed. Preludin, I believe it was called. All it did was make me want to clean my apartment to the point of ironing my underwear. So speed was never my thing. But it seemed like every boyfriend I had from 1976 to 1985 was into it big time. It's a good thing I never shared an apartment with any of these guys or I'd have died from sleep deprivation. It was fun to run with them when I had the energy, but I'd have to retreat to Joy's house, or later, to my own apartment, where I could sleep and eat some real *food* for chrissakes! The only thing these guys ever seemed to eat was Twinkies.

Anyway, after I met the Indian prince's mother, it became apparent we weren't spending the night in her house but in a little cabin out back. The minute we entered that cabin, I knew I didn't want to be there. The prince had begun a nonstop dialogue with himself that was becoming increasingly nonsensical. I sat down in a chair, trying to look calm while my heart pounded and I tried to breathe. It wasn't until twelve years later at a treatment center out in the middle of an Arizona desert that I would learn about the four primary human emotions and how to recognize them. "And how do you feel?" they were always asking me. I knew the correct answer was either "happy," "afraid," "sad," or "angry" or some combination thereof. Sometimes I'd answer "frustrated" or "uncomfortable." Then the therapist would continue in a soft and patient voice, "And what's underneath the frustration?" or "What's underneath the discomfort?" Finally I'd surrender and say "anger?" or "fear?"

Having grown up in a household where those two emotions were implicitly unacceptable—especially anger, which was out of the question as it was too unladylike—I often punctuated my answers with a question mark. The therapist would remain silent until I could say the words with more conviction. Treatment was all about learning a new language to describe your emotions. But first, you had to acknowledge them. Too bad there wasn't an Emotions 101 course at Vanderbilt to teach me all this. It sure would have saved me a lot of heartbreak, not to mention all the money it cost to go to treatment.

There were clever sayings for everything out there. If you answered "How do you feel?" with "Fine," they'd come back with "You know what FINE stands for, don't you?" Even if you didn't want to know they'd tell you anyway: "Fucked up, Insecure, Neurotic, and Evasive."

"You know what FEAR stands for, don't you?"

"False Evidence Appearing Real" or "Fuck Everything And Run!"

Sitting in that cabin that night out in the middle of West Tennessee, I may not have been aware that fear was what I was feeling. But as soon as the prince closed his eyes, I knew it was time to fuck everything and run. So I opened the door and began walking blindly out into the pitch-black darkness of the woods. There were no keys in my pocket this time so I kept on walking. There was no path, no moon, nothing. Just trees and leaves and sticks and the occasional briar bush. I was feeling my way along and every now and then I'd catch a spider web in the face. That gave me the willies.

Soon my ears began picking up the faint sound of a truck whining by in the far-off distance. So I started walking toward the sound. Every now and then I'd stop and stand in complete silence until I'd hear another one, then I'd continue on walking. The later it got, however, the longer I'd have to wait to hear the sound. Finally, I gave up and just started walking on faith for I don't know how long. Two hours, maybe three, I don't know. Then, exhausted, I stumbled into a ditch. I wanted to lie down and rest but the thought of snakes gave me all the adrenaline I needed to scurry up the embankment on the other side. There I discovered a two-lane blacktop road. Oh, the joy to be walking on pavement! Now the only question was which way to Nashville?

It wasn't long before the faint light of early dawn began infiltrating the darkness. But it was still too early, and there were too many trees to tell the direction of the rising sun. So I kept on walking. There were no cars, no trucks . . . nothing. Then I saw a farmer driving out of the woods just down the road. I began running, waving my arms. As he turned away from me onto the highway I yelled as loud as I could, "HEY!" His head jerked around and I could see he was an old man. A startled old man. He reached out to lock his door, then began pulling away. "YOU DON'T HAVE TO GIVE ME A RIDE! JUST TELL ME WHICH WAY NASHVILLE IS!" I shouted. The old man stopped again, then rolled his window down a few inches. I took a few steps toward him, then stopped at a respectful distance. "Just tell me if I'm walking in the right direction, sir. I'm trying to get to Nashville." He studied me a few seconds then motioned his head toward farther down the road. "It's thataway." A small wave of relief swept over me. It felt good to learn I'd been walking all that time in the right direction.

"I'll take you as far as I'm a-goin' thataway," he added.

We rode in silence for twenty miles or so to a town called Camden. I'd only heard of Camden as the hometown of Dianne Davidson. Dianne was a big ol' girl with a big ol' voice who'd been a regular at the Exit/In during the early days. When the old man stopped at a feed store in town, I got out and said, "Thanks for the ride!"—cheerfully—like I'd been taught to say to car-pool mothers back in grade school.

I walked through Camden following the Highway 70 signs until I was east of town. There I kept on walking while holding out my thumb. Finally a car with duel exhaust pulled over. ZZ Top was blaring from the 8-track, so I jumped in. I was in luck. The driver was a construction worker on his way to a job in Nashville. After a while he started talking a little bit, mostly about the customized gearshift in his car. I could tell he was real proud of that car. The rest of the time we listened to ZZ Top, which was his favorite band. We stopped only once when he suddenly pulled over and opened his door so he could puke his brains out without messing up his car. I could tell he really loved that car. "You okay?" I asked. "I am now," he replied. Then he drove me on in to Nashville.

I got back to Joy's at about nine thirty that morning. She was in her kitchen smoking a Vantage and drinking a Tab when I walked in. Soon as she saw me she started grinning. Said the prince had called two hours before worried to death.

"What'd you tell him?" I asked.

"I told him there's only one person he should worry about and that's whoever gets between Marshall and wherever she's going."

"Mind if I crash?"

"Be my guest."

I slept most of the day. When I awakened, it was nearly dusk. I immediately sat up and began to write:

> *If you want me*
> *You've got to want to treat me right*
> *I know you love me*
> *But I'm tired of running out in the night*
>
> *Like the sand on the shore*
> *I can shift I can soar*
> *Away in a storm*
> *And I know . . .*
> *I know a big wave when I see one*
> *I don't mind getting my two feet wet, but I . . .*
> *I like to keep 'em on the ground*
> *Come on and rock me baby*
> *Don't you go knocking me down*
>
> *If you want me*
> *You've got to want to treat me right*
> *I know you love me*
> *But I'm tired of running out in the night*
>
> *I can rock, I can roll*
> *I can bathe in a mudhole*
> *And still smell like a rose*
> *And I know . . .*
> *I know an asshole when I see one*
> *You've got what it takes to turn me on*
> *But all we ever do is get you off*
> *Come on and roll me baby*
> *We'll break the law and never get caught*

. . .

On January 12, 1977, I played "Running Out in the Night" at a CBS showcase at The Old Time Pickin' Parlor down on Second Avenue in Nashville. The club was packed with industry, New York press, and other artists. Even my parents had flown in for the occasion.

"This is a song about oral sex," I announced from the stage.

My parents either didn't hear what I said or were so shocked they went into immediate denial. They never said a word about it. A few years later, Carlene Carter played a showcase at New York's Bottom Line. In the audience were her mother, June Carter, and stepfather, Johnny Cash. After one song she said, "Well, if that don't put the 'cunt' back in country, I don't know what does." June was visibly shaken, according to reports. When I heard about it, I was relieved to know there was another woman out there talking some trash. And I was also shocked. The c-word somehow never made it into my trash vocabulary.

Joy Wahl still has an eight-by-ten publicity shot of her and Roy Blount, Jr., and Tammy Wynette and Billy Sherrill from that night at the Pickin' Parlor. Roy was in town doing an article on "women in country" for *Esquire* magazine. In the picture, Joy is whispering something into Roy's ear.

One bright morning, later that winter, Joy would be jolted from a deep sleep by the ringing of her phone.

"Hello," she answered.

"This is *Esquire* magazine, please hold."

While on hold, only one question was able to materialize amongst the cobwebs in Joy's brain: *Did I forget to renew my subscription to* Esquire? Then the voice from New York was back.

"Are you Joy Wahl?"

"Yes, I am."

"Is 'Wahl' spelled W-A-H-L?"

"Yes, it is."

"Is oral sex against the law in the state of Tennessee?"

What . . . ? This last question caused a shot of adrenaline to rush into Joy's brain, obliterating the cobwebs. She was now on red alert. Everything she had said or done in the last few months began running like a high-speed videotape in her head. Then the tape did a freeze-frame on that moment in the photograph with Joy talking into Roy Blount's ear. And it was with horror that she remembered exactly what she had said.

Now I promised Joy I wouldn't repeat it here, so I'll paraphrase. While I was up onstage singing the second verse to "Running Out in the Night," Joy leaned in to Roy Blount and said (paraphrase), "Marshall Chapman is the only person in Nashville who can sing a song about oral sex and get away with it."

Joy can be tenacious when circumstances dictate. Don't ask me how, but she managed to make a few calls, including one to Roy, and sure enough, her comment was deleted from the final published edition, replaced with some lame comment about our publishing company. As a result, the ending came off a bit disjointed. Here's an excerpt from the article entitled "Country's Angels" (*Esquire*, March 1977):

Marshall Chapman looks like a cross between Lauren Bacall and Huckleberry Finn, and plays the electric guitar like it was a machine gun, and has a voice that manages to moan and at the same time notify everybody in the area to shape up quick. I heard her sing a song she wrote called *Running Out in the Night*:

> *I can rock*
> *I can roll*
> *I can bathe in a mudhole and still*
> *   smell like a rose*
> *And I know . . . I know an asshole*
> *   when I see one*
> *You've got what it takes to turn me on*
> *But all we ever do is get you off*
> *Come on and roll me baby*
> *We'll break the law and never get caught*

(Oral sex is illegal in Tennessee.) Marshall's friend Joy Wahl has already helped her form her own publishing company.

Before closing, I'd like to say one last thing to Joy: Joy, I told Nick Tosches what you *really* said that night. He said to tell you you're a pussy and that he plans to include your comment in *his* book.

"Running Out in the Night" didn't get recorded until my third album on Epic called *Marshall* (1979). They said it could be on the album if I would clean up the second verse. So I rewrote:

> *I can rock*
> *I can roll*
> *I can hit the road*
> *And stick out my thumb*
> *And I know . . .*
> *I know a good ride when I see one*
> *You've got what it takes to turn me on*
> *But all we ever do is get you off*
> *Come on and roll me baby*
> *We'll break the law and never get caught*

Turns out, the word *asshole* bothered them more than the oral sex reference in the last four lines. But that was understandable. For how could an A&R guy in New York be expected to know that *asshole* is a term of endearment? Unless, of course, he'd done time at the Cowboy Arms Hotel and Recording Spa?

By the time I got around to recording "Running Out in the Night," a major changing of the guard was taking place at CBS in New York. So I took it upon myself to go ahead and record the words the way I originally wrote them . . . "mudhole" and all. The record was released in the fall of 1979. That January, I was dropped from the label. For better or worse, I never did like for anybody to tell me what to do.

4

Why Can't I Be Like Other Girls?

Back in 1956 I was seven
And the second grade was going real slow
I could read, I could write but learning to be white
Was nothing that I needed to know
'Cause I'd seen Elvis Presley
I was running 'round singing the blues
And I remember the words my mama said
When I asked her for them blue suede shoes

She said to me:
Why can't you be like other girls?
(Let's hope it's just a phase she's going through)
Why can't you be like other girls?
Doing what we want you to
We could give you the world
If you would be like other girls

Turning twenty-one wasn't much fun
Up in Nashville, Tennessee
I was playing guitar down at the double-knit bar
And them cats was making eyes at me
"Say, hey-hey, little miss, sing one by Kris
And I'll help you make it through the night."
But I had written this song and when he couldn't sing along
I knew I had it coming all right

He said to me:
Why can't you be like other girls?
Settled down with a kid or two
Why can't you be like other girls?
Doin' what I ask you to
I could show you the world
If you would be like other girls

Yeah, they flew me up to New York City
I was ready to rock and roll
They wined me and they dined me
Then they signed me and put me on hold
And now the man up in the city . . .
Is talking to the man in L.A.
Who's calling me down here in Mobile, Alabama
Telling me to walk this way

Saying to me:
Why can't you be like other girls?
Sitting by the phone by the pool
Why can't you be like other girls?
Doin' what we tell you to
Why can't you be like other girls?
Do you want to make me look like a fool?
Why can't you be like other girls?
Whoever told you you could be you?
Why can't you be?
Why can't you be?
Why can't I be like other girls?

When two people get together and write a song, it's called co-writing. Any more than that and it's "gang-writing." Such was the case with "Why Can't I Be Like Other Girls?" There were three of us in on that session. It was me, Joy Wahl, and Dave Hickey. Dave Hickey was my boyfriend at the time. Dave and I ran hard together from 1976 until about 1980. I probably included this song here just so I could tell you a little bit about him. To tell everything would require the combined writing skills of Marcel Proust and

Charles Bukowski. Anyway, the song was written late one night with the three of us seated around Joy's dining room table.

As I recall, it was a loud session with lots of arguing and yelling. It'd be safe to say that pharmaceuticals were involved. At one point, Dave—in a Nikita-Khrushchev-at-the-UN-inspired gesture—came down *hard* on Joy's table with the back of his boot, which caused the heel to fly off and hit him in the head. "Marshall, you absolutely can *not* use the pluperfect in a song!" he exclaimed, emphasizing the word *not* with his boot.

Speaking of boots, this was 1977 Nashville, Tennessee, where every man in the manhood-obsessed country-music business was wearing cowboy boots. Every man but Dave, that is. Dave walked around in a pair of scruffy black high-heeled boots with zippers running up the sides. "Fruit boots"—that's what Joy called them. I called them "Beatle boots." The guys in the band would invariably break into the first few bars of "It's Been a Hard Day's Night" whenever Dave walked into rehearsal.

The first time my sister Dorothy saw Dave, he was standing in front of our grandmother's house at Three Oaks smoking a cigarette, his head cocked to one side, wearing a baseball cap, black jeans, black T-shirt, black shades, and, of course, the black high-heeled boots. The contrast between Dave and the setting made such an impression on her young psyche that months later she drew a quick sketch from memory, capturing him in a way no photograph ever has. Dorothy is now an accomplished artist living in Spartanburg. For years she worked in New York as the deputy art director for *Time* magazine. This early drawing is one of my most treasured possessions. It's signed "Hickey by Chapman." I call it "CBGB's Goes to Tara."

The drawing now hangs framed on a wall in my writing room next to an autographed picture of Robert Mitchum. Now that I think about it, had Robert Mitchum had a twin brother with a *bent* extra chromosome, he would have looked exactly like Dave.

Not long ago, a friend paused at the wall, studied it for a moment, then asked, "Who's the guy in the boots?" Now there are a lot of interesting things hanging on that wall, but Dave and his boots continue to steal the spotlight.

So *what* was Dave Hickey doing standing in my grandmother's front yard in Spartanburg, South Carolina, in June of 1977? Well, the guys and I had just rolled in from Texas to do a benefit show with the Marshall Tucker Band at Spartanburg's Memorial Auditorium. My first album for Epic had been released that spring, and the press was making a big deal out of this "homecoming." It was me, Dave, five band members, and a soundman, plus a few hangers-on. For some reason—possibly to cut down on travel expenses—we all ended up staying at Three Oaks instead of a hotel. My grandmother "Nannie" had died the previous fall, and her house—all ten thousand square feet of it—was unoccupied except for my cousin Foster, who was stationed there for a semester of summer school at nearby Wofford College.

Foster seemed amused and energized by this invasion from the counterculture and in no time had assumed the role of gatekeeper. When a curious aunt or uncle dropped by, Foster managed to field their inquiries and assure them that everything was completely under control. Meanwhile, the gypsies raided the palace.

A couple of the guys got high and went up to the third floor, where they began rummaging through some of my uncles' World War II uniforms that'd been left hanging in a closet. Donning the uniforms, they proceeded to ride up and down the main staircase in an electric-powered chair that was installed back when Nannie and her sister Ditty had become too feeble to make the climb. As I stood there witnessing this *Clockwork Orange*-like spectacle, I thought I heard a strange sound in the distance, like the muffled clatter of a thousand bowling pins being scattered across a hardwood floor. It seemed to be coming from the direction of Oakwood Cemetery. Probably my Chapman relatives collectively spinning in their graves.

One last comment on Dave's boots: It's true that no self-respecting Southern man would've been caught dead in them. But they served their purpose. They kept the Nashville bubbas at bay wondering if Dave was a queer, an alien, or both . . . and the Spartanburg Weejun crowd wondering if he was a drug addict or—fate worse than death—a Communist.

Since the guys in the band were all from Texas, they naturally wore cowboy boots *and* hats. One time—I think it was our first gig in New York—Dave and I were walking along behind them as we all strolled down Bleecker Street, when Dave began to notice the guys turning the heads of some gay men on the street. Sure enough, I spotted a group smiling and nodding and nudging each other like teenaged girls picking out their favorite Beatle. Dave was cracking up while the guys were totally oblivious. Now keep in mind, this was two years before Calvin Klein discovered jeans and Madison Avenue discovered that the Marlboro Man could be used to sell a lot more than cigarettes. Later on, when the Village People burst upon the scene, I always figured the one in the cowboy getup had somehow been sartorially inspired by my band that afternoon on Bleecker Street.

Of all my ex-boyfriends, Dave is the only one I still talk to on a regular basis. He's also the only one who now has a real job *with benefits*. And he's the last one I would have expected to still be alive. He's now a tenured professor of art criticism and theory at the University of Nevada in Las Vegas, where he lives with his wife Libby Lumpkin. Libby was the original curator for Steve Wynn's three-hundred-million-dollar art collection that used to hang in a gallery at the Bellagio, Mr. Wynn's $1.6 billion hotel.

Chris and I had the pleasure of hooking up with Libby and Dave a few months before the Bellagio opened in 1998. At the time, Chris was medical director for a prison-management firm and was traveling quite a bit. This was my first time to accompany him on a business trip. He told me I'd made the travel team due to recent good behavior. I never question anybody handing me a free first-class plane ticket regardless of where it's going. Anyway, we stayed at Caesar's Palace where I lollygagged around the pool all day between massage, pedicure, and facial appointments. Chris was trying to encourage me to just "be a babe."

Being a babe is not something that comes naturally to me, but occasionally I'll give it my best shot. Like everything else, it takes a little time and practice. Sometimes I wish I could just relax and "be a babe" full time. But two days is about all I can stand. After that I get bored and start wanting to *do* something. Something real un-babe-like . . . like shooting baskets or touring Europe with a rock and roll band.

After dinner, Chris and I were delighted when Libby and Dave offered to show us the paintings destined for the Bellagio gallery. The Bellagio wasn't due to open for a couple of months, so the paintings were hanging in a small private room for high rollers just off the main floor of the Mirage, yet another Steve Wynn enterprise.

As we made our way through the casino crowd, Libby stayed on her mobile, talking with security. "We'll have to wait," she explained. "So . . . let's have a drink." At a nearby booth marked "Reserved," we ordered drinks that materialized before we could settle into the plush banquette. Meanwhile, security was checking to make sure there weren't any high rollers in the exhibit room having a bad night. One could lose a lot more than one's shirt in a room where a credit line of a million dollars was required just to walk in the door. Finally, we got the green light.

As we passed through two sets of heavy double doors, I felt like Alice stepping into Wonderland. Gone was the constant jangling roar of a thousand tourists from Des Moines pumping their tokens into the slot machines. We entered a cushioned silence that only served to heighten the visual impact of what lay before us: thirty or more paintings by some of the best-known names in art. Van Gogh, Picasso, Monet, Renoir, Modigliani, Gauguin, Manet, Miro, Warhol, Pollock . . . they were all there. While tuxedoed dealers lurked in the shadows, Libby guided us from painting to painting, pausing at each one to tell its history. Chris and I were speechless. When we finally spoke, it was in a whisper. We often find ourselves whispering whenever we experience the sacred. But the sacred was soon shattered when Dave lit a cigarette right next to the Van Gogh. I watched in horror as the painting disappeared in a cloud of smoke. Should Dave ever die and end up in a heaven that's a non-smoking environment, it wouldn't surprise me in the least to see him walk by and give God the finger. Behind God's back, of course.

After years of being ahead of his time, Dave has finally lived long enough for "his time" to catch up with him. My sister Dorothy occasionally sends me Dave clippings—articles from art magazines, sometimes *Newsweek* or *Time*—with things like "Damn! Dave is hot shit!" scribbled in the margin. He has become a hot commodity on the lecture circuit, much to his chagrin, I'm sure. Universities and museums now clamor for his services, especially since the release of *Air Guitar*, a collection of essays about art and rock and roll. I've always seen Dave as someone who finds the beauty and magic in everyday things, then articulates it in his inimitably educated street talk for the rest of us. And to think, twenty years ago, my friends and family all thought he was an alien drug pusher. Now that I think about it, if beauty is the ultimate drug, they were right all along.

I first met Dave at the Exit/In in Nashville in the summer of 1976. I'd waltzed into the bar area one night and spied Melva Matthews sitting in a booth with a stocky man wearing a fedora and a goatee. He looked like a cross between a gangster and a beatnik. Melva was managing Ronnie Milsap and Charley Pride at the time. I'd recently met her when she and Danny Flowers (who wrote "Tulsa Time") took me to a TM seminar in Melva's big shiny Cadillac. It was a spur-of-the-moment–type thing. I didn't know what TM stood for, but figured anybody driving a brand new Cadillac must be going somewhere, so I hopped in for the ride.

At the seminar, I learned that TM stood for transcendental meditation. Everything else pretty much blew over my head. As I looked around at all the people there being so serious and sitting so still—I couldn't help it—I got tickled. I felt just like I did one time as a girl back in Spartanburg at the First Presbyterian Church. My parents were off on a trip somewhere and our babysitter, old Mrs. Etters, had sent me and my brother and sisters off to church with her granddaughter, Joy Kneece. Mrs. Etters couldn't take us because she was a Baptist. For her to attend a Presbyterian service would have been just this side of blasphemy. Joy Kneece's older sister, however, had married a Presbyterian, so I guess it was okay for her to take us since her soul was already in peril. The thing is, Joy Kneece wasn't all that much older than we were, so basically we were all children sitting there in our family pew with *no grown-up supervision.* Everything went fine until just after the first hymn. That's when Harry Groblewski and his family showed up and sat in the pew directly in front of ours. Harry Groblewski was the headmaster at our school. He was short and bowlegged and as funny looking as his name. Suddenly, the pressure to be good became more than any of us could bear. One false move and we could be facing the double jeopardy of not only excommunication from the church, but expulsion from school as well.

It all started when I passed Joy Kneece a note—something about the Groblewski's youngest son Thomas—only I misspelled his name, forgetting the silent "h." When this was pointed out to me, I got tickled. And the more I tried to straighten up and return to proper church demeanor, the more tickled I got. It was like a tickle virus had taken ahold of my soul. It was contagious, too. I looked over at Joy Kneece, which was a big mistake because she was in the same condition I was. Finally, when I could hold back no longer, all my suppressed giggles burst through my nostrils in a loud sort of reverse-snort. This was followed by a cacophony of more such noises from Joy Kneece and my siblings. At this point, none of us dared look at each other. We were completely out of control and we all knew it. Our collective hysteria was shaking the pew and people were starting to stare. When it finally became obvious that none of us was going to regain any semblance of composure, we all got up, as if on cue, and ran giggling out of the church. Once outside, we kept on running until we got to Craft's drugstore a block away. We figured since we were all going to hell, not to mention getting expelled, we might as well go out in style. So we marched up to the soda counter, climbed up on the revolving stools, and ordered a round of chocolate milkshakes, which we promptly charged to my parents' account. Served them right. If they hadn't of been out of town, none of this would have ever happened.

Back to the Exit/In, where Melva Matthews is introducing me to Dave Hickey. Melva was from southern Illinois, but you'd never know it from her accent which sounded like an Italian countess speaking English.

"Marshall, this is Dave Hickey. Dave's a writer from New York."

"Oh, hi," I said, sliding into the booth. "Do you have a girlfriend?"

"Ah . . . no," he answered slowly as he stubbed out a cigarette. His head began to twist around like he was nervous.

"Do you want one?" I continued. His head twisted around some more.

"I guess so," he finally said in a little-kid voice.

He almost sounded cheerful.

Dave had been around. He was born David Charles Hickey on December 5, 1938, in Fort Worth, Texas, ". . . in the same hospital where Townes and Roger Miller were born." It was an association he was proud to claim. Over time I would discover that he'd graduated from TCU at age nineteen with a degree in English. While doing graduate work at the University of Texas, he was editor of the campus literary magazine, *Riata,* as well as the legendary humor magazine *The Ranger,* writing short stories in his spare time. (Twenty years later a collection of these would be published by SMU Press under the title *Prior Convictions*.) Larry McMurtry, in a 1967 essay entitled "Southwestern Literature?", listed Dave as "among those few whose light can be counted on to burst upon the world at almost any time now." But Dave turned his back on the Texas literary scene in 1970 to open an Austin art gallery—A Clean Well Lighted Place. A year later, he was recruited to direct the high-profile Reese Palley Gallery in New York. While there, he was involved in a nationally publicized dispute with the owners for refusing to show an exhibit of Yoko Ono's art. In short, Dave got fired. "I felt like a ship leaving a sinking rat," he proclaimed upon departure. But he stayed on in New York, where he began a stint as editor of *Art in America*. A year later, he was writing freelance for *Rolling Stone, Creem,* and the *Village Voice,* and hanging out with the Ramones.

When we met in 1976, he was still freelancing but also writing songs. He'd recently signed a song publishing deal with Glaser Publications in Nashville. Dr. Hook and Bobby Bare had recorded a few of his songs. Dr. Hook's version of his "Cooky and Lila" was playing on the radio at the time. I knew the song by heart—about two world-weary types talking over cups of coffee in a diner. It was Edward Hopper's *Nighthawks* set to words and music.

> *"Hi, Lila*
> *How 'bout a cup of coffee*
> *Take a load off, take your shoes off*
> *Here's the sugar and the cream"*
> *Cooky's been to war*
> *And Lila's been to Denver*
> *Both of them are casualties*
> *Of someone else's dream*

Had I known then what I know now about Dave, good sense would have dictated that I run in the opposite direction. I often wonder why I came on to him like I did. And what I was looking for. If it was stimulation, I hit the jackpot. But there was more to it than that. There was true love, corny as it sounds. Mix true love with youth, ambition, the drugs, and the times and you just might get some great rock 'n' roll. It's a miracle we didn't kill ourselves.

.   .   .

Joy Wahl once said that Dave was "worth his weight in gold and still more trouble than he's worth." But the most accurate insight into his psyche may have come from Joy's son, Ben. After meeting Dave for the first time, the eight-year-old turned to his mother and said, "Mom, that man's mind is stuck in teenage!"

Later on, while conferring with her on a school project, Ben said, "Mom, that's a Dave Hickey concept."

"Why, what do you mean, son?"

"Well, it's a good idea that won't work."

A lot has been said about Dave over the years and if anybody or any organization ever decided to roast him, one night would never suffice. He's a bottomless pit.

Not many figure out how to be James Dean and go on living.

One conversation with Hickey will yield more epiphanies
than a week in the desert on peyote.
—Sarah Bird (*The Austin Chronicle* October 8, 1993)

The funniest American on two legs.
—Kinky Friedman

Dave Hickey is my hero. . . . A great mind driven not by necessity,
but by desire—erudite, generous and free.
—Peter Schjeldahl, art critic for *The Village Voice*

Some people leave a trail of debris in their wake.
Dave leaves entire civilizations.
—Terry Allen, all-around West Texas artist

Dave Hickey is a friend of no one.
—A Nashville policeman (1977)

Dave would occasionally borrow my car. One time he got ticketed for running a stop sign and never told me about it. Months later, Joy Wahl got a call from the police. They'd tracked her down through my registration, which had me listed at her address. They thought my car had been stolen. Joy assured them it had not. "Well, then, who is Dave Hickey?" they inquired. "Oh, he's a friend of Miss Chapman's," Joy answered. At which point the policeman proclaimed: "Dave Hickey is a friend of no one."

Wow! Whoever lives here, doesn't want to.
—Libbo Ballenger (1978)

Libbo is a family friend from Spartanburg who once drove out to Nashville with my sister Dorothy and another friend of theirs. Dave, the band, and I were all living at the Americana Apartments at the time. I lived on the seventh floor, Dave lived on the third, and the entire band lived at the end of Dave's hall in a one-bedroom unit that came to be known as "Hellhole 305." Since Dave was out of town, it was agreed that Dorothy would stay at my place, and Libbo and the other girl at Dave's. Libbo had never met Dave and knew nothing about him. Stepping into his apartment for the first time, she took one look around and said, "Wow! Whoever lives here, doesn't want to."

After a recent conversation with Dave, I am happy to report that the man's mind is still "stuck in teenage." We were discussing birthdays. Also, I was lamenting the recent untimely death of a musician friend.

"Well, it just makes it easier to stay off drugs," Dave said.

"What do you mean?" I asked.

"Well . . ." he replied, "when all your friends start dying, the peer pressure goes down."

Leave it to Dave to find just the right comforting words.

The afternoon following our first encounter at the Exit/In, I showed up at Dave's door at the Hall of Fame Motor Inn, holding my Conair blow-dryer like a gun. I knocked a few times, then watched the security peephole darken as someone moved, then stood on the other side. After extensive fumbling with the dead bolt and chain lock, the door was finally cracked open.

"Oh, hi," Dave said, clearing his throat.

"I need to wash my hair," I announced. "Could I use your shower?"

"Sure," he said, stepping back graciously.

Dave's room was real smoky. There must've been a half dozen cigarettes of different lengths going in various locations. Some were in ashtrays. One was burning precariously on the edge of a table.

"Ah, Polish incense . . . my favorite," I said over my shoulder as I brushed past Dave on my way into the harvest gold-tiled bathroom.

Thus began one of the most intense, full tilt boogie periods of my life. Running with Dave, I began to see a world where the lights were a little brighter and the tempo a little faster. I began to see art in everyday things, not just in books and museums. It didn't matter if it was Chet Baker's horn or a *Fat Albert* Saturday morning cartoon, Dave turned me on to the treasured things in his world. Besides Chet Baker and Fat Albert, there was Bob Seger. The Ramones. The poetry of D. H. Lawrence. All of Lou Reed's songs. The novels of Donald Barthelme. The paintings of Robert Rauschenberg, Ed Ruscha, and Ellsworth Kelly. The songs of Peter Allen—in particular "Taught by Experts." The songs of Terry Allen (no kin). *The Rockford Files.* Herman Munster. Sculpture made of old shoes by Ken Dawson Little. And surfing— the ocean kind, not channel. Also, there was Tackle Scrabble. *Tackle Scrabble?* Yes, and it goes like this: First, you place the dictionary twenty feet from the board. Then, when a word gets challenged, if you can tackle the challenger before he or she can reach the dictionary, the word stays as played. Try it sometime. You might consider knee and elbow pads. Maybe even a helmet.

Dave and I wrote one song during this period that pretty much summed up our deal. It's called "We Don't Go Together (But We Do)":

Whenever I get it together
You're falling apart
When I feel like everything's over
You're ready to start
When everything's coming up roses for you
My whole world's turning into shades of blue
No, we don't go together
But we do

Late last night at the party
We were feeling no pain

I was hittin' on a bottle of booze
You were doing cocaine
When I got tired
Then you got wired
They all said Mr. Ego and Ms. Id
'll never get it together
But we did

Too many fools hang their hearts out
For a song
Then kill it with rules so other fools
Can sing along
Hear them say:
"She's too crazy, he's too clever . . .
No they don't go together"
But we've already gone

So we'll keep on going to the parties
In separate cars
While you're playing Mr. Cynical Loner
I'll be out in the bar (playing the star)
But when it all comes down
To who goes home with whom
I look around the room
On the chance that we won't go together
But we do
Do we ever
No, we don't go together
But we do
Now and forever
No, we don't go together
But we do
We're crazy and clever
And we don't go together
But we do

Some Dave Hickeyisms:

Quitters never lose and losers never quit.
It's not whether you win or lose, it's how you lay the blame.
I may be schizophrenic, but at least I have each other.
Don't let life ruin your day.

On Charity:
The more you give, the more you owe.

On Las Vegas:
The '70s with valet parking.
The only city in America where they cheat you fair.

On Writing:
Just because you're talented don't mean you're good.
Save the truth for fiction.
Enthusiasm is no substitute for craft.
Writing is hard! There are so many things you can do that you shouldn't.

The #1 Rule of Rock 'n' Roll:
You either get paid, laid, or you don't go!

The #1 Rule of the Road:
Never stand when you can sit,
never sit when you can lie down,
and eat all you can when you can.

On Drugs:
I never do more than there are.
Give me Librium or give me Meth.

On Health:
Everybody's sick. Some of us are just undiagnosed.

On seeing a 1971 orange Eldorado Cadillac with a white vinyl top, white wall tires, and temporary tags cruise slowly by J-J's Market on Division Street in Nashville at three o'clock one morning:

> That's either a Nashville pimp, a South American dictator,
> or Waylon Jennings.

ON ME:
(publicity sound bite for my first album)

> Looks like Farrah Fawcett from the back,
> Peter Frampton from the front,
> and moves well to her right.

(. . . and for my second album)
The most fun I've had since the night we gave Bo Diddley the alligator.

On one of my favorite clothing items from the mid-'80s—a bitchin' pair of pants made of black lace printed on flesh-colored stretch cotton. I wore them one night in Austin, Texas. I was running late to meet Dave and a bunch of his cronies for dinner at Abuelitas. As I approached their table, Dave acknowledged my arrival with:

> Ah, I see Marshall's wearing her Frederick's of Mars.

ON WHY EDDIE BATES SHOULD BE MY MANAGER:
He's the only man who ever got in and out of the trampoline
and the go-cart business and made money!

Eddie Bates—not his real name—was a college buddy of Dave's. He managed me for a year or so while I worked out of Fort Worth in the late '70s. He's now part of the Federal Witness Protection Program for multiple nefarious activities. I got a glimpse early on of what I was getting into with Eddie. Dave and I had been in Texas for a month rehearsing with a new band. The day before we were to embark on our first tour, I accompanied Eddie to the local U-Haul center to rent a trailer for our equipment. As we stood at the counter, Eddie flirted with the agent while she explained the terms of the agreement. After the required signatures, she handed him the pink carbon, placing the original behind the counter. As soon as her back was turned, Eddie snatched up the original, then turned and said, "Let's go."

For the next year and a half, we put over 150,000 miles on our van and almost that many on the trailer. Eddie Bates was long gone by the time we pulled in for sound check at the Agora Ballroom in Cleveland in late August 1978. The police were there waiting on us. They were not pleasant either as they confiscated the trailer and threatened us with charges. Ironically, we'd had lunch the day before in Washington at the White House with Hamilton Jordan and Tom Beard. I could see the headlines now: "Rock Singer Does Lunch at White House then Time in Cleveland Jail!" President Carter was away, vacationing in the Northwest with his family. Beard and Jordan had been at our concert the night before at a night spot near Dupont Circle called Childe Harold's. After the show, they came by our dressing room and invited us for lunch.

The next day, we arose earlier than usual in order to be on time for our luncheon appointment at 1600 Pennsylvania Avenue. After a quick tour, we were ushered into a small, private dining room where, we were told, ". . . Nixon, Haldeman, and Ehrlichman used to dine alone." Our party consisted of Beard, Jordan, the four guys in my band—Michael Dospapas, Jeff Smith, Tom Comet, and drummer Willis Bailey III—our road manager, John Harper, and me. At one point, Walter Mondale walked in carrying a telephone and set it down on the table next to Beard.

"Who is it?" Beard asked.

"Nicaragua," Mondale answered.

"Is it bad?"

"Bad?! It's a fucking disaster!"

Beard took the call while the rest of us continued our discussion on the decline of American musical culture—that is to say—on why disco sucks.

In my rock and roll scrapbook, there's a snapshot of our van and trailer parked behind five or six limousines along a private semicircular drive next to the White House. I remember it was sweltering hot that day. A couple of drivers had raised their hoods to cool the engines. It's a good thing they didn't touch our trailer.

· · ·

Not too long ago, I got a call from Bates. I hadn't heard from him in over twenty years.

"Hello, Marshall, do you know who this is?" I knew immediately.

"Hey, Eddie, how's it going?"

"Great. I just took some acid."

We talked for a long time. Mostly he talked and I listened. Even with his antinomian tendencies, it was hard not to love Eddie Bates. I'll always remember him as "the little criminal with the big heart."

One last Hickeyism:

After seeing two well-seasoned snuff queens rush Don Williams at the 1976 CMA Awards show. Both had big bosoms and big beehive hairdos. "The kind of hair you could smuggle heroin in," Dave commented under his breath. Then he winked at me and said, "Why can't you be like other girls?" After that, every time he'd see a woman with dyed hair wearing lots of make-up, or a Junior League–type in one of those A-line pink skirts with lime-green butterflies embroidered on it, he'd say, "Why can't you be like other girls?" or I'd turn to him and say, "Why can't I be like other girls?" It was our little joke. We kept threatening to write a song with that title.

Well, I could keep going and tell you how Dave and some of his friends from junior high really did steal an alligator out of the Fort Worth zoo and give it to Bo Diddley. Or about the time I tried to kill him in Baton Rouge, pushing him in front of a city bus, hoping the big front wheel would crush his jaw so I wouldn't have to listen to his shit anymore. Or about the time he was talking to Joy Wahl from a phone booth in front of the Americana Apartments and abruptly told her he had to hang up. "Why?" she asked. "'Cause there's a car full of Mexicans in the parking lot and the woman is paying her kids to stare at me."

. . .

I recorded "Why Can't I Be Like Other Girls?" twice. First on *Jaded Virgin*, my second album for Epic. And again on *Marshall* (Epic, 1979). The *Jaded Virgin* track received heavy airplay on some influential rock stations, namely WMMS in Cleveland, WNEW in New York, WRAS in Atlanta, and WKDF in Nashville. Al Kooper produced it and, even though it received *Stereo Review*'s Record of the Year Award for 1978, I was unhappy with the results. "Other Girls" *rocked* lived but the recorded version just sat there in a sea of syndrums and reverse echo. Since the song was one of the staples of our live show, I re-recorded it on my next album. That version ended up on a compilation CD entitled *Classic Country: Volume 6—Sony Ladies* (Sony Music Special Products, 2000).

"Why Can't I Be Like Other Girls" was Neil Cargile's favorite song. Neil was one of the greatest characters ever to come out of Nashville. A former fighter pilot, visionary businessman, and cross-dressing socialite, Neil often paraded—entourage in tow—into whatever club we were playing to boogie and do his thing. The first time he showed up, he was all Brooks Brothers from the waist up. But from the waist down, he had on a plaid kilt with panty hose and gold lamé spike heels. As we launched into "Why Can't I Be Like Other Girls," Neil shimmied right up next to me onstage and began singing along in his off-key gravelly voice. When the applause died down, he yelled out to the crowd, "I play her song every morning while I'm getting dressed!" With each subsequent appearance, Neil seemed to cross over more and more, sartorially speaking. The last time he showed up, there was no more Brooks Brothers and no more kilt. He was in full regalia in a slinky full-length red satin dress with lots of dangling jewelry and accessories. I'm sure the diamonds were real. I forgot to look at his feet.

5

Don't Leave This Girl Alone

"Don't Leave This Girl Alone" was written around midnight on June 12, 1978, in Atlanta, Georgia. Earlier that evening, I'd gone to my first Rolling Stones concert. I'd been hearing the Stones' music on radio and records for years, but nothing prepared me for the real, up-close experience of seeing them live. They just blew me away.

The show was at the 3,900-seat Fox Theater, the first "small venue" stop on a North American tour geared mostly for 50,000-seat stadiums. With Keith's legal problems looming over the band's future, rumors were flying about a breakup. "This Could Be the Last Time" would have been a good name for the tour. The Stones added to all the speculation by running ads under assumed names. For the Fox show, they were billed as The Cockroaches. All this intrigue, combined with a chance to see The Greatest Rock and Roll Band in the World in an acoustically perfect and intimate setting like the Fox, created a ticket-buying frenzy unseen in Atlanta since the 1939 premiere of *Gone with the Wind*. The show sold out in less than an hour.

The day the Stones rolled into town, my band and I were finishing up a three-night engagement at Rose's Cantina, a club on Spring Street, not far from the Fox. By the time we'd heard about their show, it was sold out. Scalpers were reportedly getting five hundred dollars a ticket.

While we were loading out at Rose's, a guy we all knew as "Bear" approached us with a single ticket he was willing to part with for $70. It was a good ticket, too: seventh row—dead center. Since all my guys were chomping at the bit to get back to Nashville and their girlfriends, the ticket was mine for the taking. So I wrote out a personal check and handed it to Bear. He looked at me like I was crazy. "It's good," I said. "Don't worry about it."

. . .

The next day, while checking out of the hotel, I called an old friend, a guy I'd once gone out with who'd since married and settled down with a good woman and their five children from previous marriages. They were now living in a big old rambling house in nearby Ansley Park. If the truth be known, I'd fallen madly in love with this guy about five years earlier and was *devastated* when I heard he'd married. At the time, I wanted to blow my brains out, but instead I wrote a song called "A Woman's Heart (Is a Handy Place to Be)." It was my first major "cut" in the music business.

In Nashville song-publishing circles, there's an expression: "It ain't final 'til it's vinyl." Sometimes an artist will record twenty or more songs, then choose ten or twelve for the album. When I first heard that Crystal Gayle had recorded "A Woman's Heart (Is a Handy Place to Be)," I was excited, but not nearly as excited as when I first heard it on the radio. I promptly ran down to BMI where they cut me a check for a thousand dollars. In those days, BMI would grant songwriters an advance against future royalties. It was like a bank loan with no interest. The practice has long since been discontinued, but it was fun while it lasted.

Anyway, this influx of cash did much to jump-start my broken heart back into action. Of course, everybody knows time is the great healer, but I've found that money helps too. Sometimes I think we songwriters have it made. Our hearts get broken . . . we write about it, which saves us a shitload in psychiatrist fees . . . then we get royalty checks in the mail for doing something we'd've done anyway. For me, it's like getting paid to breathe. Not bad work if you can get it.

The thing that struck me most about the Rolling Stones show—other than the sheer energy coming from the stage—was how incredible their new songs were. A veteran band will often lose an audience the minute they start playing the new stuff. But not the Stones. They performed eight songs from their new album in *succession* in the middle of the show. Sandwiched between "Honky Tonk Women" and "Brown Sugar," these new songs more than held their own. I'll never forget Ron Wood and Keith Richards stalking the stage with their guitars during "Miss You," each with a lit cigarette going between curled lips. You know the facial expression . . . the one you only see on lead-guitar players. Are they feeling pain? Or contempt. Irony?

Sometimes it's hard to tell. Anyway, I watched in fascination as the two slithered up to join Jagger for the mock-BeeGees falsetto chorus. Both waited until the last second to free their mouths of the cigarettes so they could sing "Oo-ooh Oo-ooh Oo-oo-ooh / Oo-ooh Oo-ooh Oo-oo-ooh / Oo-ooh Oo-ooh . . . Ye-aah." As if on cue, they spit-launched their cigarettes like two little skyrockets out into the audience, then laughed in acknowledgment as a couple of fans snatched the flaming souvenirs out of the air with their bare hands then triumphantly stuck them in their mouths and began puffing away. It was a rock and roll moment. The Stones do it better than the rest. They make *every* moment a rock and roll moment, and that's why they're the greatest rock and roll band in the world.

After the show, I was probably in a mild state of shock. I can remember spilling out of the theater with the crowd, then trying to move away as quickly as possible. Once free of the teeming herd, I started walking in my natural stride. I needed to walk. I was wired to the gills. During the show, a certain illicit substance kept making its way along our row, where it would invariably pass right under my nose. In keeping with the spirit of the occasion, I naturally partook. There are certain things in certain situations that you just do and don't think about.

As I made my way north along Peachtree Street, I passed fewer and fewer people until it was just me walking all alone on the sidewalk. Probably not the best part of town to be doing this in, but I wasn't afraid. I was too wired to be afraid. There was no way I was going to get mugged. I was Freddy Kilowatt. If anyone so much as touched me, they would be electrocuted. Besides, there was no room in my body for fear. I was too full of what I'd just seen and heard.

One song in particular kept working its way through the maze of memory, feelings, and everything else making up what I was in that moment. The rhythm of the song was in perfect sync with the rhythm of my footsteps. It was a song from the concert. I'd only heard it once, and already it was a part of me. Soon I was singing out loud "I'll never be . . . your beast of burden / I've walked for miles . . . my feet are hurtin."

This was not my first time to spontaneously burst into song. Once, in the second grade, I got sent to the principal's office for singing Elvis Presley's

"Too Much" in the hallway while classes were in session. This was 1957 at Pine Street Elementary School in Spartanburg. I'd excused myself to go to the restroom and, while walking back down the big empty corridor, out of the blue I started singing at the top of my lungs: "Well, a-honey I love you . . . ah-oom . . . too much / I-I need your lovin' . . . ah-oom . . . too much." I wasn't trying to cause a disturbance. It's just that I could hear the echo of my footsteps reverberating down the hall, and it sounded kind of spooky and exciting all at the same time. So I started singing. It just seemed like the natural thing to do. Then when I heard my voice, I couldn't believe it. That high-ceilinged public school corridor made me sound like I was in a recording studio in Memphis. And the louder I sang, the more I sounded like Elvis. By the time I got to "Now you got me started / Don't you leave me broken-hearted 'cause I love you . . ." I was really rocking. Imagine my surprise when I looked up and saw teachers' heads sticking out of doorways all the way down the hall. It was like looking in a mirror with another mirror directly behind you where the image seems to repeat forever. Every teacher had the same expression and none of them was smiling. Especially Mrs. Laramore. She was my teacher. Mrs. Olga Laramore. She was as no-nonsense as her name and as old as Methuselah. She'd been teaching second grade at Pine Street for as long as anyone could remember. After our class, she retired. I don't know if my rendition of "Too Much" played a role in her taking retirement or not. She seemed strong enough as she half-dragged me down to the principal's office that day.

After that, I was real careful about where and in front of whom I sang. For the next few years, I only sang in the basement at home and only when Lula Mae Moore was down there ironing. I'd slick my hair back, then go gyrate around the ironing board, doing my best Elvis, until Lula would squeal with delight: "Ooh chile! You are something else!" Through all this I learned a valuable lesson . . . and that was: Know your audience.

After the Stones concert, I finally made it to my friends' house in Ansley Park. As I walked up to their front porch, I noticed all the lights were out. They'd long since gone to bed, leaving the front door unlocked so I could let myself in. As I entered the hallway, I immediately stumbled over a piece of furniture. "Shit!" I whispered. I felt like a sonic boom in a China shop. Then it hit me. *A drink. That's what I need. Only where the hell am I gonna find one here at the Waltons'?* "Goodnight, John Boy. Goodnight, Mary Ellen. Goodnight, Ben. Goodnight, Erin. . . . **Goodnight, Freddy Kilowatt!**" The Waltons were upstairs dreaming of angels while I was downstairs trying my damnedest not to break furniture or electrocute the cat.

I removed my shoes and padded into the kitchen where I began poking around. Finally I found a bottle of white wine in the pantry. Then a jelly glass in a cabinet. I managed to set both down on the counter without breaking either one. Then I opened the refrigerator and removed a blue plastic ice tray from the freezer. I was so wired, and the house was so quiet, that the slightest little noise seemed unbearably loud. I was trying to "keep things down to a dull roar," as my mother used to say. We'd be in our playroom in Enoree and hear Mother yell out from another room, "Y'all try and keep it down to a dull roar!" We didn't know what a "dull roar" was, but we knew to pipe down or suffer the consequences.

That night I thought I was doing a pretty good job keeping quiet. That is, until I turned the water on in the sink. When that water came into contact with the frozen ice tray, the crackling noise had me jumping out of my skin. "Be . . . Jeez-sus!" I whispered through clenched teeth. I felt like I was shooting off fireworks.

Finally, my jelly glass of wine-on-the-rocks was all assembled. After a few good swigs, I moved over to a wall phone and dialed up Hickey.

"Hey," I said after he answered Hello.

"Marshall?"

"Yeah . . ."

"You sound fucked up."

I started crying. Crying is one of the things I do best. Chris is the first man to understand that sometimes I cry just so I can breathe.

"I can't believe how good they were," I blubbered into the phone. By now, I was crying for a lot of reasons: I'd just seen the greatest rock and roll band in the world; I was alone with no one to talk to; their band was gone; my band was gone; . . . I was having major separation anxiety. I wanted to be with Dave but instead I was crashed out at the Waltons with John Boy and the gang. Plus, it was more than just seeing the greatest rock and roll band in the world. It was seeing the greatest rock and roll band in the world play one of their greatest shows ever. This I heard from Peter Rudge at a meeting later that fall in New York. Rudge had been with the Stones' organization for years.

Al de Marino at Epic had arranged for us to meet and talk about management. In talking, I mentioned the Fox show in Atlanta. "Ah, yes. *That* show," he said. "The boys all said that was *the one* for the tour, if not for all time."

Anyway . . .

"They're a good band," Dave said, nonplussed. "Now try and get some sleep and I'll see you tomorrow."

Before hanging up, we exchanged "I love you's," but I could tell Dave was a little annoyed that I was so wired. Hell, he *stayed* wired. Talk about the pot getting pissed off at the kettle for being black.

After talking to Dave, I wandered into the Waltons' living room where there was a guitar leaning against a chair. I picked it up and started playing and singing as quietly as I could, which wasn't easy to do. I was feeling way too much and it was all too real. *Quick. Grab a pencil . . . a piece of paper . . . anything.* A song was on its way and I could no more stop that baby than could a ten-centimeter dilated mother-to-be. Fortunately, it was a quick and uncomplicated delivery.

I went to a rock and roll show
At the Fox last night
I've never felt anything yet
That felt so right
I stood on my seat
The beat knocked me off of my ass
And back on the street
Yeah back on Peachtree Street
I started moving
I started moving real fast

I started thinking to myself . . .
You know rock and roll music
Makes me want to lose it all
I can't keep my hands off of nothing
That's gonna turn me on
I try to use my head
But then I follow my hands instead

Oh you better not leave
This girl alone too long

Don't leave this girl alone
Don't leave this girl alone
You better not leave this girl alone
Too long
The boys in the band
They are homeward bound
Now there's no love to be lost
And no love to be found
She's gonna get in trouble
If she don't get out of this town
Get out of town!

You know it's been too long
Since I felt real close to you
Too much on my mind
Just trying to do the thing that I do
And when we ever get back together
Oh, I want you . . .
I want you to sing this song
You better not leave
This girl alone too long

Don't leave this girl alone
Don't leave this girl alone
You better not leave this girl alone
Too long

The next morning, the Waltons all bounded downstairs to find me crashed out on their living room sofa. Freddy Kilowatt unplugged. Later, a couple of us drove over to the Majestic for a big breakfast. The sign out front said "Put the South in Your Mouth!" After that, I rode the hound on back to Nashville, a tired but happy camper.

. . .

"Don't Leave This Girl Alone" was the closing song on my third album for Epic. Pete Drake was the producer. Even though it was a rock album, I begged Pete to play his pedal steel guitar on that one cut.

Oftentimes, a producer who is also a musician won't play on a project that he or she is producing. Pete was a world-renowned steel guitar player, having played on Tammy Wynette's "Stand by Your Man," Charlie Rich's "Behind Closed Doors," and Bob Dylan's "Lay Lady Lay." The steel guitar has a mournful sound that is strongly associated with country music. Pete was adamant in his refusal, but eventually I wore him down, and I'm glad I did. I loved the results and I think he did too.

6

Texas Is Everywhere

There ain't a cowboy at the stockyards
In Fort Worth, Texas
There ain't a cowboy at home on the range
They've all gone to Wall Street
Up in New York City
And I find that a little bit strange
You see they've got Dallas on TV
Willie Nelson in the movies
And the Lone Star's on Fifth Avenue
And there's cowboys in Calvins
Drinking Miller Lite in taverns
Selling Texas to me and to you

I don't have to go to Texas
I don't have to go down there
Why should I go down to Texas?
Texas is everywhere

Now there's songs about cowboys
Growing up to be babies
Then doping and singing the blues
And if Billy Joe Shaver
Ain't doing the singing
Then somebody is lying to you
We got Dallas on TV
Willie Nelson in the movies

And the Lone Star's on Fifth Avenue
And all the Cowboys in Texas
Why they play football on Sunday
And God help 'em should they ever lose

I don't have to go to Texas
I don't have to go down there
Why should I go down to Texas?
Texas is everywhere
I'll just turn on my radio
Turn my TV to HBO
Texas is everywhere

This song was written faster than any song I ever wrote. Not that I'm one to be thinking about the clock when I set out to write a song. I've always subscribed to the Willie Nelson school of time management: "Time'll take care of itself, so just leave time alone." But it's a fact that some of my songs have taken years to write while others have come quickly—as in an hour or two. This song squirted out in about fifteen minutes, mainly because that's all the time I thought I had to write it in.

1980

It was a time when country music had taken a turn for the tacky. Before then, if a person wore jeans, they were either Wrangler's or Levi's. Then along comes Calvin Klein and suddenly there's all kinds of jeans—Jordache, Christian Dior, you name it. And in different colors, too. Some with *white* top stitching. It was enough to make me want to gag. *New to the game? Buy 'em stone washed and your jeans will make you look like you've been riding a horse out in the wind and sun all your life!* Madison Avenue got in on the action, and before you could say yippee-ay-ay-yeah, the cowboy image was popping up everywhere, selling everything from cars to beer. On Fifth Avenue, a club called the Lone Star Café had a huge banner out front proclaiming—in the words of Billy Joe Shaver—TOO MUCH AIN'T ENOUGH. Every March 2, they'd have a big whoop-de-do in celebration of Texas Independence Day. Wall Street types in pinstripes wearing Tony Lamas and Stetsons would pack the joint.

This national craze for all things Texas shifted into high gear with the 1980 release of *Urban Cowboy*. The movie starred John Travolta and Debra

Winger and was filmed in and around a large nightclub just outside of Houston called Gilley's. Country singer Mickey Gilley was one of the owners. Jerry Lee Lewis *and* Jimmy Lee Swaggart are Mickey's first cousins. With bloodlines like that, he could've been the Unabomber or president of the United States.

Gilley's claimed to be "the largest honky-tonk in the world." After the release of *Urban Cowboy,* it became the most popular tourist stop in Texas—more popular than the Astrodome and the Alamo combined. Speaking of the Alamo, I once stayed across the street from that historic landmark at the old St. Anthony Hotel in downtown San Antonio. This was 1974. I was in town, compliments of the Roger Miller Show. I'd been asked to substitute for one of Roger's background singers for an upcoming tour of New Zealand and Australia. They'd flown me in to start learning the ropes. It was my first time on the road with a band.

After the show, Roger had us all pile into limousines that whisked us off into the night, instead of back to the hotel. Next thing I knew, we were barreling along some unlit Texas highway at about ninety miles an hour. Eventually, we came upon hundreds of pickup trucks parked in what looked like the middle of nowhere.

"Where are we?" I asked no one in particular.

"John T. Flores' Country Store," came the answer.

Holy Shit! I thought to myself.

Until that moment, I'd thought John T. Flores was something out of Willie Nelson's imagination. Turns out Willie was even more real than I'd originally suspected.

> *Now John T. Flores was a-working*
> *For the Ku Klux Klan*
> *At six foot five*
> *John T. was a hell of a man*
> *He made a lot of money*
> *Selling sheets on the family plan*

Visions of burning crosses flickered in my mind as we pulled into the drive. Then I saw a little outdoor stage, and there was Willie Nelson and his band playing music, surrounded by picnic tables of ranchers and cowboys and old folks and hippies and families with sleeping babies bundled up.

Everybody was smiling and swaying along to the music. To my great relief, not one of them was wearing a sheet.

Willie had no idea we were there until he turned around and saw that Roger had replaced Paul English on drums. I was so full of adrenaline that I ran up to Willie and picked him up like a trophy, and just held him up there for a while . . . guitar and all. I once read where Dylan Thomas did that to Katherine Anne Porter at a party in New York City because he admired her writing so much. That may or may not have played a role in my behavior, but Willie, as usual, seemed to take it all in stride. It was one of those nights of music and happiness and life all coming together, and everybody trying to stretch it out as far as they could.

I don't remember leaving John T. Flores' or going to bed that night. But I do remember being awakened the next morning. I was dead asleep in my room at the St. Anthony, and the telephone was ringing. After extensive fumbling around, I managed to put the receiver to my ear. When I realized who was on the other end, I nearly dropped it again. It was Roger Miller.

"Hey . . . oh, how ya' doin'?" I mumbled.

"I don't know," he answered. "I just realized I forgot to remember the Alamo." With that, he laughed that "Dang Me" Woody Woodpecker laugh of his and was gone.

I was twenty-five years old. This was my first big-time tour. I'd just started writing songs. Roger Miller was one of my heroes. In the next moment I heard a little voice say, *Fasten your seat belt, Maah-shul. 'Cause, honey, you're fixin' to go for a wild ride.* Little did I know. But that's a whole nother story.

So where are we? Oh, yes . . . *Urban Cowboy* . . . Gilley's . . . the biggest thing in Texas since the Alamo. Okay. So every day after five, the parking lot at Gilley's would start filling up with pickup trucks carrying not only oil field workers, but stockbrokers and lawyers and accountants and whatnot. Everybody wanted in on the action. The suits and corporate types would be changing into jeans and cowboy boots out in the parking lot before ambling on inside. After downing a few longnecks, they'd line up for a chance to pit their manhood against "El Toro," a mechanical bull used by rodeo riders for training. Soon, these mechanical-bull honky-tonks were popping up like neon mushrooms all across the United States and Canada. But in Texas, where bigger is better and biggest is best, Fort Worth would soon unveil a honky-tonk even bigger than Gilley's called Billy Bob's.

Texas may own the market on all things big, but nobody can touch Nashville when it comes to tacky. The Urban Cowboy phenomenon sent shock waves through the country music industry. Suddenly, labels were more interested in Hollywood than hillbilly. Nashville became Nashvegas. Forget Willie and Waylon and the boys. Let's hear it for Lee Greenwood and Alabama! Bobby Braddock ("D-I-V-O-R-C-E") and I wrote a spoof about this whole phenomenon in a song called "Hillbillies Ain't Hillbillies Anymore":

> *Hillbillies ain't hillbillies anymore*
> *They're wearing polyester suits from Christian Dior*
> *They've forsaken Merle and Willie*
> *For the video rental store*
> *Hillbillies ain't hillbillies anymore*
>
> *Good 'ol country Muzak's here today*
> *Who needs a steel and fiddle anyway?*
> *They've got rural synthesizers*
> *Demographic analyzers*
> *Two promo men just flew in from L.A.*
>
> *Hillbillies ain't hillbillies anymore*
> *They don't get wild and crazy like before*
> *Nothing's been the same*
> *Since Dr. Rippy closed his door*
> *Hillbillies ain't hillbillies anymore*
>
> *No wonder country music sales are low*
> *Why they even moved Hank Williams' house to Music Row*
> *Jones straightened up his act*
> *Dolly's never coming back*
> *No wonder country music sales are slow*
> *Hillbillies ain't hillbillies anymore*

A few nights later, Braddock and I played a benefit at the Tennessee Performing Arts Center. In a light moment, I recited the words to our song. People went nuts. The next day, both dailies called requesting lyrics. *The Tennessean, The Banner,* and *Billboard* all ran articles.

Tacky has always been one of my favorite words. I can't tell you what it means, but I know it when I see it. Too much make-up is tacky. VPL—as in "visible panty line"—is tacky. Track mansions are tacky. Polyester is tacky. Tanning beds are tacky. Plastic flowers are tacky. The death penalty is tacky. *The death penalty?* Yes, the death penalty. I actually heard someone say that on network TV one time. I was watching a political talk show and this William F. Buckley type was going on and on about why we should have the death penalty. He was obviously well educated and making sure that everybody knew it. I didn't think he'd ever stop talking. Finally, it was the other man's turn. I heard the moderator say, "Well, Reverend, let's hear *your* views." I immediately sat up and took notice because right there on national TV was everybody's favorite Southern Baptist agitator, my good buddy Will Campbell. The camera panned to Will's face, which was scrunched up like he'd just gotten a whiff of bad shrimp. Finally he said, "Well . . . it's *tacky*." The moderator and Mr. Erudite Republican looked at each other, then cleared their throats. "Excuse me?"

"Tacky," Will repeated. "The death penalty is tacky."

Mr. Erudite looked at his watch. Mr. Moderator was trying to keep things rolling.

"And what exactly does 'tacky' mean, Reverend?"

"Well . . . it's a word we use in the South that describes anything that's artificial and unnatural," Will explained, ". . . that goes too far . . . you know . . . tacky."

Mr. Moderator looked over at Mr. Erudite. They both shrugged while the network cut to a commercial break.

Dolly Parton once said, "It cost a lot of money to look this cheap!" She should know. But no matter how tacky Dolly tries to look, she will always be cool. Sometimes you can be so over-the-top tacky that you end up cool.

There was one trend during this wasteland period that bothered me more than all the others combined—men getting their hair frizzed. Had I known the exact date, I would have hung a black wreath on my door the day Porter Wagoner and Conway Twitty forsook their pompadours in favor of this tonsorial plague. One frizz job and they went from looking like sexy truck drivers to little old ladies at the mall.

Frank Dycus, a songwriting buddy ("Marina Del Ray") from Hard Money, Kentucky, not only frizzed his hair but dyed it *orange*. On top of that, he started wearing an orange jumpsuit. But Dycus never lost his hillbilly charm. Like Dolly, he took tackiness to such heights that he ended up cool. Soon, everybody was calling him "Disco" . . . "Disco Dycus."

By early fall 1980, Hickey had gone back to Texas and I'd taken up with yet another songwriter with a penchant for speed. Tom Newby, my road manager at the time, once labeled all my boyfriends from 1976 to 1985 as "forty-year-old pear-shaped speed freaks." Actually, there were only two, but who's counting. Anyway, this particular boyfriend—we'll call him "Jazz"—was speeding his brains out one day and it was starting to drive me nuts. We were holed up in my place at the Americana, where he'd been talking nonstop for days. At one point, I opened the refrigerator and made some comment about being out of milk. With that, Jazz jumped up and offered to go get us a half-gallon at J-J's Market. Since J-J's was a block away, I figured he'd be back in fifteen minutes or so. Basking in the peace and quiet that followed his departure, I picked up my guitar and started strumming a nice waltz rhythm in 6/8 time. It felt good and before I knew it, "Texas Is Everywhere" just popped out. Like I said earlier, it was a fast delivery. The subject matter surprised me. I would have thought I'd write something a little more personal and soulful. The last thing I expected was a period piece about the cowboyization of America.

For a while, I kept an eye on the door, expecting to see Jazz walk in any minute. But the minutes soon turned into hours, and the hours to days, and still no Jazz. This was not the first time something like this had happened, so I wasn't overly concerned.

Two and a half weeks later, I heard a knock at my door. I looked through the peephole and, sure enough, there was Jazz . . . with a case of Heineken and a five-year-old child from a previous marriage I knew nothing about.

I was laughing when I opened the door.

"Where's the milk?" I asked.

"Damn!" he said, "I knew there was something I forgot!"

7

The Perfect Partner

Look over here there's a girl
You've never seen her before
Her eyes are looking straight at you
Across the crowded dance floor
Ooh ooh she's smiling
What a beautiful sight
I've got a funny feeling
She's gonna dance with you tonight

She could be the perfect partner
She can take it in her stride
She won't try to lead or follow
The perfect partner at your side

Ooh you've got to take a chance
You've got to let somebody move you
It can happen at a dance
When there's a rhythm you can groove to
Ooh here she comes boy
She's coming straight to you
She's gonna ask you if you want to dance
Now what you gonna do?

She could be the perfect partner
She can take it in her stride

She won't try to lead or follow
The perfect partner at your side

The worst that can happen
Is she steps on your toes
But 'til you take that first step with her
How will you know . . . know . . . know?

She could be the perfect partner
She can take it in her stride
She won't try to lead or follow
The perfect partner at your side

"The Perfect Partner" was a breech baby. Unlike most of my songs, which started with the very first line, this one started with the bridge, which is toward the end of the song. I was sitting at the breakfast table one morning and, out of the blue, began singing: ". . . the worst that can happen is she steps on your toes / but 'til you take that first step with her / how will you know? . . ." and I thought, *Umm . . . this doesn't sound like a verse . . . and it sure isn't a chorus . . . maybe it's the bridge.* After that, things just sort of fell into place.

I am usually more interested in the rhythm, lyric, and "feel" of a song than in the melody. But every now and then, a good melody will present itself, and I'm always delighted when that happens. There've been times I'll wake up in the middle of the night dreaming a beautiful melody and, if at all possible, I'll lean over and sing it into a tape recorder kept on my nightstand for just such moments. Sometimes I can't get conscious enough to do this and I fall back asleep. If so, I may or may not be able to remember it the next morning. Or it may come back weeks later while I'm doing the laundry. Or it never comes back, and it's lost forever.

Song ideas often come when I'm driving alone. Many's the time I've nearly wrecked my car while furiously jotting down lyrics on a yellow legal pad propped up on the steering wheel. Once, in the late '70s, I half-carved the words *Don't let it go to your Nose!* into the light tan upholstery of a rental car with a ballpoint pen. "Don't let it go to your nose," coupled with "You'll never know a skunk from a rose," eventually became a song—one of only two co-written with Joy Wahl and Dave Hickey. But this time, there were no fights, just lots of hilarity.

Today, I caught you flying by
Your nose held high, well so was I
And I could tell by the crazy way you flew
You don't get down and get high the way we used to

Don't let it go to your nose
Don't let it go to your nose
You'll never know a skunk from a rose
If you go and let it get to your nose

Then you, you looked 'round that nose at me
I said, "I see your highs they don't come free"
Then you said, "Au contraire, my dear, laissez-faire"
Now don't you talk that French at me like you done been there

Don't let it go to your nose
Don't let it go to your nose
You'll never know a skunk from a rose
If you go and let it get to your nose

While you're out sniffing the wind
Don't you try and pretend
You know the way that it's blowing
You're just trying to be cool
But like a new kid at school
Your insecurity's showing
Hey! don't you know you got to be whoever you are
Let it go to your nose
You're gonna lose a certain je ne sais quoi
Do you follow so far?

Don't let it go to your nose
Don't let it go to your nose

You'll never know a skunk from a rose
If you go and let it get to your nose

A few years ago, I started receiving royalties for "Don't Let It Go to Your Nose" from France of all places. Curious as to who, besides me, would be interested in such a song, I asked the administrator for Enoree Music to do some investigating. Turns out, some band in France had recorded another song with the same title. It was a mix-up, and the royalties stopped soon thereafter. Sometimes it pays to keep your mouth shut.

These days, with cell phones and answering machines, it's easy to record spontaneous ideas. Occasionally, while traveling or running errands, I'll dial home and sing song ideas into our Memory Call® answering service. Sometimes, I even leave little pep-talk messages for myself like *Maah-shul, dahlin'. We love you. We all love you . . . 'cause you try so hard. Hang in there, girl!* I've often wondered, when Chris checks our service and hears one of these, what he must think.

But back to "Perfect Partner." After I wrote the bridge, I knew I had to answer the question: *How will you know?* How will you know *what?* The answer came immediately: *that she could be the perfect partner.* Then it was Bingo! I knew I was on to something. This is one of the most exciting moments in the creative process. In answering that one question, I discovered not only the title of the song, but the first line of the chorus. So I naturally wrote the chorus next:

She could be the perfect partner
She can take it in her stride
She won't try to lead or follow
The perfect partner at your side

The verses came last. By then, I could visualize the scene. A girl sees a guy at a dance and thinks he might be "the one." She wants him to notice her, but if he doesn't do it soon, she's thinking she might ask *him* to dance. The cool thing about this song, the thing that makes it work for me, is how the singer is the narrator and she's also the girl. It's like the singer is having an out-of-body experience. She looks down on this scene, sees herself and sees this guy, and she's trying to direct traffic.

One time in 1986, I was visiting Key West and ran into Shel Silverstein. Shel and I'd known each other for years, ever since we met at Johnny Cash's studio in the mid-'70s. We'd always talked of writing together, so I was delighted when he invited me to drop by his place for an afternoon song-writing session.

Shel's house was hidden away in the old part of Key West. From the street, it looked like the kind of place Boo Radley would have lived in, had Boo Radley been a pirate. It was dark and weather-beaten and surrounded by a jungled garden. When I arrived for our session, I was shown through the house to the back, where a narrow boardwalk disappeared into foliage. As I walked along the boardwalk, I felt like I was stepping into a Rousseau painting.

The walkway snaked all through the garden, and every now and then, there'd be a little pavilion where you could sit down. There must've been two or three of these, hidden away like little secrets, throughout the garden. Shel and I sat down in one and began swapping stories and songs and ideas. I was having a great time, but then suddenly everything changed. I had just finished singing "The Perfect Partner" when, out of the blue, Shel turned professorial on me. Told me I should change "She could be . . ." to . . . "*I could be the perfect partner.*" There I was, singing him one of my best songs, and he starts *critiquing* it—unsolicited. I hate when that happens! I wanted to say *Fuck you, you imperialistic asshole! Let me critique some of your silly misogynistic songs and see how you like it!* But instead, I quietly gathered up my things, made up some story about another appointment, and hit the street.

One of the most satisfying times for a songwriter is those first few moments after you finish a new song, when you sing it aloud for the first time from beginning to end. All the fine tuning is done and it sounds and feels just right. When I sang "The Perfect Partner" that first time, it felt so good, I started crying. I must have been a sight, sitting there at my breakfast table, singing all alone, big ol' tears splashing in my Cheerios.

A truly original and beautiful melody is a rarity. As more and more songs are created, the pool of possible melodies gets smaller and smaller. After all, there are only eight notes to choose from. Think about it. Language, on the other hand, is changing all the time. New expressions are born with every generation and sitcom. A lyricist, writing in English, has over 340,000 words to choose from—not counting specialized words—and that's twice as many as in any other language. I only recently learned this. It has something to do with William the Conqueror and the Battle of Hastings in 1066.

It's hard to say where a good melody comes from. Heaven? . . . the collective unconscious? . . . the music of the spheres? . . . outer space? . . . past lives? Some say "There's nothing new under the sun." I once read an interview where Bob Dylan said he ripped most of his songs off from Robert Johnson. And, for all we know, Robert Johnson may have ripped his off from his mother. *Ripped off* is a harsh term. But it's true we are all *influenced.* So where did "The Perfect Partner" come from? It's hard to say. But if I had to speculate, I'd say it came from the Pawley's Island pavilion, where I spent countless teenage summer nights, swaying to the music of the Drifters, dreaming and hoping that true love would one day be mine.

Sometimes when I perform "The Perfect Partner," I'll introduce it saying: "This next song was written because I wanted this ol' boy to love me. I figured if I wrote a beautiful enough song, he would be so smitten that he wouldn't be able to resist. But resist he did . . . and it broke my heart. Then Jimmy Buffett recorded it on his *Last Mango in Paris* album, and next thing I know, royalty checks are pouring into my mailbox. So I moved out of my little cinderblock apartment and bought me a nice high-rise condominium. Meanwhile, the guy I wanted to love me ended up in the federal pen for not paying his income tax. It all just goes to show . . . you just never know. And knowing what I know now? If I had to choose between the guy or the money? Forget it. I'm taking the money. After all, happiness is wanting what you have, not having what you want. Can I have a witness? Do I hear an Amen? Thank you."

Buffett and I have been pals for years. We first met in Austin, Texas, in the summer of 1975. I'd flown down with a crowd from Nashville that included Don Light, Buffett's personal manager. Jimmy was playing a club called Castle Creek. My three most vivid memories from that night are: (1) the curb on the street outside the club: It was so high that if you parked your car too close to it, you couldn't open the door. I remember sitting on the hood of our rental car, with my feet propped *up* on the curb, drinking my first long-neck beer. This was my first trip to Texas and I'm thinking *Wow, everything in Texas is so big, even the curbs!* (2) how packed the club was: This was before the Coral Reefer Band . . . before "Margaritaville." It was just Jimmy and a guitar player, a guy he kept introducing as Marvin Gardens; and (3) how crazy the audience was for Jimmy. They knew all the words to his songs and were singing along at the top of their lungs. I'd never seen a solo performer work a crowd like that. I thought, *Umm . . . this guy's on to something.*

After the show, we all retired to a laid-back club where a pickup band, featuring Jody Payne from Willie's group, was playing songs like "Faded Love" and "Rose of San Antone." There were couples gliding around on a dance floor, doing the Texas two-step. Jimmy was splayed out in a big easy chair next to the bar, having a beer . . . just kicking back after his show. When Don Light introduced us, I didn't know what to say, so I asked him to dance. His eyes got big as saucers. "No way, man," he said. "You're way too tall!"

Ten years later, Jimmy asked *me* to dance. It was late one night in the console room at Sound Stage Studios in Nashville. A crowd of us was stand-ing/sitting/lying around listening to the final mix of *Last Mango in Paris.* Now anyone who's ever been around a studio console knows there isn't much room for dancing. But when "The Perfect Partner" came on, Jimmy started waltzing me around, skillfully navigating us between the speakers, chairs, console, and bodies. At one point, he dipped me all the way to the floor and back. Now I am six feet tall, and Jimmy is more than a few inches shorter. How he managed to dip me all the way to the floor and back without some-body breaking something is beyond me. The man is strong.

Earlier that day, I'd received a phone call from Mike Mooney, a longtime Buffett aide-de-camp, instructing me to bring a toothbrush and change of clothes to the studio that night. There was no real explanation, just some-thing about Jimmy wanting to take the writers somewhere. With Jimmy you never know what's going to happen next, mainly because he doesn't know. At least, not until the last minute. So it's best to be ready at all times, because something *will happen,* and it could very well be the adventure of a lifetime. He usually has three or four courses of action ready to go at any given moment, so if you're hanging with him, it's best to hang loose.

Anyway, back to the studio. As soon as the playback was over, Jimmy, Will Jennings, Mike Utley, and I were quickly ushered out of the building into the MCA parking lot, where a limousine was waiting. I had no idea where we were going, but wherever it was, we were going in style. Next thing I know, we're bouncing across a runway at the Nashville airport. When at last we stopped, the door nearest me opened, and I was simultaneously hit with a cool rush of night air and the high-pitched whine of a Lear jet warming its engines not ten feet away. The driver offered me his hand, and I held on to it as I stepped from the car up into the jet's plush interior. I don't think my feet ever touched the ground.

Moments later, we were rocketing up into the late-night sky. 340,000 words in the English language, but none to express how I felt in that moment. The g-forces had me nailed to my seat. The only thing moving was the smile slowly spreading across my face.

No one but Jimmy and the pilots knew our destination. I've said this before and I'll say it again: When you're going in style, it doesn't matter where you're going.

Forty minutes later, we began our descent. I glanced down to see a string of lights shimmering across a big black void, which I soon realized were the lights on the causeway over Lake Pontchartrain. *Ah, New Orleans! Laissez les bons temps rouler!* I began thinking about the last time I had been there. It was 1982 and I had driven across that same causeway with my band, The Road Scholars, in a 1975 Ford Econoline van, pulling a U-Haul trailer. We were coming in to New Orleans to play a club called Tipitina's. The drive from Nashville had taken about ten hours. My reverie was interrupted by the jet's wheels touching down on the runway at Lakefront Airport.

Things were happening so fast, it was hard to tell if I had just awakened from a dream, or if this *was* the dream. Dinah Washington's "What a Difference a Day Makes" began playing in my mind, followed by Gram Parsons singing "Oh Lord grant me vision, oh Lord grant me speed." I don't know what kind of speed Gram was singing about, but I sure liked this kind. Fifty minutes ago I'd been in Nashville. Now I was in New Orleans. We went up, leveled off, then came down. Just like that. Smooth as silk. I was thirty-six years old, and this was my first ride in a Lear. Flying Delta would never be the same.

That year, Buffett asked me to join his band for a summer tour of North America. Ten years later, I found myself on the roster of his record label. I'd recorded a live concert at the Tennessee State Prison for Women and when Jimmy heard the tape, I was offered a contract. Things with Jimmy and me seem to run in ten-year cycles. Who knows what will happen in 2005, but if any of it involves Jimmy Buffett, I hope I'm hanging loose.

Jimmy has known success in many different arenas. Aside from music, he's a bestselling author, a restaurateur (he insisted "blackened hotdogs" be included on the menus of his Margaritaville restaurants), a retailer (the Margaritaville stores are adjacent to the restaurants), a playwright (he co-wrote and produced the musical *Don't Stop the Carnival* with Herman Wouk), and a philanthropist. He also once owned a minor league baseball team with Bill Murray—the Miami Miracle—which later became the Florida Marlins. His accomplishments revolve around his legendary live performances and the flock of "parrotheads"—as his fans are known—that show up summer after summer in amphitheaters across America. In the off-season, his fans breed more parrotheads—called "parakeetheads"—causing his numbers to swell every year. He has toured every summer for over thirty years, and his popularity continues to grow. He's an unprecedented phenomenon in the music business, and it's fun to see a guy like him win. He is married to Jane Slagsvol, a beautiful woman and South Carolina native I've known longer than I've known Jimmy. Jane has impeccably good taste, and I once accused her—to her face, of course—of being a modern-day Ladybird Johnson . . . out to beautify America . . . one house at a time.

Occasionally, someone will ask "What's Buffett like?" and my patented answer is this: "Jimmy is one-third musician, one-third P. T. Barnum, and one-third Huey Long." But he's also a generous and loyal family man, friend, *and* employer. Sometimes I laughingly refer to him as "the only boss I ever had in the music business." It's easy to surrender whenever I find myself in his inner circle. For Jimmy is always cooking up something in that big pot of life-gumbo he keeps going, and sometimes it's just plain fun to be an ingredient. *He ain't heavy, he's my brother . . . and he ain't selling nothing he ain't living.*

Well, I put off writing this chapter for four months because, after the chapter on Hickey, I just didn't have the strength to write about any more boyfriends on speed. But now that I've regained it, I have a confession to make: "The Perfect Partner" was inspired by my boyfriend after Dave, and yes, he too was a speed freak. Now, don't get me wrong. Speed freaks can be very lovable. But if you are contemplating falling in love with one, here's my advice: It's okay to live in the same apartment complex, but *never, ever* share the same apartment. This is very important. Also, you will need to keep a list of important numbers taped on the wall next to your phone. This list should include a sympathetic doctor, the nearest emergency room, a friendly bail bondsman, his next of kin, and Frances Preston's private line. You will also need an updated version of the *Physician's Desk Reference* on hand at all times. And, if you are not on speed yourself, then you will need a lot of energy to keep up with him, so it helps to be young. If you are over thirty-five, forget it. And always remember this: No matter how much he loves you, he will always love speed more. So *never, ever* get between him and his speed.

I usually weigh around a hundred and forty-five pounds, but during this period, I stayed at about a hundred and twenty. A model friend in New York once asked me what diet I was on. I told her I was on the *stress* diet. It's not what or how much you eat but *who* you eat with that counts.

During these years, I could spot and identify a hit of speed from a mile away. Especially Desoxyn, which was Speed Freak Boyfriend #2's drug of choice. I could always tell when he was high on that one. He'd do things like smash his guitar against a hotel mirror . . . or throw his briefcase through a plate-glass window at the Spence Manor that ended up in the neck part of the guitar-shaped swimming pool six floors below . . . or jump out of my van in the middle of traffic in Nashville's Hillsboro Village only to start ranting and raving and banging his fists on the window of a Metro police car in the next lane. Once I took him to Spartanburg to meet my parents and he stayed in the shower the whole time we were there. Later, my mother discovered our family Bible vandalized. "Judge not, that ye be not judged!!" had been underlined with a heavy red marker complete with exclamation points. Another time I took him to Hilton Head to meet my sister Mary and her family. He paced around in their den all night long. The next morning, just before dawn, my brother-in-law was easing out of the driveway to go duck hunting, when he spotted Speed Freak #2 in a grove of palmetto trees with a shovel, digging up their cable line. Later, my sister discovered the cover of their current issue of *Rolling Stone* defaced with the inscription "A Rolling Stone gathers no truth!" scrawled across the cover. Then there was the time I was returning home to my apartment from the grocery store, and I looked up to see SFB #2 hacking at my front door with an ax. All I could think was *"Here's Johnny!!"*

After the ax incident, I wrote a song called "Go On 'bout Your Bidness":

Well you wrecked my car
Then you tried to hide it
Put an ax to my door
Because you got excited
Cut the cord to my cable TV
Said you were paranoid

You made my sister cry
You said she was a snob
When all she did was try
To make you feel at home
And now you wonder why
Nobody wants to mess with you

Go on 'bout your bidness
Yeah go on 'bout your bidness
Go on 'bout your bidness
Nobody wants to mess with you

You think the whole wide world is
Out to get you
That a monster girl, Lord, she
Wants to eat you
When it comes to squirrels
You're sitting at the top of the tree

You think the FBI is
Spying on you
That BMI is

Lying to you
Well I hate to tell you baby
But we've all got better things to do

Go on 'bout your bidness (about your bidness)
Go on 'bout your bidness (about your bidness)
Go on 'bout your bidness
We've all got better things to do

One night, I was performing "Go On 'bout Your Bidness" live with my band. We were rocking out toward our usual climactic ending when all of a sudden, as if on cue, we all pulled back into a quietly tense and pulsating rhythm. After a few bars, I started singing "Caught in a trap / Can't get out / Because I love you too much, ba-a-by!" as we seamlessly launched into the old Elvis Presley classic. The audience went nuts. From then on, we always did it that way. Also that night, a songwriter for whom I have enormous respect came up to me after the show and said, "Marshall, I can't get over how *active* your imagination has become in your writing lately. Especially in that new song 'Go On 'bout Your Bidness.'"

"*Imagination?*" I replied. "*What* imagination? I don't have time to imagine anything. That shit happened!"

Before I go any further, I must say that SFB #2 never once hit or physically hurt me in any way. When he wasn't on speed, he was one of the kindest, most tenderhearted human beings I've ever known . . . with an innocence the rest of us weren't born with. But when he got high . . . look out! Things got so crazy so fast it's a miracle I didn't get killed.

One more SFB #2 story and I'll stop. We were riding along in my van— I was driving—when I looked over and noticed him smiling off into space, looking so incredibly happy that I couldn't help but wonder what was going on. Turns out, he was so wired that his brain was picking up radio waves and the station he was receiving was playing Aretha Franklin singing "Chain of Fools." So in that moment, he truly believed he was Aretha Franklin. Hell, who *wouldn't* be smiling?

Not long ago, I was watching *Larry King Live*, and I nearly fell out of my chair when I heard Larry's guest Jean Harris—the former headmistress and ex-convict—say that she'd been strung out on "something called Desoxyn" for years and that her former lover, Dr. Herman Tarnower—the Scarsdale Diet guy—had prescribed it for her. *Holy Shit!* I thought. *He must've run out!*

I recorded "The Perfect Partner" on my fourth album, *Take It On Home* (Rounder, 1982). But it was Buffett's version on *Last Mango in Paris* (MCA, 1985) that inspired the following letter from an ad agency in Miami:

Gentlemen:

We request permission for the Arthur Murray Studios to reprint the lyrics to the song "The Perfect Partner" in a privately circulated, noncommercial, newsletter-type publication we call the Murray Go-Round *that goes to our 300 franchised studios worldwide. We would like to share the thoughts that the lyrics express to our staff, teachers and students alike, and give whatever credits you require.*

Thank you.

Sometimes people ask me what I do.

"What exactly do you do?" they say.

"I make something out of nothing," I reply.

And that's pretty much it. One minute I'm sitting at the breakfast table staring off into space, and the next thing I know, that space has been filled with a new song and I'm crying in my Cheerios. Add Jimmy Buffett and Arthur Murray to the mix and people are dancing all over the world.

8

Betty's Bein' Bad

Betty's out bein' bad tonight
Betty and her boyfriend
They had a big fight
She found out what everybody knew
Too many cooks spoil the stew
She don't care what nobody thinks
She's gonna be bad 'til the whole town stinks

Betty's bein' bad
Betty's bein' bad
She's bein' bad, bad, bad
She's out bein' bad
Betty's out bein' bad tonight
Betty and her boyfriend
They had a big fight

She went home when she found out
Said pack your bags
I want you out
Her boyfriend thought she was talking jive
'Til he saw her standing with a .45
A .45's quicker than 409
Betty cleaned the house for the very last time

Betty's bein' bad
Betty's bein' bad

She's bein' bad, bad, bad
She's out bein' bad
Betty's out bein' bad tonight
Betty and her boyfriend
They had a big fight

Now if you go out
And you see Betty
Don't scream and shout
Unless you are ready
You are ready to rock
Ready to roll
'Til hell freezes over and you . . .
Catch a cold
Betty's not mad
She's just gettin' even
Betty's bein' bad
It's her way of leaving

Betty's bein' bad
Betty's bein' bad
She's bein' bad, bad, bad
She's out bein' bad
Betty's out bein' bad tonight
Betty and her boyfriend
They had a big fight

Bye, bye Betty, good-bye
Bye, bye Betty, good-bye
Bye, bye, bye
Betty, good-bye

"Betty's Bein' Bad" was written on July 31, 1984. I remember the date because I had a demo session booked the next day. We ended up tracking "Great Big Crush," "Daddy Long Legs," and "Bad Debt" as planned, then threw down a quick version of "Betty" as sort of an afterthought. Of course,

Betty turned out to be the favorite. Often in music, as in life, things that aren't planned turn out best. There's more space for magic that way.

This particular session was special for a lot of reasons, one being that all four songs were eventually covered by other artists. Rick Bedrosian, a bass player from upstate New York, recorded "Great Big Crush" on his first solo album; Tanya Tucker included "Daddy Long Legs" on *Girls Like Me*; "Bad Debt" ended up on *Cleaning House* by Saffire, a group of singing housewives out of Chicago better known as "The Uppity Blues Women." And last but not least, was Sawyer Brown's version of "Betty."

I wrote quite a few songs that year with the word *bad* in the title. Besides "Betty's Bein' *Bad*" and "*Bad* Debt," there was "*Bad* Bones," "Big *Bad* Mama," "Too *Bad* to Be True," and "Alabama *Bad*." It was a good year for bad songs.

It was also a good year for bad behavior. But not in any premeditated kind of way. Let's just say I was at loose ends and running out of rope: "Betty's bein' bad / It's her way of leaving." But in my case, "bein' bad" was also a way of grieving.

My father had died the previous November and through that experience, I decided: (1) I had to get off the road and (2) I had to break up with my boyfriend (SFB #2). So I did both of those things. Which left me with way too much time on my hands.

After a depressing Christmas in Spartanburg, I returned to Nashville in January 1984 with no band, no boyfriend, no plan . . . no nothing. I was completely at a loss. Then one morning, I got up early and decided to walk over to a little waffle place just off 21st Avenue North, near the construction site for the new Vanderbilt Plaza Hotel. It was freezing cold outside, with a mixture of sleet and snow blowing in my face. I was the only soul on the street.

The waffle place was your basic waffle place: a single long counter of revolving stainless steel stools with a kitchen hidden away in the back. It was a daytime version of Edward Hopper's *The Nighthawks*.

The place was empty except for one customer, a man, sitting at the next-to-the-last stool to my right. Normally, I would have taken a seat to the left, as far away from this stranger as possible. But then the sun suddenly burst through the clouds, sending a bright shaft of light onto the very last stool, the one between the man and the wall. For a moment I stood transfixed.

Now what do I do? Reason and instinct began to converse in my mind: *Go left, young lady,* said the voice of reason, *and sit at one of those many empty stools where you can have your breakfast in peace and then go on about your business. And, by the way, that man over there is probably a pervert.* Then the voice of instinct: *Girl! do you want to freeze your ass completely off? Then you'd better go sit it over there in that sunlight, where you can do yourself some good. And forget about that man. 'Cause whatever he is, he ain't as big as the sun. Now go on!* As usual, instinct prevailed. And like a cat, I began moving toward that last stool like it was my very own sunlit pedestal.

As I sat down, a waitress came out of the kitchen and without asking poured me a steaming cup of hot coffee. "Thanks," I said, cradling the cup in both hands. When she returned, I ordered up some waffles with a side of bacon cooked crisp. As I sat there eating my breakfast, I could tell that the man next to me was trying to keep a respectful distance, but it was hard, seeing as we were shoulder to shoulder and the only two people in the place. Finally he broke the ice with "You're Marshall Chapman, aren't you." It was more of a statement than a question. He sounded a little shy. I glanced over at him for a second, long enough to see his eyes, which looked sincere and kind.

"I hope so," I mumbled. "I've got her clothes on."

We began to talk. His name was Steve Carter, and after a while, he was telling me about a family he knew that lived in San Pedro, a small fishing village on Ambergris Caye, an island off the coast of Belize. Their last name was Paz and their place was called the Sea Breeze Hotel. The Paz family lived on the third floor, renting the second out to tourists, mostly scuba divers and fishermen. On the ground floor, there was an open dining/bar area with a kitchen, where tasty meals were prepared daily by Eduardo, the cook. The house stood not ten feet away from the clear, blue waters of the Caribbean. At low tide, you could see white caps all along the horizon as the sea broke over the Great Barrier Reef, which ran about a half mile offshore. The more Steve Carter described this place that sounded like some kind of paradise, the more entranced I became. Later, he would hand me a piece of paper where he'd written the name Steferino Paz along with a phone number. "Good luck," he said. Then he turned and was gone. Two days later, I was on a plane heading south.

Thus began one of the great adventures of my life. Mainly, because I was traveling alone. There is something exhilarating about traveling completely alone in a third world country. Especially if no one there knows who you are, and no one you've ever known knows *where* you are.

My journey from Nashville to San Pedro took three flights, with connections in New Orleans and Belize City. The airport in New Orleans is always funky by American standards, but nothing could prepare me for the Belize City airport, where live goats and armed soldiers swigging bottles of Belikin beer milled about freely in the terminal. From there, I was one of only two passengers to board a small commuter plane for Ambergris Caye.

After a forty-minute flight across water, our plane bounced to a landing on a sandy grass runway, then taxied up to the San Pedro terminal, a weather-beaten wooden structure sitting up on four cinder blocks. The terminal door was open, but there was nobody inside . . . or anywhere else, as far as I could tell. It was like a ghost airport. Finally, a battered orange pickup truck rattled into view. The man behind the wheel turned out to be Steferino Paz. I was surprised to see him and wondered how he knew to meet me, since I'd told no one my flight schedule. I had planned to catch a cab, which was a joke, because there weren't any cabs . . . or any paved roads, for that matter. Vehicles of any kind were a rarity on this tropical island. Anyway, I later learned how Señor Paz knew to meet me. It wasn't so hard to figure out. He knew my date of arrival because I'd made my reservation with him for the Sea Breeze. He also knew something I didn't know: My flight was the only inbound flight for the day. I guess he assumed I wouldn't be arriving by boat. Anyhow, I was glad to see him.

As he picked up my suitcase, he looked over my shoulder a couple of times like he was expecting to see someone else. Finally he asked, "Where is your husband?" I got the impression that people in Ambergris Caye were unaccustomed to the sight of a woman traveling alone.

My first morning in San Pedro, I awoke to the sound of the laughter of children as they played in the street. I spent most of the day walking around the village, getting my bearings . . . just looking around. That evening, back at the Sea Breeze, I sat down to a delicious dinner of steamed langouste, a kind of lobster with no claws that is indigenous to the local waters, and fresh heart of palm salad. Heretofore, I'd only had canned heart of palm; the fresh version was out of this world. After dinner, I walked down the main drag to the town square, which was really more of a town rectangle in the form of a regulation concrete basketball court where a spirited game was in progress. A few locals were sitting about on benches, visiting with each other, pausing occasionally to take in the action. The players were young men who looked to be in their twenties. I took a seat on one of the benches and settled back to watch. The men played hard, but they didn't have the moves I'd grown accustomed to seeing back in the States.

When the game was over, five or six little boys rushed out on the court to try their hand at dribbling and shooting the ball. They were having fun, so I joined them, rebounding their air balls and bounce-passing them back so they could have another go. Finally, one little boy managed to get his off-balance push shot to go in, much to his delight and the delight of his buddies. They all shouted and squealed in their excitement. I wanted to shout, too, but I remained low key. I got the impression that people here were unaccustomed to the sight of a woman on a basketball court.

The next evening proved to be more of the same. The men played their full-court game for an hour or so, then left it to me and the little boys to play mop-up.

On the third evening, I decided to show up early, in time to walk out on the court with the men as they warmed up before their game. I just stood there until one of them threw me a ball, which I promptly pulled up and shot from about eighteen feet out, breathing a sigh of relief as the ball swished through the net. As the shoot-around continued, I took a few more shots and watched as they all went in. I was *feeling it*—no doubt about it— and soon could hear a murmur rise up from the crowd every time one of mine went in.

When it came time to play, there were eight of us on the court. My presence seemed to make some of the guys uneasy. Their eyes shifted around until they focused on this one guy who appeared to be the leader. He looked back at them with an expression that said *Don't worry about it* as he began organizing everyone into two teams—shirts and skins. He was a shirt, and there were a few smiles, including my own, when he indicated I'd be playing on his team.

For the next hour and a half, I played and ran my heart out. I was a thirty-five-year-old woman in fairly good shape, but after four or five times running the court with these guys, my lungs began to feel like they'd been punctured with an ice pick. But that didn't stop me. I just kept on running until finally I got my second wind and the pangs went away.

It was nonstop basketball. No intermission, no time-outs, no substitutions, no nothing. Just run, run, run. When it was all over, I walked off the court straight into the Caribbean, where the water felt like cool velvet on my skin.

After wading in up to my waist, I turned and fell backward, completely immersing myself. Then I laid back, my hands clasped behind my head like a pillow while I floated effortlessly on the saltwater. As I watched the steam rise from my body, a slow and involuntary "aaa-ah" escaped in a whisper from somewhere deep in my lungs. I have no memory of the Presbyterian baptism I received as a little baby back in Spartanburg, *but this . . .* I thought to myself, *I will always remember this.* And in that moment, I pronounced myself baptized in the name of basketball and fresh heart of palm salad and everything else that was sweet and good in this world.

The next evening and every evening thereafter, I showed up to play in the big game. I became somewhat of an attraction for the locals, who began filling the square to watch the "crazy gringo girl" play basketball. Every time one of my shots went in, they'd all shout their approval. Once, a fight broke out between two of the players on my team. They were yelling at each other in some Spanish/Creole/Mayan dialect that I couldn't understand. The leader guy came over and explained to me in English that the one was mad at the other because he thought the other was throwing me the ball too much. After that, I consciously tried to dish out rather than shoot. My reason for playing wasn't about scoring anyway. I just wanted to run myself into oblivion so I could sleep that night and not worry or think about what I was going to do with the rest of my life.

San Pedro was one of those "time-out" periods when magical things happened pretty much every day. The island population was a mixture of natives and colorful dropouts from abroad. There were one or two couples, but most of the dropouts were guys traveling alone. I was the only single woman. We were all at the end of some sort of rope: getting over a bad divorce, running from the law, corporate burnout . . . you name it. Then there were those guys one just instinctively knew never to ask anything about what they did. Like this one guy from Corpus Christi. Rumor had it he was living on counterfeit one-dollar bills.

I met one guy—a foreign correspondent for *Time* magazine named Bruce—who was taking a breather from covering the nearby Guatemalan conflict. Bruce had a buddy named Art from Austin, Texas, and the three of us would sit out on the mahogany dock in front of the Sea Breeze—yes, *mahogany* dock. I was amazed to learn that nearly all of the docks on Ambergris Caye were made of mahogany. Mahogany trees in Belize are like pine trees in Georgia; they're everywhere. Anyway, the three of us would sit there sipping our rum and sodas in the late afternoon just shooting the breeze. I would ask Bruce a leading question like "In all of your travels, what's the weirdest thing you've ever seen?" Then I would sit back and relax while he regaled us with stories of Calcutta; Nicaragua; G. Gordon Liddy; the monkey parlors in Bangkok, where patrons *eat* monkey brains while the monkeys are still alive(!); and the jails in Thailand, which have *bars* in them, not only the kind they use for cells to keep the prisoners in, but the kind where visitors can order a drink. That's right. Prison bars open to the public. Tourists dropping by to take in the spectacle of the prisoners and drinkers taunting each other.

Some nights, I would play chess with Steferino's son, Mito, who tended bar in the dining area. Or backgammon with Mito's sister, Adelita, who waited tables. Other nights, I kept to myself, writing letters and reading Graham Greene novels. One was called *A Burnt-Out Case*. I could identify with the protagonist, a guy named Querry, who'd lost his drive and ambition and was seeking refuge in the Congo. How I envied Querry. How I wished I could lose myself forever in Belize. To hell with drive and ambition. But it was only a dream. On some level, I knew the time would come and I'd be heading back to Nashville to try and get something going once again. I'd been knocking around the music business for over ten years and all I had to show for it was a pile of press clippings. Fame had come quickly, but fortune had yet to kick in. *Maybe things'll be different this time. Maybe I should forget about a recording career and just concentrate on writing. Nashville, Smashville, Trashville . . . whatever you are. Sometimes I wish you'd just leave me alone!*

I had been on the island four or five days when I became aware of a wiry young black man lurking in the shadows everywhere I went. He seemed to be following me. Sometimes I'd look his way only to see him drift back into the shadows. Finally, one night he came up to me and said, "I am watching you. You are a puzzle. I protect you. You don't worry." His name was George Estrada and he was from Jamaica. For the rest of my time in San Pedro, George stayed in my peripheral vision. If I went to my room to nap, he would sit outside my door and meditate. He was so muscular and wiry he could do push-ups with his arms extended straight out in front of his head, supporting himself only on his toes and *thumbs*. He was proud to show off this feat for me and I was duly impressed.

I stayed in Belize the entire month of February. This was 1984, a pivotal year for the village of San Pedro. It was the year it officially became a town. It was also the most prosperous year ever for the local lobster trade. Since then, I've heard that tourism has overtaken the fishing and that there're now over twenty hotels, where there used to only be one, south of the square where I played basketball. I've also heard there's a new, modern airport. I often think of going back, but I'd rather keep it in my mind the way it was.

After Belize, I returned to Nashville healthy and tan but still without a plan. Since I had written a batch of new songs, I did the only thing I knew to do: I put a band together. With Glenn Worf playing bass, Nick DiStefano on drums, Dwight Scott on keyboards, and Fred Williamson, Jr. on lead guitar. We began performing around town. To kill time on my nights off, I'd sometimes go barhopping with my friend Barbara South.

Barbara was a feisty woman who carried a pistol in her purse. Her boyfriend, Joe Harbin, ran an after-hours establishment over near the fairgrounds. Barbara was a trip without a suitcase. I never knew what she was going to do or say next.

One night I was awakened by the phone from a dead sleep at about three A.M.

"Hello," I answered.

"I've shot Joe," announced a voice that sounded an awful lot like Barbara's.

"What?"

"I shot Joe."

"Why'd you do that?"

"Aw . . . he was just sittin' there in my kitchen pissin' me off so I shot him," she answered matter-of-factly.

"Is he okay?"

"Yeah . . . just scared him a little bit, that's all. The damn bullet grazed the top of his head where he didn't have any hair anyway. But . . . damn! . . . you oughta see my storm door. That bullet blew every bit of the glass out of the top half of that door!"

Relieved no one was hurt or killed, I said, "You know, next time you go cleaning your windows, you might try using some 409."

"Yeah, but with a Magnum .357, you only have to clean 'em once."

"I heard that."

"Who's Betty?" That's a question I get asked a lot. The Betty of "Betty's Bein' Bad" is a composite of a lot of feisty women I happened to know at the time. A list would include Barbara South, Alice Randall, Elaine Wood, her sister Martha Claire, Virginia Team, Marcia Beverly, my sister Dorothy, Diana Haig, Helen Bransford, and myself. But there *was* and *is* a Betty, and she definitely was in the mix.

I first met Betty and her husband, Bobby Herbert, in the basement of a Nashville club called The House in April 1971. I was a senior at Vanderbilt, with graduation only a month away. With no plans to marry or work in a bank, I knew I had to do something quick to keep from going back to South Carolina, so I joined the local musicians' union and started singing and playing my guitar in bars.

The House was my first paying gig ever. There was a piano bar in the basement where a singer named Buck Fells performed nightly. I started out playing happy hour, but pretty soon was filling in for Buck whenever he wanted to take a night off. Not ready to carry the load by myself, I enlisted my classmate Woody Chrisman to accompany me on guitar and fiddle. Later, I was joined by local musician Willo Collins, who sang and played guitar and banjo.

Buck seemed to know the words to every song ever written. For the ones he didn't know, he'd consult a song sheet where he'd written out lyrics with the chord changes. He must've had over a hundred of these in a stack by his piano. He was kind enough to let me make copies of any I wanted to learn. My repertoire was limited to James Taylor, Simon and Garfunkel, old bluegrass songs, and some Everly Brothers and Big Joe Turner. I needed to work up some of the more popular songs of the day if I wanted to stay employed.

The first night I played The House, there was a couple in the back of the club kissing and carrying on. It was Betty and Bobby. Whenever I mention this now to Betty, she denies it, saying "Hell, we'd been married too long to be acting that way!" But it's true. I don't forget things like that. Soon they were passing me notes, things they'd jotted down on cocktail napkins. Not song requests, like most of the patrons did, just inspirational quotes from F. Scott Fitzgerald, things like that. I could tell they were well educated even though Bobby was dressed like a homeless person. Betty had a twinkle in her eye and dimples in her cheeks that told me she knew something. They intrigued me.

As I began performing more around town, Betty and Bobby would often show up, and pretty soon we became friends. On my nights off, I'd meet them for dinner in the basement of the old Jimmy Kelley's or at the Gerst Haus and then we'd hit the town. We'd go hear Millie Jackson or dance to The Ink Spots or take in a boxing match at the fairgrounds or drop in on Jack "Cowboy" Clement at his tree house apartment or attend an art opening . . . we were always doing something. Betty used to laugh and say, "Bobby would go to the opening of a door!" I'd never met anybody that loved life as much as Betty and Bobby Herbert.

I soon learned that Bobby was from an old Belle Meade family. His grandfather had founded Herbert Materials. They made bricks. Bobby had graduated with honors from M.I.T., but instead of returning to the family business in Nashville, he ran off to Greece to write the great American novel. He finished the novel, then decided it wasn't any good and threw it into the Aegean Sea. Shortly thereafter, he fell in love with an Italian woman and married her. In Bobby, she thought she'd found her Rhett Butler—her ticket to America—and had visions of moving into Tara. Instead, she ended up in a duplex on 21st Avenue South in Nashville, Tennessee. Disappointment soon set in, and before long she left Bobby and their baby and returned to Italy.

The first time Betty saw Bobby, he was walking down the street crying with a big hole in his sweater. It was love at first sight. They began seeing each other. Betty had five children of her own from a previous marriage, but that didn't deter Bobby. (He later adopted her two youngest, who later became my godchildren.) Betty and Bobby married on April Fool's Day 1967. That morning, Betty went to a beauty parlor to get her hair done. While there, she overheard a woman gossiping: "Bobby Herbert is *never* going to marry that Betty Looney with all those babies. She is out of her mind to think he's ever gonna marry her." With that, Betty pushed her dryer hood up, turned to the woman and said, "I sure hope you're wrong 'cause I'm supposed to meet him at the courthouse at noon!"

The Herberts became my surrogate family. I'd go to their house on Jackson Boulevard for Thanksgiving and Christmas or to their cabin at Rock Island, eighty miles east of Nashville, for Easter and the Fourth of July.

Betty was well read and always turning me on to some new writer, poet, or even a songwriter. The first time I heard of Willie Nelson was from Betty. She'd read about Dripping Springs in the *New York Times,* then announced, "Next time that Willie Nelson plays Nashville, we're going to go hear him."

In the early '80s, Betty's son Kelley Looney played bass in my band The Road Scholars. One night, we were playing a Nashville club called Cantrell's, and Betty and Bobby showed up after driving back from Betty's father's funeral in Decatur, Alabama. During our break, one of the Cantrell's regulars said, "Marshall, you sure do attract some strange people at your shows!"

"What do you mean?" I asked.

"Well . . . there's a lady in a pink linen dress and pearls back there standing on a table screaming 'Raise Hell in Dixie!!' at the top of her lungs."

Whenever Betty would start having too much fun, Bobby could usually be found standing at the bar with a lost look on his face. "Hey, Bobby, where's Betty?" someone would ask. In a soft voice, with a strange mixture of fear and pride, he'd answer: "Betty's bein' bad." Sometimes he would just stand there muttering "Betty's bein' bad" to no one in particular.

Minutes before writing "Betty," I'd been curled up in a fetal position on top of my bed at the Americana Apartments. I was so depressed I couldn't move. I was also real nervous about my recording session the next day. Had I prepared enough? Did I have the right musicians? Plus, there was a man in New York who called himself Generalissimo Snowflake bankrolling the session. *Generalissimo Snowflake? Have you lost your mind? Girl . . . what have you gotten yourself into* this *time?*

I had met Generalissimo Snowflake earlier that year through my friend Diana Haig. Diana and Generalissimo had been friends for several years, ever since they'd met at the 1980 ASCAP awards dinner in Nashville. To hear her tell it: "I had just moved to town and didn't know a soul, so I went to the ASCAP dinner hoping to meet some people. I had long hair back then, and I felt someone behind me pull my hair really hard. I mean *really* hard! So I turned around (in my party dress) and there was Generalissimo with his son, Michael, and he said, 'Oh! . . . well, since your hair is real, then you can sit at our table!'"

. . .

I met Diana the following summer at Cantrell's, where I was headlining and she was playing bass for the opening act, Fred Koller and the Stereo-types. Fred and I were songwriting buddies and the Stereotypes were his first Nashville band. I had arrived early to catch their act and couldn't help but notice Diana, who seemed to be having more fun than anybody. My first thought was: *When did Betty Boop start playing a pink paisley bass in a rock 'n' roll band?!* Diana had on a cute little polka-dot dress with a big bow ribbon in her dark curly hair and the biggest smile on her face I'd ever seen. The contrast between her and the other musicians was almost comical. It was like she was playing in Technicolor and they were in black and white. How she managed to play that pink paisley bass—it was a Fender, and Fenders are notoriously heavy—and smile that great big smile, all while prancing about in a pair of very high heels, sidestepping cords and monitors and all the other things that can trip you up onstage . . . well, it was just an amazing thing to see. She was a one-woman fun house.

After their set, I was milling around with the usual backstage crowd when Fred introduced me to Diana. We became instant friends.

Diana was born Diana Reid Haig in Reidsville, North Carolina. In the South, you often meet people with the same name as the town they're from. I grew up with a guy named Tom Moore Craig from Moore, South Carolina, and went to grade school with a girl named Jo Willa Gramling from Gramling, South Carolina.

When the time came for college, Diana chose Sarah Lawrence in Bronxville, New York. She studied music, literature, and art history under such luminaries as Ed (E. L.) Doctorow and Joseph Campbell. After graduating with honors at age nineteen, she drifted down to Manhattan, where she became pals with Johnny Thunders and played bass in a band that featured Stu Boy King of the Dictators. Stu Boy prided himself on being "the loudest drummer in rock and roll."

Diana left New York for Nashville in the fall of 1980, just a few days before CMA week and the ASCAP dinner where she had her tonsorial first encounter with the great Generalissimo.

By 1984, Diana was writing and directing a variety show-with-music called *Belle Meade Beach* for the local-access cable channel. She was also working in the publicity department at MCA Records with Kay Shaw (now Kay West, food editor for *The Nashville Scene*, Nashville's alternative weekly).

Kay was a *Belle Meade Beach* regular. Her segments were called "Listening to Kay." With no prompt cards or script, she would just launch into a stream-of-consciousness tirade about whatever was bothering her that day—be it Nashville drivers, germs, or men who perm their hair. The camera would fade her in, then fade her out, with her talking the entire time. This would happen two or three times a show, which left the impression that this woman *never stopped talking*. It was a clever and original bit . . . sort of a Jane Curtin meets Chatty Cathy.

Diana had an uncanny knack for persuading her friends in the music business to do things on her show they wouldn't be caught dead doing anywhere else. For instance, she talked me into wearing a *swimsuit* her mother had worn in the 1945 Miss America pageant, while I sang a song Dave Hickey and I wrote called "Don't Make Me Pregnant." The suit was a metallic blue Esther Williams number with fringe all around that shimmied when I walked.

Video copies of *Belle Meade Beach* were constantly being pitched to places like Gaylord Entertainment (for The Nashville Network) and to Viacom, who liked the show well enough to program it on their Long Island cable system. Somehow a copy ended up on the desk of Leon Brettler aka Generalissimo Snowflake.

Leon was a respected player in the music business. A longtime board member and treasurer at ASCAP, he was also president of Shapiro-Bernstein, one of the older, more established New York song-publishing companies. Shapiro-Bernstein owns the copyrights to some of the most celebrated songs in American music . . . songs like "In the Mood," "Ring of Fire," "You're Nobody 'til Somebody Loves You," "Oh! My Pa-Pa," "Harlem Nocturne," "The Glory of Love," "Beer Barrel Polka," and "Wolverton Mountain," just to name a few.

Anyway, Generalissimo—that is, Leon—was so taken by my *Belle Meade Beach* performance of "Don't Make Me Pregnant," that he immediately called Diana and told her that he wanted to meet me. Imagine my surprise when Diana called, asking if she could give my number out to a man named

Generalissimo Snowflake. "He's very energetic!" she said in her breathy Marilyn Monroe voice.

Next thing I know, my phone is ringing: "Hello," I answered flatly. "At-ten—*tion*!!" booms the voice on the other end. "At ease, Field Marshall Chapman. You are hereby commissioned by me, Generalissimo Snowflake, as reigning supreme commander of the Green Army, to join me for lunch during my upcoming official visit to the Nashville post!"

I didn't know what to think. Had Diana not briefed me about the guy, I would have hung up immediately thinking it was a crank call. Instead, I found myself not only agreeing to meet him for lunch, but starting to speak the lingo: "Request permission to be dismissed, sir!" I heard myself shout at the end of our exchange.

For our first meeting, I picked Generalissimo/Leon Brettler up in front of the Vanderbilt Plaza Hotel in my blue van. Lunch was my call, so I decided to take him on the "Franklin Lunch Tour." That's when you drive thirty miles south from Nashville to Franklin, pick up your barbeque sand-wiches at the One-Stop, go two doors down to the Dairy Dip for some chocolate-chip milkshakes to go, then drive west along Highway 96 until you come to a road that leads to the Old Natchez Trace, which runs along the Harpeth River back to Nashville. A stop is made at some scenic spot along the river where the barbeque sandwiches and chocolate-chip milk-shakes are ingested. Then you drive slowly back to Nashville. That's the Franklin Lunch Tour. But on this day, with Generalissimo, the Franklin Lunch Tour was served up with a twist. Instead of stopping along the Har-peth, we took our lunch to the old Confederate cemetery, surrounded by battlefields where the Battle of Franklin—the bloodiest battle of the Civil War—had been fought a hundred and twenty years before. The military set-ting was not lost on Generalissimo. After lunch, we visited the Confederate Museum. I thought the young girl at the front desk was going to faint when Generalissimo announced his intention to *buy* the museum.

Leon Brettler was one of the most eccentric people I'd ever met. He looked to be about sixty years old, was large in stature and well-groomed in a New York kind of way. He also possessed a kind of sick bathroom humor, always telling jokes that I never thought were funny. His boisterous enthusi-asm for his own jokes, however, was never diminished by my lack of enthusiasm. "Generalissimo Snowflake" was the title he gave himself as head of the Green Army, a secret organization whose mission was to get more money for publishers and songwriters. It was a game he played—or was it? One could never be sure—with certain "enlisted" friends from around the world. Diana was Drill Sergeant Haig of the Nashville Post. I was commissioned as Field Marshall Chapman. Once you were inducted, there was nothing you could do about it. And your first order of business better be to get a bigger mailbox because your volume of mail was about to increase dramatically. I was soon inundated with letters from Green Army headquarters, i.e., Shapiro-Bernstein in New York. Whatever caught the Generalissimo's attention, he would copy all members of the Green Army by mail. Each mailing had "Attention!" and "Via Con Diós" rubber-stamped numerous times all over the envelope. In green ink, of course.

Generalissimo was brilliant, and I think the Green Army was something he made up to keep himself entertained. He was also tenderhearted and enjoyed helping struggling artists realize their dreams. If he found you interesting—and you were down on your luck—he might "adopt" you for a while until you got back on your feet. He was sort of a Robin Hood figure in the music business. His credo could have been: "Collect from the record companies, distribute to the songwriters." In explaining his name, he'd say "*Generalissimo* means 'supreme commander.' A generalissimo answers to no one!" As for the "Snowflake" part, he'd shrug. "What can I say? Snowflakes always melt eventually."

A few months after our first meeting, I received what turned out to be an important call. "Attention!! At ease, Field Marshall Chapman. I hereby command you to go into a recording studio ASAP! There you will record three or four of your new songs to the best of your ability! You will hire whoever you need in the way of engineers, musicians, background singers, et cetera. If you want to hire a horn section, then by all means, hire a horn section. You are not, I repeat, *not* to worry about anything because you are under my orders and I am THE Generalissimo Snowflake, reigning supreme commander of the Green Army! And, finally, you are to send all invoices to Green Army headquarters here in New York. Do I make myself clear, Field Marshall Chapman? At ease, dismissed!!" *Click.*

I was flat broke at the time and couldn't believe what I was hearing. I kept waiting for the other shoe to drop as in "all you have to do is just sign over your publishing" but it never did.

I'll never forget that session. Lou Bradley was brought in to oversee things. Lou had just produced John Anderson's huge hit "Swingin," which I just loved. It was a different sound for country radio. John's voice was unusual enough—many have compared it to the sound you get when you run a vocal track *backward* through the tape machine. But the horns were what really made it cook. A country hit with horns is about as rare as a pop hit with steel guitar. The only other country hit I can think of that had horns was Johnny Cash's "Ring of Fire." Since "Swingin" was overdubbed and mixed at John D. Loudermilk, Jr.'s newly renovated Nashville Sound Connection, Lou and I decided we would record there, with John D., Jr., at the board. Jerry Whitehurst from the *Nashville Now* band played piano and was session leader. Jerry had played piano on J.J. Cale's recording of "After Midnight," and I had always enjoyed working with him whenever I appeared on *Nashville Now*. Larry Sasser, also with the *Nashville Now* band, played steel guitar. Dale Sellars played electric guitar; Jerry Carrigan, drums; and Henry Strzelecki, bass. Later, we overdubbed horns using a horn section led by saxophonist Norm Ray. The *Nashville Now* singers (Donna Rhodes, her brother Perry, Ned Wimmer, and Jana King) added background vocals. Then we mixed it all down.

It was my first time to record in nearly three years. No wonder I was nervous. No wonder I was curled up in a fetal position the night before. My mind was going a mile a minute. I couldn't control it. I started thinking of all the different ways people kill themselves . . . *anything to stop this anxiety! . . . this fucking ache in my heart!! . . . this goddamned loneliness!! . . . this black motherfucking hole that I can't seem to crawl out of!!! And so what if you get a fucking record deal! That's when your heartache* really *begins!!! They'll own your ass! You crazy fool!* My mind was like a bad neighborhood, and once again, I'd gone in there alone.

But wait! Hold everything! Just when I thought I couldn't stand it any longer, the voices suddenly stopped. It was like someone had opened a window to my brain. And music was blowing through the curtains like fresh air. This music had a familiar beat. *What is that riff? I know that riff!* Then the lyrics started coming. They were coming so fast I was scared to go get my guitar in the next room. *Leave it there! Don't break the spell!* So I grabbed the nearest thing I could find, which was a piece of shirt cardboard from White Way Cleaners. With a brown felt pen I started writing in big bold letters: "Betty's out bein' bad tonight / Betty and her boyfriend they had a big fight /

She found out what everybody knew / Too many cooks spoil the stew . . ."
At this point, I'm thinking *Man, this is cool! Just keep writing, baby, just keep
writing.* And then I was laughing as it suddenly dawned on me where I'd
heard that riff. It was something from my childhood, a commercial for
shortening bread I used to hear on the radio: "Mama's little babies love
shortening, shortening. . . . Mama's little babies love shortening bread! She
went home when she found out / Said pack your bags I want you out / Her
boyfriend thought she was talking jive / 'Til he saw her standing with a .45
/ A .45's quicker than 409 / Betty cleaned the house for the very last
time . . ." *Holy shit! Don't anybody touch me now 'cause I am hot!* Thirty minutes later, "Betty's Bein' Bad" was a song. I walked into the other room,
picked up my Martin guitar, and played it for the first time from beginning
to end, singing into a little microphone hooked up to my Realistic cassette-
to-cassette recorder. Afterward, it was too late to call anybody, so I went to
bed. Peaceful sleep fell over me like a blanket and I dreamed of angels.

I re-recorded "Betty's Bein' Bad" in 1986 for *Dirty Linen,* the first album
released on my own Tall Girl Records (motto: "We're too tall to sell ourselves short!"). The album got picked up in Germany by Line Records for
European distribution. Robert Christgau gave it an A minus rating in his
Village Voice Consumer Guide. "It's her best album by a mile and a half," he
wrote. "The singing is relaxed and aware, the writing sharpest when it means
to cut a little, as on 'Betty's Bein' Bad' ('Betty's not mad / She's just gettin'
even / Betty's bein' bad / It's her way of leavin'). May she glorify her Pignose
amp forever."

On Halloween Eve 1993, I recorded a concert at the Tennessee State
Prison for Women. "Betty" was one of fourteen songs from the concert that
ended up on *It's About Time* . . . (Margaritaville/Island, 1995).

I first performed "Betty" on TNN's *Nashville Now* in April 1985. Jimmy
Buffett was guest-hosting for Ralph Emery. Jimmy had called me early on,
saying, "Look, Marshall. I've asked Reba (McEntire) to be one of my guests,
but if she can't do it, I want you. Okay?" Well, lucky for me, Reba couldn't do
it, so I was on. Jimmy's other guests were John D. Loudermilk and Dan

Fogelberg. The show ended up having the highest viewer rating ever on TNN. But more important to me was what happened after the show. Lynn Shults, an A&R man for Capitol, had been in the studio audience that night. Afterward, he came up and introduced himself, then asked for a cassette copy of "that song you sang about Betty bein' bad." He wanted to play it for a hot new group called Sawyer Brown. Of course I tried to talk him out of it, thinking it'd be better for a *girl* group. Thank goodness his enthusiasm was stronger than my skepticism. Next thing I know, Sawyer Brown not only recorded it, but Capitol released it as the first single off the album. By the end of the year, "Betty" was sitting at the top of the charts. Sawyer Brown's version spawned a few covers, including one by some Swedish guy who, naturally, sang it in Swedish.

A year later, I nearly fainted when the first big royalty check arrived from BMI. I didn't know what to do, so I drove out to Jackson Boulevard and showed it to Betty. "My God, Marshall," she said. "Do you know what this means? You are a woman of means . . . you hear me? . . . a woman of *means.* You will never have to ask a man to buy you *anything!*"

A year later, I went to the BMI dinner to pick up my award for "Betty," accompanied by my sister Mary and songwriter Will Jennings. I had been at a loss as to what to wear, but Marty Stuart saved the day. When I asked to borrow one of his rhinestone jackets, he said, "Why, of course you can, darling! I've got one here that'll light you up like a Christmas tree!"

Marty once inspired a song that I wrote with Will Jennings called "Rockabilly Sweethearts." I'd run into him at Rosanne Cash's thirtieth birthday party. He was wearing a fabulous rhinestone jacket with wagon wheels embroidered all over it. The jacket had once belonged to Buck Trent, who for years played banjo in Porter Wagoner's band, the Wagonmasters. Marty was married to Rosanne's sister Cindy at the time, and they looked so cute and so in love, that I later wrote in my journal: "What a cute couple! They look like a pair of rockabilly sweethearts."

> *He got a rhinestone jacket*
> *From Porter Wagoner's band*
> *She's wearing high-heel sneakers*
> *And a-holding his hand*
> *They're doin' the duck walk to Memphis*

In the full moonlight
They're gonna check into the Peabody
Hotel for the night
They're rockabilly sweethearts
Syncopated love
Rockabilly sweethearts
They got every single record
In the Sun catalog

He got his hair piled up
In a pompadour
She got them long legs moving
Out across that floor
They got no bags
Just an old guitar
The Fender Stratocaster
Got 'em where they are
They're rockabilly sweethearts
Syncopated love
Rockabilly sweethearts
They got every single record
In the Sun catalog

They take the elevator ride
To the thirteenth floor
They got lucky there once
Now they're looking for more
The windows and the curtains
Open in their room
They're gonna sing their song
To the cat in the moon
They're rockabilly sweethearts
Syncopated love
Rockabilly sweethearts
They've got every single record
In the Sun catalog

"Betty" was nominated for Country/Rock Song of the Year at the 1987 *Music City News* National Songwriter Awards Show. In 1999, "Betty" was featured in a country-music revue called *Good Ol' Girls* that played to packed houses across North Carolina and Virginia. The show was the brainchild of singer/songwriter Matraca Berg and featured not only my and Matraca's songs, but adapted passages from the novels of Lee Smith and Jill McCorkle. *Good Ol' Girls* is touring again, so you never know; Betty could end up bein' bad on Broadway.

One of my most prized possessions is an autographed picture of Scotty Moore playing guitar with Elvis. It was taken during the filming of *Loving You* as part of a photo shoot for *Guitar Player* magazine. It was Scotty's first cover shot, and he and Elvis are really cutting up. Elvis had just pushed Scotty to the front, so it would look like Scotty was the star and Elvis his backup. The photograph is inscribed: To Marshall— "Scotty's Bein' Bad" (I think!) Yours, Scotty Moore. Later, he told me, "I always loved that 'Betty's Bein' Bad.' It may be my favorite." I walked on air for a week.

A few years ago, I was informed by BMI that "Betty" had logged over a million performances. So how many listening souls does that include? There's no telling, but wondering about it keeps me dreaming.

I reach for the stars
It's the least I can do
I may never hold them
But I dream that I do

I'm a dreamer
I believe in things nobody can see

9

Goodbye, Little Rock and Roller

Once there was a little girl
Unlike any in the world
One night she looked inside her soul
And all she saw was rock and roll
Her dad bought her an old guitar
He never dreamed she'd be a star
She worked her fingers to the bone
On that Sears and Roebuck Silvertone guitar

She played that guitar all day long
Then put her feelings into song
Then sang her songs for Lula Mae
Who said, "Child, you've got just what it takes."
We all knew she'd leave somehow
To find the world she dreamed about
She never turned around that day
To see her sister wave to her and say

Goodbye, little rock and roller
Gee it sure was good to know ya
Goodbye, my little rock and roller
Goodbye

She hitchhiked to Hollywood
Like everybody knew she would
She put a rockin' band together

They made plans, they cut a record
The rest was history they say
She took off down the fast highway
People came from miles around
While every night she burned 'em down

All the fortune and all the fame
And all the lights around her name
And every night was now or never
The road just seemed to go forever
And all her dreams that had come true
They didn't thrill her like they used to
She never thought she'd grow to hear
A voice inside her strong and clear sing

Goodbye, little rock and roller
Gee it sure was good to know ya
Goodbye, my little rock and roller
Goodbye

She found a place down by the sea
The place was called Serenity
There she learned that life goes on
Life is more than just a song
You'll never guess what happened then
She met a gentle man named Ben
Together they made love so real
They made a baby girl they named Lucille

She rocked Lucille to sleep each night
Then sang her lullabies she'd write
She thought her heart would break in two
The first time she heard, Mom, I love you
And then one day her baby girl
Walked outside to find her world
She never dreamed she'd see the day
She'd be fighting back the tears to say

Goodbye, little rock and roller
Gee it sure was good to know ya
Goodbye, my little rock and roller
Goodbye

I started writing "Goodbye, Little Rock and Roller" aboard an American Airlines jet that had just lifted off from L.A. International Airport. It was Thursday, May 8, 1986. I know this because I was keeping a journal at the time. I was on my way back to Nashville after eight days in Los Angeles, where I'd been hanging out writing songs. Acting on a tip from Emmylou Harris, I had stayed at the Shangri-La, a wonderful old Art Deco hotel that overlooks the bay at Santa Monica. It was built in 1939 and still had the charm of that era.

The Shangri-La was my kind of hotel. It had a touch of the exotic but with a faded, no-frills kind of elegance. The rates were reasonable due in part to the lack of air-conditioning. The spacious rooms were naturally cross-ventilated by windows and balconies that opened to the fresh salt air. My room was on the fifth floor. From there I could look out and see the green of grass and palm trees in Palisades Park, and off in the distance, the purple mountain majesty of the Santa Monica Range as it sloped down toward the infinite blue where the Pacific Ocean meets the sky.

All the rooms at the Shangri-La were accessed from open hallways rising up from a central courtyard garden. The first time I walked along one of these hallways, it was after nightfall. I had just checked in and was following the bellhop to my room. Even though I was groggy from travel, I couldn't help but notice a soft breeze carrying a sweet and exotic fragrance. For a moment, I stopped and closed my eyes. "What is that wonderful smell?" I asked.

"It's is the night jasmine," replied the bellhop.

I must have looked confused.

"The blooms, they only open at night," he explained.

"Oh, I see," I said, then thought to myself, *Whew! I must really be jet-lagged.* For I had misinterpreted "jasmine," thinking he'd said "jazzmen," as in jazz musicians, and this had turned my thoughts to The Rolling Stones. Maybe Keith Richards and Mick Jagger had this nocturnal flower in mind when they wrote "Sunshine bores the daylights out of me." Don't ask me why, but I suspect John Denver would never have stayed at the Shangri-La.

.   .   .

The staff at the Shangri-La was polite in a European kind of way. If you needed assistance, they provided it. Otherwise, they left you alone. Call slips were placed under the door. There were no flashing red lights on the phones. The hotel operator, speaking with a heavy Middle Eastern accent, might respond to an incoming call with "Miss Chapman wishes not to be disturbed. It would please me to take your message."

Which reminds me of a story my mother tells from her days as a student at Converse College in Spartanburg. She was trying to place a call to *her* mother in Lilesville, North Carolina. This was just before the war, around 1938 or '39. Lilesville was and still is a very small town—small as in 386 people. The one telephone operator worked from a little room above the post office. The room had a big window that looked down on the main street. The interchange went something like this:

"Hello, operator? I'd like to place a call to my mother, Mrs. Fayette J. Cloud in Lilesville, North Carolina."

The Spartanburg operator then rang the operator in Lilesville.

"I have a person-to-person call here for Mrs. Fayette J. Cloud."

"I'll be happy to ring the house, operator, but Miss Chaney . . ."—everybody around Lilesville called my grandmother "Miss Chaney"—"Miss Chaney's not there. She drove by here about ten minutes ago on her way to her hair appointment." Then there was the time the operator said, "I'm sorry. I can't ring Miss Chaney until after three o'clock. She's taking a nap."

But back to American Airlines. As the plane leveled off at its cruising altitude, I began to settle down in my seat. I was hoping to get an hour or two of shut-eye before landing in Nashville. After eight days in Los Angeles, I was fried. Besides, I'd been up since 4:45 that morning, in time to shower, pack, check out of the Shangri-La, drive to the airport, return my Alamo rental car, check my luggage, and board the flight. God, I hate early morning flights. In fact, I hate early morning anything. A psychic once read my chart armed only with the knowledge of the date and time of my birth, and her first comment was "You're not a morning person, are you?" Duh!

But sleep would not come. My mind kept flashing back to the events of the past few days. Plus, I was ovulating. I've said this before and I'll say it again. If you haven't ovulated at forty thousand feet, then you are missing out on one of life's great experiences.

Mainly, my mind was on the night before. I had driven up the Pacific Coast Highway to Malibu to have dinner with my current love, a Texas songwriter who shall remain anonymous. For the past two years, we had been involved in a tumultuous affair. We'd had a thing for each other ever since Dave Hickey had introduced us in 1977. We'd kept in touch over the years, but in the winter of 1985, things started heating up in a major way. That January, we found ourselves living together on a two-stateroom trawler called *The Magic* in Key West, compliments of Jimmy Buffett. I don't know if it was the moon, the stars, the ocean, the Cuban food, the writing sessions with Jimmy, the sunsets from the deck at Louie's Backyard, or *what*. All I know is by the time we left Key West, I was head over heels in love.

There was, however, one drawback. This Texas songwriter had a Texas wife. But not to worry. He would soon be divorced. At least, that's what he told me. And what he told my mother when we visited my family that Fourth of July . . . and told Betty Herbert . . . and my sister Mary . . . and anyone else when the subject came up. But there was one person he failed to tell. You guessed it. His wife.

It's funny. Dwight Scott, who was playing keyboards in my band at the time, mentioned one night between sets how he'd met this love of my life fifteen years earlier in Nashville. "What was he like?" I asked. "Oh, I don't know," Dwight replied. "He had this notebook full of songs and . . . oh yeah, I do remember this. He was in the process of getting a divorce."

Hello? Is anybody home?

After Key West, the Texas songwriter leased a condominium in Nashville, and we ended up spending most of 1985 together. Our affair culminated in mid-December with a trip to New York City, where we met up with Steve Winwood and his new Tennessee girlfriend, Eugenia Crafton, who later became Mrs. Winwood. Steve was overseeing the final mix of his *Back in the High Life* album. The four of us stayed at the Gramercy Park Hotel and every night we'd go out to dinner and then out on the town. Everybody was in love and we were living the high life. It was big times in the Big Apple.

From New York, the Texas songwriter and I flew south to visit my sister Mary and her family in Hilton Head. From there, we took day trips to Savannah and Beaufort, driving the old back roads in our rental car. I've always loved those old roads. One minute you're driving through a long, dark tunnel of live oak trees strewn with Spanish moss, then, just when your eyes have adjusted to the dark, you're suddenly thrust into the blinding light of an open marsh with dazzling blue skies and glimpses of the ocean. I've always felt more of a kinship with this part of the South Carolina low country than with the Piedmont region where I grew up. There's something majestic and mysterious about it that draws me back time and time again. I can envision living out my final years in a high-tech sharecropper's shack on some secluded barrier island between Georgetown and Savannah.

When Christmas Eve rolled around, the Texas songwriter flew back to his wife and California, leaving me in Hilton Head to spend Christmas with my sister. Before boarding his flight, he once again assured me he would soon be divorced and we would be together at last. "Hang on, Sloopy," he said.

The next morning, Christmas, I arose bright and early and tiptoed down the hall to look in on my sleeping nieces—Catie, age six, and Frances, who was almost three. As I approached their rooms, I unfortunately walked into a door frame and banged my head really hard. I was unaware of the extent of my injury until I saw their startled faces, their eyes big as saucers. "Ooh, Aunt Marshall, you're bleeding! Yuk!!" Within minutes, Mary arrived with an ice compress, and then it was off to the emergency room.

My family always shines during times of high stress. And with style, too. Mary threw on a full-length sable coat over her pajamas, then slipped into a pair of black Belgians without breaking stride. This was no time to be lacing up shoes.

At the ER, a nurse started asking me all the usual questions: name, address, date of birth, insurance, and so forth, while my sister was doing her usual running commentary. When Mary is "on" she is in a class with Richard Pryor, and she was definitely "on" that Christmas morning in the ER. She was cracking me up. "Stop making me laugh," I begged. "It hurts to smile." Even Nurse Ratched was starting to loosen up and get into the act. At one point, she peered at me over her clipboard and said, "Now, Miss Chapman, how'd you come to walk into a door frame on Christmas morning?"

"Well," I drawled, trying to stay calm while the doctor was stitching me up, "I guess you could say I was blinded by love."

My comment was met with a blank stare.

"Write that down," I said.

So she did. In the space where it says "Describe injury," she had written "full thickness laceration of right temporal area." Now she added "Patient walked into door frame. Says she was 'blinded by love.'"

After Christmas, there were daily phone calls from California with divorce progress reports. Then the calls thinned out to once every few days or so. Then they stopped altogether. I couldn't believe what was happening. I was out of my mind with grief and despair. This was worse than the death of my father. At least that had some finality to it. This was like a living death that I could not accept. Cleopatra had nothing on me. I was the undisputed Queen of Denial.

So five months later, I fly out to California and check into the Shangri-La. Yeah, yeah, I know. I was out there on business, writing songs and meeting with the guys at Bug Music, the company that administers my song catalogs. But who was I kidding? Certainly not myself. I was there to see him. Period. So I did. We got together numerous times, and I was as crazy about him as ever. But one thing was different. I no longer believed him when he talked about leaving his wife. I didn't know what I was going to do, but I knew whatever it was, I couldn't count on him. Also, if I got real honest with myself, I knew that my greatest fear was not that he *wouldn't* leave his wife, but that he *would*. I mean, why would I want to live with a chain-smoking alcoholic? But my mind didn't like to go *there* very often.

Two days before I left Los Angeles, I wrote a song called "Do You Love Too Much?" Every line was a question—just like my life.

Do you try to change your lover
With the power of your touch?
. . . Do you love too much?

Are you driven and obsessed?
Do you want to be possessed?
. . . Do you love too much?

Do you measure everything
By the pleasure of your pain?
. . . Do you love too much?

Do you look for someone else
So you don't have to see yourself?
. . . Do you love too much?

It's a love epidemic
And it's going around
You may be afflicted
So you better take this down . . .

. . . Do you love too much?
. . . Do you love too much?
. . . Do you love too much?

Okay. So it's my last night in Los Angeles and I'm driving up the Pacific Coast Highway to meet my Texas love for dinner at a place called Alice's Restaurant. As it turned out, it was also sort of a "last supper" for the relationship. I would not see this man again for another two years.

Alice's Restaurant was built up on a dock with big glass windows all around. The setting was romantic in a dramatic kind of way. Inside, diners sat at candlelit tables while just outside, big swells of ocean went rolling by. You could hear the muffled sound of the waves as they crashed and churned against the boulders on the beach. The whole scene made me think of Burt Lancaster and Deborah Kerr rolling in the surf in *From Here To Eternity*.

On this particular night, tsunami warnings had been posted on the front door, adding to the drama. I'd never heard of a tsunami. Back in South Carolina where I grew up, all we ever had were hurricanes. But I soon learned that a tsunami was an unusually large tidal wave produced by undersea volcanic eruptions or earthquakes that would sometimes wipe out entire villages, not to mention restaurants standing precariously out over the ocean.

I stopped and read the "eat at your own risk" disclaimer, which basically stated that the restaurant would not be held responsible if we all got swept away. *Yeah? Well, bring it on!* I thought to myself. The idea of being swept away by a big tidal wave, I found strangely appealing. Since I seemed incapable of ending this Greek tragedy of a romance on my own, an ocean earthquake sounded like the perfect deus ex machina.

Dinner was pleasant enough. The wine certainly helped keep the reality of our situation at bay. I was able to enjoy my halibut with caviar sauce and, later, the flan with decaf coffee while our conversation centered safely around songs and ideas for songs. We started writing one called "China Kind of Love," inspired perhaps by the Far Eastern threat of the tsunami: "You've got a China kinda love / it seems so far-off, distant and strange / like I'm lost in a foreign mountain range / you've got this great big wall / and what goes on on the other side / nobody knows at all / A China kind of love." We monkeyed around with this idea for a while, then later I mentioned something about "Goodbye, Little Rock and Roller." But the minute I said it, I knew it would be a song that I would write alone.

After dinner, as he walked me to my rental car, the futility of our situation blindsided me, and I started crying uncontrollably in the parking lot. I cried so hard, I got sick to my stomach. He tried cheering me up by cracking jokes, but I was inconsolable. I just couldn't bear the thought of him going home to his wife and me flying back to Nashville alone. I was still crying as I drove my rental car back to the Shangri-La with the radio tuned to a Spanish-speaking station on the AM dial and the volume cranked all the way up. I was hoping the noise would drown out my pitifulness.

Then a song came on where a man was singing *"Adiós . . . adiós . . . adiós . . ."* Over and over again he sang *"Adiós"* while in the background the stifled sobs of his abandoned lover could be heard along with the music. And that's when I heard a little voice that wasn't coming from the radio. *Marshall,* it said. *Listen, Marshall. It's over. I repeat. It is over. Give it up, girl. Get on with your life. Can't you hear what the man is singing? Spanish people wouldn't lie to you about something like love. You are going to die if you don't let go of this man.*

But it would be another five years of misery and therapy before I could extricate myself. At one point, I even checked into a treatment center out in the middle of an Arizona desert. When I think about those days now, it is hard for me to believe that I damned near lost my soul over some Texas songwriter. Lord have mercy!

I've often wondered why this guy had such a hold on me. As far as I can figure, it was a combination of two things: (1) I fell for him when I was thirty-six years old. Maybe in my mind, I was fast approaching the "last chance to settle down and live happily ever after" exit. (2) After my father died in 1983, this guy had been among the first to call offering condolences. Drowning in grief, I may have mistook his offering for a lifeline. Because, Lord knows, I grabbed on for dear life.

Once back at the Shangri-La, I began to pack and organize my gear for early departure. Before retiring, I took half a Restoril with half a Xanax and was out by midnight.

So there you have it. My state of mind, not to mention body chemistry, as I cruised along over America at forty thousand feet.

When sleep would not come, I finally gave up and had a cup of coffee. If I was going to be awake, then by god, I was going to be *awake*. The caffeine seemed to liberate the right side of my brain because the next thing I knew, I was furiously jotting down lyrics on an American Airlines cocktail napkin: "Once there was a little girl / Unlike any in the world / One night she looked inside her soul / And all she saw was rock and roll . . ." *Oh, okay I get it . . . This must be "Goodbye, Little Rock and Roller." Cool.*

I completed the first verse and was taking notes for the second when finally I crashed, caffeine and all. I was completely out by the time we touched down in Nashville. The stewardess had to wake me up so I could get off the plane.

That weekend, in between unpacking, checking in with friends, and playing a gig, I kept writing on the song. I couldn't believe how it kept going on and on. Finally, on Sunday, Mother's Day, I wrote the last two verses:

> She rocked Lucille to sleep each night
> Then sang her lullabies she'd write
> She thought her heart would break in two
> The first time she heard, Mom, I love you
> And then one day her baby girl
> Walked outside to find her world
> She never dreamed she'd see the day
> She'd be fighting back the tears to say
> Goodbye, Little Rock and Roller . . .

By the time I got to the "Mom, I love you" part, I was crying my eyeballs out.

I've often described "Goodbye, Little Rock and Roller" as a "folk song about rock and roll rejuvenation." And I'm often asked if the song is autobiographical. Well, the answer is yes and no. My Dad never bought me a Silvertone guitar. But he did buy me a Gibson when I was fourteen and later a Martin D-28. But when I was *fifteen,* my best friend's brother—her name was Tricia Troup and his name was Bob—let me have his Silvertone guitar and amplifier while he was away for the summer. The guitar was blue and silver, and the silver part sparkled. I loved that guitar with a passion. I immediately started playing blues and rock and roll bass riffs on it. The first riff I ever learned was the one from "What I'd Say" by Ray Charles. After that, it was Chuck Berry's "No Money Down." It's funny how an instrument can affect the kind of music you play. On my Gibson, I'd strum country, bluegrass, and folk. But plug me into that Silvertone, baby, and I became a full-tilt boogie child. A little rock and roller all the way.

During that summer of the Silvertone, I spent the month of June working as a junior counselor at Camp Pinnacle, which nestled in the Blue Ridge Mountains near Hendersonville, North Carolina. It would be safe to say I was the first junior counselor ever to show up with an electric guitar. Ukuleles had always been the musical instrument of choice, and on balmy evenings, campers and counselors alike would sit cross-legged around the campfire strumming away, singing "Kumbaya" and "Twenty-six Miles Across the Sea."

The first time I plugged in Bob Troup's metallic blue-and-silver electric guitar and sang "I'm like a one-eyed cat peeping in the seafood store . . ." well, everybody just kind of went wild. The people that ran the camp were Baptists, but since I was "that nice Chapman girl from Spartanburg" they didn't seem to notice much. The thing is, I had no idea what a "one-eyed cat peeping in the seafood store" was. I thought the song was about a real cat, like the kind that goes *meow,* and he's licking his chops while peering in the window of a seafood store at the display of dead fish on ice. That was good enough for me. The sexual explicitness of the lyrics went right over my head, and I would imagine over the heads of the reigning Baptists, or I'd of been out of there.

. . .

Camp Pinnacle had a wonderful old open-air gymnasium, where we'd go every night after supper for that evening's entertainment. Every night except Sunday, that is. On Sundays there was a somber vespers service at a campfire site in the woods behind the gym. But on the other nights, when they weren't showing us movies like *Bambi* or *How Green Was My Valley*, there would be organized talent shows.

There was a raised stage at one end of the gym that even had a backstage door *and* an electrical outlet. The outlet was used to run the projector on movie nights and a little 45-rpm record player on "cabin show" nights. It was also convenient for plugging in an electric-guitar amplifier.

Camp Pinnacle had twenty-four cabins. Each cabin had four bunk beds and four single beds for ten or eleven campers with a counselor and sometimes a junior counselor. On cabin show nights, two or three cabins would take turns presenting little skits. Then there was the Miss Pinnacle contest. Bert Parks and Atlantic City had nothing on this production. Especially in the emotional department. I remember the year Mozelle DePass was crowned Miss Pinnacle. During the talent segment, she sang a credible rendition of the theme song from the movie *An Affair to Remember*. The music, combined with the memory of Deborah Kerr getting hit by a taxicab just outside the Empire State Building, where she was to meet Cary Grant, had us all crying so hard that there was no way the judges could vote for anybody but Mozelle. She won by a landslide.

Another big night at Pinnacle was Coronation, which was basically a popularity contest. The camper who got the most votes was crowned Queen, the second most King, and on down through the ranks of the court, whose members represented every sport and activity offered at Pinnacle. But for sheer entertainment, nothing could top the skits on cabin show nights, or the annual show put on by the counselors and junior counselors. Of course, counselors had the advantage of having a place where they could rehearse in private. There was a building called "The Lodge" just up the hill from the gym, where only counselors could go. It was also the only place at camp where cigarette smoking was allowed.

I went to Pinnacle for seven summers. Four as a camper, one as a junior counselor, and two as a counselor. The year I was a junior counselor, The Lodge was where I kept Bob Troup's electric guitar and amplifier. But what

I remember most were the brainstorming sessions we'd have before a show. We'd be sitting around perfecting the art of French inhaling our cigarettes until somebody came up with a good idea. Then we'd get to work putting together a script, deciding who was going to play what, planning scenery, and so on. We would work on those shows for days using whatever props were available: sheets, ketchup, flashlights, pillows, tree limbs . . . you name it.

Most of our "plots" were inspired by Disney movies or rock and roll songs that told a good story. One such song was "Little Egypt," which was a big hit that year for the Coasters. "Little Egypt" told the story of a stripper of the same name who did "the famous dance of the pyramids." She walked, she talked, and crawled "on her belly like a reptile." At least that's what she did until she had so many children she was forced into early retirement.

> Let me tell you people Little Egypt
> doesn't dance there anymore a–wo woh
> She's too busy mopping and
> a–taking care of shopping at the store a–wo woh
> 'Cause she's got seven kids and all day long
> they crawl along the floor a–wo woh

At that point, seven campers wearing diapers and sucking on makeshift pacifiers would come scurrying out across the stage on their hands and knees.

Sometimes it was hard to tell who enjoyed these skits more—the audience or the performers. Sometimes production would come to a halt because the performers would be laughing too hard to continue.

Another rock and roll song that inspired our dramatization was "Running Bear," the Native American version of *Romeo and Juliet,* Juliet being "Little White Dove" and Romeo "Running Bear." Their respective tribes did not approve of their union, so poor Running Bear and Little White Dove drowned trying to reach each other across "raging" waters. They were swimming furiously toward each other when the current pulled them under just as "their hands touched and their lips met."

Death was always good for a dramatic ending. As for cause of death, drownings were okay, but car wrecks were the best:

> Oh where oh where can my baby be
> The Lord took her away from me

She's gone to heaven so I've got to be good
So I can see my baby when I leave this world
We were out one night in my Daddy's car
We hadn't driven very far . . .

Daddy's car gets totaled. The girl dies in the boy's arms while he kisses her one last time. He then makes a lover's vow of chastity until they can be re-united in heaven. "Teen Angel" was another song with basically the same plot.

Teen angel, can you hear me?
Teen angel, can you see me?
Are you somewhere up above?
And am I still your own true love?

"The Hero" was another vehicular tragedy set to music. In this song, "Johnny" is the hero of his high school football team, and his girlfriend, Sue, "the lucky girl that's gonna marry him / soon after graduation day."

My sisters and I once sang this song at a wedding reception for our next-door neighbor, whose name was, of course, Johnny. Needless to say, the marriage did not last. The thing I loved most about this record was the dramatic recitation toward the end. A girl is telephoning Johnny's girlfriend, Sue, to tell her the awful news.

"Hello, Sue? Sue?! Have you heard the news? The bus turned over coming home from the game, and everybody was killed!"

"Not my Johnny!!" Sue gasps.

"*Everybody!*" sobs her friend.

Years later, I would be standing in front of my first Roy Lichtenstein at the Museum of Modern Art in New York. It was a large painting of a frame from a romance comic strip, depicting a distraught young woman with tears flooding out of her eyes. The talk balloon could very well have read: "Not my Johnny!!" As I stood gazing at the canvas, the recitation from "The Hero" played in my mind like a soundtrack for the painting.

Anyway, after the bearer of the bad news blurts out "*Everybody!*", the music kicks back in with a chorus of voices singing "He was a he-ee-ee-ro, he was a he-ee-ee-ro . . ." This is repeated over and over again as the record fades. I always loved the screeching tires and broken-glass sound effects in the background music of these records.

After one of our car wreck skits, there would usually be a couple of ketchup bottles missing from the Camp Pinnacle dining hall. But the only time we *really* got in trouble was after an updated '60s version of *Peter Pan*, which we called *Peter* Pot. In preparing for this production, somebody sawed a hole in the middle of the stage floor so the "little lost boys" would have a place to go.

I often label "Goodbye, Little Rock and Roller" a "*semi*-autobiography." Yes, there was a Lula Mae, but no, I did not sing her songs I would write. But I *did* sing her the songs of Elvis, the Shirelles, and Big Joe Turner and whoever else was on the radio in those years. This was way before I ever wrote a song.

And, yes, I once hitchhiked to Hollywood, but it was to see this guy I was in love with, not to put a band together. However, five years later—in 1978—I *did* cut a record in Hollywood with my band. In fact, we were recording at the Record Plant the day the famous fire broke out that destroyed Studio C. Fortunately, we were working in B.

The fire got a mention in *Rolling Stone,* complete with a picture of our producer, Al Kooper, and Jaded Virgin bassist Tom Comet standing in front of the Record Plant, where dark, billowing smoke can be seen rising from the roof. They had just spilled out onto North Sycamore Avenue, where a bunch of us, myself included, were forming a line to salvage master tapes from the Record Plant archives. We might as well have been rescuing Rembrandts from the Louvre. Boxes containing master tapes of some of the best-known names in rock passed through our hands. Every now and then I would glance down and see one marked "Linda Ronstadt" or "Sly and the Family Stone." I remember seeing *"Hotel California"* on one, and "John Lennon" on another. I nearly fainted when I realized I was holding a box containing a master tape from Stevie Wonder's *Songs in the Key of Life.*

The last two verses of "Goodbye, Little Rock and Roller" are completely fictional. As far as I know, there's no place called "Serenity" down by the sea. But there is—or there used to be—a place called "Tranquility" on Pawley's Island. I used to fantasize about living there.

And no, I never had a baby, much less one named Lucille. But *had* I ever had a baby, Lucille would have definitely been in the mix for a name. God knows, there are enough Marshalls and Marthas in my family to sink a battleship. Better to bestow a child with the energy and spirit of a Little

Richard or a B.B. King than drag it down with a name used over and over by a string of dead Presbyterians. A baby named Lucille just might have a chance in this world that's getting crazier every day.

As for a "gentle man named Ben," most people think that came from the Disney movie or the TV show *Gentle Ben*. And maybe subliminally it did. But the truth is, I wrote "You'll never guess what happened then / She met a gentle man named . . ." and "Ben" just seemed to fit.

"Goodbye, Little Rock and Roller" will always hold a special place in my heart. I truly believe I was on the verge of losing my soul when I wrote that song. It gave me my life back. Some writers say they write to find out who they are. I once said in an interview, "My songs are smarter than I am," and ofttimes they are. I have written songs and not known what they meant until years later. And then I've written songs that were downright psychic.

So who knows? Maybe one day I *will* have a baby and name her Lucille. Stranger things have happened. But nah . . . if there's to be a Lucille wandering around in my future, it will most likely be a one-eyed cat. The kind that goes *meow*.

. . .

I recorded "Goodbye, Little Rock and Roller" twice. First for *Inside Job* (Tall Girl, 1991), then later on *It's About Time* . . . , the live album we did at the women's prison. I hadn't planned to sing "Goodbye, Little Rock and Roller," but when we got an encore, I decided to do it. It was a last minute, spur-of-the-moment–type thing.

The idea to do a concert at the prison was never mine. I did not wake up one morning and think, *Ummm . . . I believe I'll go play a concert in the maximum security compound at the Tennessee State Prison for Women.* Here's what happened.

In April 1989, I received the following letter from Warden Eileen Hosking:

Dear Ms. Chapman,
   I had the pleasure of hearing you perform again recently at the Bluebird and thoroughly enjoyed your performance. Unfortunately, my work is such that I never really leave it behind and it occurred to me that your work and

the way you present yourself might be of both entertaining and modeling value to the women here at the Tennessee Prison for Women.

We have been fortunate to have had a number of well-known performers to donate concerts here in recent years. I don't believe we've had a woman performer lately, however, whose talents and person are as powerfully projected without glitz and amplification. Also, some of the issues inherent in your songs are very significant issues in the lives of the inmates here, whether or not they accept that.

What I'm after, of course, is a free performance here at the prison. I can certainly understand if you are unable to do one. Unfortunately, we are unable to offer you money and quite frankly, I have no idea how you would be received.

Do know, however, that there are several staff members who have followed your career and enjoyed your music over the years. We thank you for that.

Sincerely,
Eileen R. Hosking
Warden

The letter was dated March 31, 1989.

I wanted to respond right away, but I just couldn't. I had been released from treatment only a few months earlier and was still feeling a little fragile and raw around the edges. Also, whenever I even thought about picking up the phone, the words *no idea how you would be received* played in my mind like one of those sky messages at the beach. The idea of being inside a prison was scary enough. But the idea of *bombing* inside one was more than I could bear.

The letter sat on my desk for four years. Every few months or so, I'd pick it up and think about responding, then set it back down. By August 1993, the letter's white paper and envelope had begun to yellow with age. And I was beginning to wonder if *I* had started to yellow with age.

Then one morning, I woke up and decided I was bored. I needed something to shake me up. I was feeling way too complacent and it was starting to get on my nerves. I needed to take a risk. So I picked up the letter and read it one more time. Then I picked up the phone. I dialed Warden Hosking's number at the prison.

Whoever answered informed me that Warden Hosking had taken a maternity leave and was no longer there.

"Is there a number where she can be reached?" I asked.

"We can't give that information out, but you might try the telephone directory. She may be listed."

"Thanks," I said.

I found an "E. R. Hosking," and since it was the only Hosking listed, I dialed the number.

"Hello," answered a female voice.

"Is this Eileen Hosking?" I asked.

"Yes, it is."

"Well, ah, this is Marshall Chapman and I'd like to talk to you about doing a concert out at the women's prison."

There was a long pause, then she laughed, "You sure do take your time answering your mail."

We chatted briefly. She suggested I call an associate warden out there named John Organ. So that's what I did. I called him the minute we hung up. Otherwise, I might have had time to talk myself out of whatever this was I was doing, and I didn't want to do that.

John Organ had a friendly voice and was very enthusiastic about the prospect of my playing the prison. We scheduled a meeting for the following Tuesday in his office.

"Have you ever been inside a prison?" he asked.

"No," I replied.

"Well, when you come out, I'll take you on a tour. It's a pretty interesting place." Then, "By the way, I'll need your driver's license number and date of birth."

"Why do you need that?" I was curious to know.

"It's just for security measures," he replied.

"What kind of security measures?"

"Well, they have to make sure you haven't committed a felony or tried to smuggle contraband into the prison, things like that." I couldn't tell if he was pulling my leg or not.

"If I have," I answered, "I am unaware of it."

He laughed. "That's what they all say."

That Tuesday, as I was driving out to the prison, I tried to imagine what a concert there would be like. *Maybe a songwriter's thing would be the way to go. I could call Ashley (Cleveland), Pam (Tillis), and Emmylou or Rosanne and do a women's in-the-round. That way, I wouldn't be up there by myself, and I'd be less likely to freak out. Calm down, Marshall. This is just a fact-finding mission. You don't have to do or decide anything. Just stay in the moment and everything's gonna be all right.*

As I walked into John Organ's office, I was surprised to see a framed autographed copy of one of my old publicity pictures hanging on his wall. Turns out John had been a huge fan for years. This serendipitous discovery had me once again believing in that old Presbyterian concept of predestination, and I felt myself begin to relax.

We sat there and talked about music for a while. John was a fan of many Nashville-based recording artists, including Emmylou Harris, Dave Olney, Tom Kimmel, Beth Nielsen Chapman, Nanci Griffith, and Jonell Mosser. I love it when my preconceptions get blown out of the water. Never in my wildest dreams did I think I'd be discussing the music of Dave Olney with an associate warden at a state-run prison. Garth Brooks, maybe, but not Dave Olney. John Organ was about as far from your stereotypical Southern male prison warden as you could get. He was distinguished-looking, smart, articulate, and worldly. But best of all, he had great taste in music!

"You ready to take a tour?" His voice brought me out of my reverie. "I'll show you the performance space, then we can visit one of the living units. That'll give you a chance to meet some of the inmates."

We went through a couple of checkpoints, then entered a large treeless courtyard surrounded by red brick buildings. The buildings were connected by covered walkways. The largest building was the gymnasium to our left. As we walked toward it, we passed a couple of inmates who exchanged hellos with John. Then I noticed a few others milling about in the courtyard. I felt like they were all aware of our presence even though most of them were looking the other way. That's the first thing that struck me about being on the inside. No matter who you are, someone is always watching.

Another thing that struck me was how normal all the inmates seemed. They just looked like women you'd see at the mall. The only difference was their clothes. They all wore faded blue work shirts with TN DEPT OF CORRECTION stenciled across the back and dark blue pants with the same thing stenciled on white stripes running down the outside seams. A few wore work boots, but most had on white sneakers.

The most noticeable thing about the exterior of the gym was the accordion-shaped roof. It reminded me of the Sydney Opera House. But since the gym had been built in the mid-'60s, I figured the roof design was a leftover from the funky, space-age architecture of the '50s. Still, it made me want to go inside and check out the acoustics.

The interior was basically a large basketball court painted on a wooden floor with a raised stage at one end and bleachers rising up almost to the ceiling at the other. I climbed a few stairs to the stage, then turned to face the big empty space. I tried to imagine what it would be like looking out at an audience full of inmates. *This might work,* I thought to myself. I liked the space. It felt just right.

Then I stepped down off the stage and walked out onto the middle of the floor, where I stopped for a moment. I snapped my fingers and couldn't believe the sound I heard. Like a rifle shot with lots of reverb. *My god,* I thought. *What a great place to play rock and roll!* And in that moment, I knew. I was somehow going to do a show there. And I was going to do it right. Round up The Love Slaves, bring in some good sound, and with these acoustics, hell, we might as well record it.

John Organ liked the idea and already had a few possible dates in mind. One was Friday, October 29. The prison was planning a big graduation ceremony that evening for twenty-seven inmates receiving their G.E.D.s. He thought a concert would be a nice reward for those who had worked and studied so hard. Sounded good to me.

We left the gym and walked across the courtyard to one of the older cell blocks. As the outside security door opened, it made such an eerie, loud scraping-metal sound, that the hairs stood up on the back of my neck. I was told it was one of the older doors in the compound. "The new ones are electric operated and much quieter," John explained.

A few months later, I would return to capture this spine-tingling sound with Donivan Cowart, our recording engineer. The opening and closing of that door ended up being the first and last thing heard on *It's About Time . . .*

The night before the concert, The Love Slaves and I played a club in Nashville called 12ᵗʰ & Porter. That way, we could run down our hour and a half prison set in front of a live audience in case there were any kinks that needed to be worked out. I'd invited John Organ to this preview in hopes of getting some feedback. John had recently told me about a band that they'd had some problems with.

"What kind of problems?" I asked.

"Well, they did some inappropriate things in front of the inmates."

"Like what?"

"Let's just put it this way," he explained. "What started out as a band playing music turned into a burlesque show."

"Really?" I said, then laughed. "Well, you're lucky this isn't fifteen years ago or you might have gotten the same thing from me!" I was thinking about a gig I'd played in McDonough, Georgia, back in 1980. There had been little or no advertising, and as soon as I took the stage, I realized there were only two people in the audience, and both of them were drunk. The only other living thing out there was a dog with an infected ear. We were in the middle of "Rock and Roll Clothes" and I was so bored and disappointed—not to mention a little drunk—that I stripped off my T-shirt and got down on the stage floor and started doing the Alligator. The drunks were too drunk to notice, and the dog kept scratching his ear, but the guys in the band loved it. Afterward, the club owner told me I'd never work in that town again. "Could you put that in writing?" I slurred.

After our set at 12th & Porter, I walked over to John Organ at the bar and said, "Well, what do you think?"

He took a long sip from his drink, then said, "You know that third song you sang . . . the one about the guy hanging around you like a bad debt?"

"Yes."

"Well, by the end of that song, you'll have 'em." He took another sip, then added, "Many of our maximum security inmates are in there because they killed their bad debts."

I wrote "Bad Debt" in 1984, after back-to-back experiences with Speed Freak Boyfriends 1 and 2. The first time I performed it was for a benefit at a Nashville club called Bogey's. The crowd response was incredible. John Prine came up afterward and said, "Marshall, when are you gonna stop picking on us?!"

You hang around me like a bad debt
You haven't taken out the garbage yet

I must be crazy I'm the one that let
I let you hang around me like a bad debt

The night I met you you were looking good
I took you home with me and fixed you some food
We kissed and hugged until the morning light
Now how was I to know that your intentions weren't right

That was three years ago now you're still here
Stretched out on my couch drinking all my beer
I'm paying all the bills while you watch TV
I think it's time I underwent some psychotherapy

Bad debt
Bad debt
You hang around me like a bad debt
You haven't taken out the garbage yet
I let you hang around me like a bad debt

I'm gonna find a man that really works
I've had it up to here with clowns and jerks
If he can't play the guitar that's okay
In fact I would prefer it if it was that way

Bring me a doctor, lawyer, Indian chief
J-O-B is how I spell relief
I want somebody with a little backbone
You know . . . a MAN with a PLAN and a PLACE OF HIS OWN

Bad debt
Bad debt
You hang around me like a bad debt
You haven't taken out the garbage yet
I let you hang around me like a b-b-b-b-b-b-b-b . . .

Bad debt
Bad debt

I've had it up to here with bad debt
I'm gonna write you off so I can forget
I let you hang around me like a . . .

At this point, the band would take off with Eddie and James exchanging guitar solos. Then John would gather us all back in with a little drum roll, and then *pop!* the volume would drop out, leaving only the pulsating rhythm of a double heartbeat every other bar. After a few measures of this, I would slowly begin to "gather myself" before launching into a stream-of-consciousness rampage directed at an imaginary bad debt stretched out on an imaginary couch somewhere between me and the audience. No two rampages were ever alike, and the intensity level always varied, depending on the state of my hormones and their relationship with the moon. If I happened to be ovulating on a full moon, chances were good that all hell would break loose.

"Gathering myself" usually involved taking a sip from a bottle of Evian, unstrapping my guitar and setting it down on its stand, removing my jacket, reapplying my lipstick, wiping my brow with a white hand towel, and generally lah-de-dah-ing around on stage while the band continued its pulsating rhythm. When the anticipation level of the audience reached a certain level, I would then make my way back to the mic and, with one hand on my hip, start in with something like:

Hey baby!
Why don't you get your BIG FAT
LAAARD ASS
Off of that couch just one time
Just one time! . . .
I'm talking to YOU, Lard Ass
Move! I said, MOVE!!
Yeah, I want to see some of that garbage go moving
Out the . . . BACK door
And while you're at it
Why don't you just take it on down to the recycling center
Uh, huh . . .
And while you're there . . .
You might as well recycle that laard ass of yours . . .

Hell, there's enough lard in there to fry chicken
For the entire county!
Put it to work, baby!
Move it!
I said . . . Move it!!!

John Organ was right. The next night at the prison, I was about halfway through "Bad Debt" when I realized the inmates were starting to really get into the swing of things. By the time I finished lard-ass-takes-the-garbage-out, it was sheer pandemonium.

The fourth wall had come down, and I could feel the connection. The inmates and I were now soul sisters on the highest plane. From then on, everything I said or did was punctuated by comments from a chorus of black women led by an inmate named Diane, who was celebrating her birthday that night.

"I heard that, Maah-shul!"

"You go on now, girl!"

"Raise the roof, Maah-shul, so we can get out of here!"

I couldn't say five words without them yelling out something, and I was loving every minute of it.

"Now there was this lady . . ." I would begin, and before I could say another word . . .

"What *kind* of lady?"

"I don't know but she had *definite* ideas," I answered.

"I heard that!"

At one point, about fifty minutes into the show, I knew Donivan would soon have to change the tape. We had talked about this beforehand, wanting to make sure the change took place between songs instead of in the middle of one. So we decided I would check in with him before launching into "Bizzy Bizzy Bizzy," which was the longest song in the show. "How much time have we got?" I asked him, meaning how much time left on the tape. Before he could give me a thumbs up, one of the inmates yelled out, "Don't worry about time, Maah-shul. We got *all the time in the world*!"

Fortunately, Donivan had placed a couple of microphones out in the audience and had kept the tape machine running not only during the show, but before and afterward as well. The first time we listened to a playback, we couldn't believe some of the things we were hearing on the two audience tracks. Our favorite was a comment made while the inmates were filing in before the show. Amidst the shuffling feet and scraping chairs, a voice can be heard saying "Who in the hell *is* this honky bitch?"

This comment didn't make the CD, but I had fun telling people I was considering *Who in the Hell* Is *This Honky Bitch?* for the title. I don't know about you, but if I saw a CD called *Who in the Hell* Is *This Honky Bitch?*, I would buy it in a heartbeat.

As Donivan and I listened to the rough tracks that first time, sitting at the console in Brian Ahern's Enactron truck studio, one thing was for sure: The Love Slaves and I had only been a catalyst. The inmates were the show.

The last song on our set list was "Betty's Bein' Bad." That night, after I sang the last chorus, I thanked everybody, then set my guitar down while The Love Slaves continued to rock. Usually, I make my exit when they start singing "Bye-bye Betty Goodbye." But on this night, I turned and walked out toward the inmates. There are no words to describe how I felt in that moment. As I looked into their faces and shook their outstretched hands, I experienced something I'd never experienced in over twenty years of performing. The volume of love and appreciation was deafening. Finally, I turned around and exited to the back of the stage. Tommy Spurlock, our monitor engineer, was there to help me down the stairs and back across the hall to the classroom that served as our dressing room.

From there, I could hear the band finishing up and the thunderous applause that followed. Then, one by one, The Love Slaves—James Hollihan, Eddie Angel, Jackie Street, and John Hammond—filed in. For a moment, we just stood there looking at each other, our eyes dilated with adrenaline. We all looked like we'd just gotten off a wild ride at the fair. We waited for the applause to die down, but instead of dying down, it seemed to grow stronger. Finally, as if on cue, we all turned and headed back for the stage. When the audience saw us, they went nuts. They were revved up and ready to rock. But I had other plans.

"This is a song I wrote on Mother's Day," I said after things finally began to settle down.

It's hard to believe that an hour and a half earlier, I had been so nervous standing around in our dressing room that I decided to *glue* my picks on with Crazy Glue. I had never tried this before, but had once seen this permanent adhesive used to close a gash in Stevie Ray Vaughan's thumb so he could rush back out and finish a show. This happened backstage at the old Orpheum Theater in Memphis, where we had all convened to tape the pilot for a PBS series called *American Caravan with Lonnie Mack*. The Orpheum was where a young Elvis Presley had once worked as an usher in the early '50s.

I figured if Crazy Glue was good enough to stop the bleeding for Stevie Ray, it sure as hell could keep my picks on.

James Hollihan, the most detached of all The Love Slaves, was watching with interest as I applied the glue.

"What are you doing?" he asked. James was not the type to ever get in anybody's business.

"My picks keep sliding off so I'm gluing them on," I replied.

"Have you ever done that before?"

"No."

"How you gonna get them off?"

"I don't know," I replied. "I'll worry about that after the show."

In the weeks preceding the show, I was constantly asking John Organ questions. I've always been that way. When Chris and I first got together, he called me The Question Lady. Anyway, I wanted to be as informed as I possibly could before walking out on that stage to stand before two hundred inmates. And there was a lot to know.

I learned that the inmate population was 52.6 percent white, 47 percent black, and less than one half of 1 percent for "all other," which included Hispanics and Native Americans. I learned that the average age for an inmate was 31.7 years. I learned there was one inmate serving a death sentence. Her name was Gaile Owens.

Gaile and two other inmates, Barbara Tole and Deborah Knapp, had been allowed to bring a platter of fruit to our dressing room that evening. Barbara was editor of an inmate-published quarterly called *A Look Inside . . .* She had received special permission to interview me before the show.

"If we could do it afterward," I told her, "that would be better. I'm way too nervous to talk to anybody right now."

Fortunately, permission was granted and we got to talk. The first thing Barbara said was, "I knew I'd like your show the minute you turned down my interview request because you were 'way too nervous.' I'm thinking 'Wow, this woman doesn't waste time beating around the bush. She just tells it like it is.'"

"Yeah," I laughed, "and sometimes it gets me in trouble."

Barbara was intelligent and had a lot of spunk. She liked music and had written a few songs herself. I enjoyed our interview and the article she later wrote for the paper.

Three years later, Barbara Tole would slash her arms and bleed to death alone in her cell. She left behind a two-page typed note that said in part: "In life we hold on to everything. In preparation for death I wonder why I ever believed that anything other than love was important."

I was devastated when I heard the news. Barbara's friends organized a memorial at the gym and asked me to sing. I didn't have to worry about *what* to sing because they had printed up a program that listed three of my songs: "Happy Childhood," "In the Fullness of Time," and "Goodbye, Little Rock and Roller." Her cell mate, Linda, told me "Goodbye, Little Rock and Roller" had always been Barbara's favorite.

Gaile Owens and I have been pen pals over the years. She was sentenced to death in 1986 for "accessory before the fact—murder." In other words, she hired someone to kill her husband.

Statistics show that women who kill their husbands receive longer sentences than men who kill their wives. There are many reasons for this. A man who kills his wife usually does so in a fit of rage. Come trial day, he is full of remorse. And understandably so. For he has killed the person who took care of his kids, cleaned the house, fixed his meals, washed his clothes, and made love to him on demand. So there he is, up on the witness stand boohooing his eyes out, and the judge, usually a man, is boohooing right along with him. So maybe the guy gets twenty years and is out in four.

A woman, on the other hand, usually kills her husband to stop the abuse. She is living in terror, and it gets to the point she thinks there is no way out. She waits until he is asleep, then shoots him in the head. Or maybe, as Gaile did, she hires someone to do the job. Her crime is cold, calculated, premeditated. The judge is not amused. In fact, he is downright threatened. Down comes his gavel. Life imprisonment! Or in Gaile's case, death by electrocution.

Just recently, another Tennessee woman was sentenced to only ten years for the same crime as Gaile's. I understand that life isn't fair, but I feel like

Gaile's sentence was too harsh and that she has paid her debt to society. Today, she leads a productive life within the prison system, serving on various boards and councils, helping new inmates with orientation. She made a horrible mistake many years ago. She acknowledges it. The State of Tennessee has certainly acknowledged it. And I sympathize with her husband's family. But killing her won't bring him back. There's enough killing in the world without state-sanctioned executions.

Some people see the light and make changes. Others never do. This was never better illustrated than in an article I read in an issue of *A Look Inside* . . . . The question was raised: "What have you learned since your incarceration?" Some of the answers reflected a newfound sobriety and wisdom gained from various programs and ministries within the prison system. It was easy to tell the ones who were on the path to rehabilitation. Then there were the others, one of whom exclaimed, "Next time I rob a liquor store, it won't be in the state of Tennessee!"

Back to prison statistics: I learned that 27 percent of the inmates were in for murder or murder-related offenses. About 20 percent were in for cocaine possession and/or other drug charges; 35 percent for burglary, robbery, and theft; 10 percent for assault and aggravated assault; and the rest for everything from forgery, fraud, and embezzlement to arson, rape, and kidnapping.

I also learned some new terminology. For example, a prison guard is never referred to as a "guard" on the inside. He or she is called a "C.O.," as in "correctional officer."

And I learned that there is much more shame connected to being a woman in prison than being a man. As a result, women get fewer visitors. Come visitor's day at a men's facility, there are codependent women lined up all the way out in the parking lot waiting to bring food, clean socks, sex, and whatever else they think their men need.

John Organ told me about one Christmas morning he was working out at the women's prison and by the time he'd left at noon, only two inmates had had visitors. "It was pretty sad," he said.

But the saddest story of all is the mothers. They either don't ever or rarely get to see their children. In a 1995 survey given to all inmates at the Tennessee State Prison for Women, *81.2* percent said they had children.

. . .

So when I introduced "Goodbye, Little Rock and Roller" saying "This is a song I wrote on Mother's Day," the compound suddenly became very quiet. Of course, to lighten the mood, I went on about how I was ovulating at the time, then digressed into a discourse on the *h*-word, that is to say, *hormones.* "They're here. They are powerful. They are *not* going away."

Then I started singing the song. By the time I reached the last verse, where the mother is telling her daughter goodbye, that big ol' gym got so quiet you could've heard a pin drop. Then something happened that I will never forget for as long as I live. I glanced down and noticed two inmates on the front row with their arms around each other, their heads resting together, nodding in time to the music. They were both looking right at me, smiling, but with tears streaming down their faces.

Later John Organ thanked me for doing "Goodbye, Little Rock and Roller" for the encore. "That was a perfect choice," he said. "Usually after a concert, the inmates get so riled up we always have a few write-ups. But there were none after your show. It was like church. They all filed back to their cells in a peaceful and orderly fashion. I've never seen anything like it. Usually, somebody's mouthing off about something. You sure made our job easy."

I don't know about that. I just know that I went home that night and curled up on the sofa with Chris and cried and cried. "Why are you crying?" he asked. "I don't know," I said. "It's just they're locked up in their cells now, and . . . well . . . I miss them."

The next week I received some wonderful mail. A letter from Penny Ellis, Warden Organ's secretary, said, "It was more than a concert. It was a spiritual awakening." And this from Warden Organ: "I do not think many people know how much you put into that evening. The preparation time, the coordination, the cost of equipment, and the courage to stand up before the toughest audience in Nashville . . . on behalf of the staff and residents of the Tennessee Prison for Women, I thank you. It was wonderful."

But the best mail came from the inmates. Gaile Owens programmed a huge computer foldout that said: YOU WERE GREAT!!! THANKS MARSHALL CHAPMAN! flanked by printed images of two electric guitars, along with appreciative handwritten notes from thirty or so inmates. I was overwhelmed.

Some were articulate, written with a sure and steady hand; others were scrawled and barely legible. Even now, whenever I look at that banner, it stirs my heart.

Two more things on "Goodbye, Little Rock and Roller" and then I'll close. First of all, it's the longest song I ever wrote. And . . . well, I'll say this to Barbara Tole wherever she is:

"Hey, Barbara. It's my favorite, too."

10

Girl in a Bubble

Men who hate women
The women that love 'em
Women that love too much
It's so complicated
I'm afraid to go out
Afraid to get back in touch
So I turn to Andy Griffith
And The Lucy Show
'Cause every time I watch the news
They remind me that the world
Is turning hard and cold
And then I end up getting the blues
I'm just a girl in a bubble
Staying out of trouble
That's all

I had a lover last year
I thought the coast was clear
Then he blew up in my face
I went a-rockin' and a-reelin'
Out a-lookin' for the feeling
Wasn't nothing there to take his place
I spent a whole lot of money
At a funny farm
People, I had a blast
I was playing Ping-Pong

From dusk 'til dawn
Until they made me go home at last
Now I'm a girl in a bubble
Staying out of trouble
That's all

Flying on a Lear jet
With Jimmy and the Jet Set
Settin' ourselves on fire
We hit the high seas
Off the Florida Keys
On a loveboat named Desire
The fast lane's a nice place
To visit for a while
But I wouldn't want to live there
I got to get back
To where I once belonged
Now I'm so happy just to be right here
A girl in a bubble
(Staying out of trouble)
Girl in a bubble
(Staying out of trouble)
Girl in a bubble
(Staying out of trouble)
. . . that's all

"Girl in a Bubble" was written one amazing weekend in the fall of 1986. I use the word *amazing* because I wrote four songs that weekend. It was the most prolific, intense songwriting span I had ever experienced. Maybe it was a coincidence, maybe not, but I had spent the weekend in a dreamy, soft state—the aftermath of my first (and next-to-last) Ecstasy experience. And the songs just came pouring out, one after the other, beginning with "Girl in a Bubble."

I had first heard about Ecstasy in the summer of 1985 while spending a couple of weeks with two friends in Bridgehampton, New York. Bridge-hampton is one of several resort villages that make up the Hamptons on Long Island's South Fork. It's about ninety-five miles east of Manhattan.

My friends, whom we'll refer to as Mildred and Kit, had rented a house there for the season.

The house turned out to be "party central" for the area, and the hottest topic of conversation that summer was this new drug called Ecstasy. At the time, Ecstasy was legal. Psychiatrists had been using it for years to help couples headed for divorce so they could talk to each other instead of trying to kill each other. But by the end of 1985, Ecstasy's popularity as a recreational drug was so great that the DEA quickly moved in and declared it illegal.

There were lively parties nearly every night at the house in Bridgehampton, with people like George Plimpton, Alana Stewart, Jann Wenner, Michelle Phillips, Jack Nicholson, and assorted Kennedy cousins drifting in and out. Now I don't mean to imply that any of the above were partakers, but Ecstasy was definitely *the* buzzword that summer for those living on the edge. My friends were into it big time and took perverse pleasure in describing its effects to me in detail. Kit in particular would say things like "Chapman, you're missing out, baby!" or "What are you saving yourself for . . . Christmas?" It was all good-natured ribbing. We'd been friends long enough for them to have become accustomed to my voyeuristic ways. So I never partook—at least not that summer—but I *was* intrigued.

Kit would also tease me unmercifully whenever I pulled one of my disappearing acts before a party, which I did routinely, retreating to my room with a book to hide out until most of the guests had gone. I was reading Colette that summer . . . and still lovesick over the Texas songwriter. Partying was the last thing on my mind.

But the teasing went both ways. I remember one time Mildred and I were playing Scrabble in the dining room while Kit was upstairs entertaining a gentleman caller. It was early afternoon, and we were well into our game when suddenly we heard an unusual noise coming from above. It sounded like a dentist with a damn drill up there. We were both thinking, *What in the hell is going on?* as we looked up at the ceiling, then looked at each other, then back up at the ceiling again. Mildred had just formed the three-letter word *two*—as in the number two—with the *w* falling on a triple-letter dark blue premium square.

"Challenge!" I cried out.

Mildred looked at me like I'd lost my mind.

"Two *(twŏh)*?" I continued, unaware of my phonetic mispronunciation. "That's not a word. I challenge!"

Then I realized my mistake.

Maybe I'd been distracted by the noise from upstairs or suffered a flash attack of alexia—a word blindness caused by playing Scrabble for so long you can't see the forest for the trees. Whatever the cause of my blunder, it was soon forgotten as the buzzing noise from upstairs resumed, this time accompanied by peals of laughter. Soon the giggles were replaced by low moans that kept gaining in pitch and volume as the buzzing noise continued, until it all culminated with a loud shriek beseeching a deity. At that point, Mildred and I knew one thing for sure: Though there were seven unplayed letters sitting in each of our trays, Scrabble, at least for the afternoon, was officially over.

A few minutes later, Kit descended the stairs with her paramour de jour and, after seeing him off, announced she was ready for a swim. She and Mildred and I were in the habit of taking long daily swims in the ocean. So we grabbed our towels, bundled into Mildred's car, and headed for the beach. I rode up front with Mildred, while Kit writhed about in the backseat, looking like the cat that just ate the canary. The sky was gray and overcast, and a northeaster was beginning to blow.

"I'll bet the ocean's cold as shit!" Mildred exclaimed.

"Not if Kit goes in first and heats it up for the rest of us," I said loud enough for Kit to hear me in the backseat. "It's the least she can do."

A year later, in the fall of 1986, I was still lovesick . . . and still curious about Ecstasy. I was thinking, *Hell, I could* use *a little ecstasy in my life right now. It might be just what I need. And besides, I'm an artist. It's my duty to check these things out.*

So I did.

According to the DEA, Ecstasy, or methylenedioxymethamphetamine (MDMA), has a "stimulating, analgesic, and hallucinogenic effect in humans." In other words, it's a pharmaceutical cocktail of the best speed, opiate, and acid you'll ever have. It energizes in a smooth way, giving the user "a heightened sense of awareness and a feeling of increased empathy or closeness to others." Of course, it has its dangerous side effects—like brain damage, for instance—but my heart had been hurting for so long that my brain was the last thing on my mind.

I decided to share my first Ecstasy experience with a photographer friend we'll call "Damien." Damien lived above his studio in an old warehouse building in downtown Nashville. I arrived there one Thursday evening armed with four 100-mg tablets procured from a friend who happened to be the founder and CEO of a successful independent record company.

As the sun was going down, Damien and I each took half a tablet, then waited twenty minutes or so before taking the other half. I'd been cautioned by veteran partakers that I might experience a mild wave of nausea as the drug begins to take effect . . . and I did. But it was a small price to pay for what waited on the other side. For the next six hours I was in a blissful state unlike anything I had ever known. The pill totally obliterated all fear and pain.

At one point, I remember lying flat on my back, looking down along my body and I literally "saw" the pain that had been in my heart rise up out of my chest and move over into my peripheral vision. And the pain had a voice. It said, *Marshall, I am going to be over here for a while, so enjoy yourself because I'll be back.* Later, I heard another voice that may have been the voice of some higher power, I don't know. But it said, *Marshall, I know you feel great right now, and you* deserve *to feel this way. But this drug will kill you if you take it on a regular basis, so you be careful. Also, I want you to hear what I'm about to say, so listen up!* It is possible *for you to feel this way without taking anything. So just hang in there girl, and I promise that one day you will* naturally *feel this good.*

Ecstasy is not a sex drug; that is, it's not something you take to have sex with someone you're not in love with or don't know very well. I've heard that it is difficult for male partakers to achieve ejaculation. Only recently, an artist friend was describing it as a "yin drug." Yin as opposed to yang. "It makes you expansive, sensitive, vulnerable," she said. "It's the most powerful love drug there is." Of course, she was referring to the pure, therapeutic variety prevalent in the mid-'80s. Today, the real article can still be found, but black-market Ecstasy is often a cheap cocktail of other drugs with a greater emphasis on speed.

. . .

Damien and I just laid there and held each other while we listened to music and talked about everything under the sun: our work, our dreams, our friends, Nashville, Austin, England, family, music, art, therapy, and love. We came to the conclusion that love was the ultimate drug. We were lying in the dark in his upstairs living area, and at one point, I remember being mesmerized by the light coming up between the wooden planks in the floor. Of course, it was just the light from downstairs, but I thought I was seeing a miracle . . . like the Holy Grail or something. I just thought that light was the most amazing thing I'd ever seen.

Damien and I remained in this blissful altered state throughout most of the night. Come morning, as the pills' effects began to wane, he arose and began stirring in the kitchen. Soon we were enjoying warm cups of English tea and toasted fresh bread with marmalade. Later, we ventured out to a nearby park to walk his dogs.

Shelby Park is Nashville's oldest public park. It sits on a hilly tract of land along the Cumberland River, just east of downtown, and is home to some of the most ancient and beautiful trees in the metropolitan area. I remember trying to hug a particularly large and craggy bur oak. It was like trying to hug a wall. My long, outstretched arms couldn't begin to reach around its massive trunk. So I just leaned into it for a while, probably trying to absorb its strength, because Lord knows I would need it as I made my re-entry back into the real world.

The morning was overcast and misty with cool temperatures, sympathetic weather for the mild hangover I was now experiencing. An Ecstasy hangover isn't like a drinking hangover. No headaches or nauseous aftereffects. I didn't feel *bad*. I just felt drained in a pleasant kind of way. I had been well counseled by my veteran friends: "It'll last two or three days," they said. "You won't feel sick or anything, but you will feel 'soft,' and you should surround yourself with beauty. Take the phone off the hook and just take it easy. And drink lots of fresh orange juice with teaspoons of sugar . . . and though you won't be hungry, try to eat something . . . comfort food." It was sound advice.

After Shelby Park, Damien and I went our separate ways. As I drove back to the Americana, I noticed a steady rain had begun to fall. It was still falling when I got to my apartment, so I walked over to the nearest window and opened it as wide as it would go. For a while, I just stood there breathing in the cool, moist air. *Aaah . . . October . . . how I love you! . . . the pungent*

smell of your wet brown leaves . . . mother earth replenishing herself . . .
aaahh . . .

1986 was a rough year emotionally. I just couldn't figure out how to be happy. I was still laboring under the false assumption that something outside of me could do the trick—the right boyfriend, the right pill, the right record deal, the right vacation, the right whatever. Also, I was living proof that money can't buy happiness, because in 1986, the money was finally coming in.

The year before had been my most successful to date. Nine of my songs were recorded by other artists, including four by Jimmy Buffett. There was a Tanya Tucker cut, and of course "Betty," a huge hit for Sawyer Brown. Then, out of left field, comes a *wrestler* named Hillbilly Jim. Doc Pomus and I wrote a song for him called "Don't Go Messin' with a Country Boy."

Doc Pomus was a dear friend and mentor who helped keep my spirit alive from the time we were introduced in 1977 until his death in 1991. We first met when he came to see me perform at The Other End in New York. My first album for Epic had just been released, and the record company brass was out in full force. After my show, they all poured into my dressing room. "Doc Pomus is here! He *loved* the show, Marshall. . . . He wants to meet you! . . . a legendary figure . . . blah, blah, blah . . . wrote 'Save the Last Dance for Me!' . . . 'Little Sister' . . ." and on and on it went.

I'd seen the name Doc Pomus on some of my all-time favorite records: The Drifters ("Save the Last Dance for Me," "This Magic Moment"), Elvis Presley ("Little Sister," "Suspicion"), Ray Charles ("Lonely Avenue"), Dion and the Belmonts ("Teenager in Love"), The Coasters ("Youngblood"), plus many, many more. Other than that, I knew nothing about him.

When we met, I was somewhat taken aback. Doc was an imposing man. He must have weighed three hundred pounds, his massive body confined to a wheelchair due to a childhood bout with polio. He had a gray beard and wore tinted glasses, a big Stetson hat, and fat rings. He was Ironsides meets Santa Claus meets the Mafia. He looked frightening but had a Buddha-like presence that could fill a room. There was something so vulnerable and soulful in his eyes that I was drawn to him immediately. It was love at first insight.

Later, whenever I would go to New York, I would always check in with Doc. I was among the last to visit him at NYU's Tisch Hospital before he finally succumbed to lung cancer. I was massaging his right hand when the nurse came in and told me my time was up. As I turned to leave, I heard a rasp whisper: "We'll save the other one for later."

Doc once told me, "Maah-shul, if anybody ever tells you they know somebody just like you, you tell 'em I said they're a goddamned liar 'cause there ain't nobody even *close* to being you in this whole wide world." *Okay, Doc. Whatever you say. But the same goes for you.*

Before Bridgehampton, I was in the City for a few days, so naturally I called Doc. As soon as he gave me the green light, I jumped in a taxi and headed for his building at 253 West 72nd. As I breezed into his apartment, Doc, as usual, was sitting up in bed, talking on the phone.

"I've got just the right person standing right here in my apartment," I heard him say. "She's a terrific songwriter . . . yeah, from Nashville . . . knows all about country music . . . yeah, no problem . . . okay . . ." Finally he hung up.

"What's up?" I asked.

"You're not gonna believe this shit," he said. "They're wanting a song for some wrestler, a guy named Hillbilly Jim. It's Cyndi Lauper's people. They're doing an album of singing wrestlers. They've got Hulk Hogan and everybody. But they want a theme song for this Hillbilly Jim guy. Something like 'The Ballad of Davy Crockett.' You up for it?"

"I guess," I replied. I'm thinking, *Only in America could something like this happen. After all, this is the country that gave the world Tiny Tim, Mrs. Miller, and Alvin and the Singing Chipmunks. So why not singing wrestlers? Makes perfect sense to me.*

Doc and I finished the song in a couple of hours. A courier was dispatched to pick up our rough demo. And just like that, "Don't Go Messin' with a Country Boy" was on its way to the recording studio and the radio airwaves of the world.

A few days later, Doc called me in Bridgehampton.

"Joel Dorn just played me the final mix of our song," he said.

"How's it sound?"

"It sounds real stoo-pid. We'll probably make a shitload of money."

And we did. The song ended up on an album called, oddly enough, *The*

Wrestling Album, and it sold a bundle. I may be the only songwriter in Nashville receiving royalties from the World Wrestling Federation.

It usually takes BMI and the record companies about a year to collect and distribute money to writers and publishers. So by October 1986, the checks were coming in. Big checks, too. The biggest checks I'd ever seen. Checks with commas between the numerals. I called it "beyond rent money."

Since being on my own, I'd only lived in three places: a condemned neighborhood, my car, and the Americana. Now my accountant was telling me I needed to *buy* a place.

I'd begun the process of looking around, keeping notes in a yellow legal pad, which was the same pad I picked up and began filling with lyrics as the October rain continued its steady drone outside my open window.

I still have that yellow legal pad today. It stays in a chest where I have been throwing cocktail napkins, scraps of paper, and legal pads filled with lyrics ever since I first started writing. Many of these scribbled ideas become songs. The rest are either (1) waiting to become songs, or (2) have a snowball's chance in hell of ever becoming anything. I got the idea for keeping a "treasure chest" of lyrics from Harlan Howard, dean of Nashville songwriters and writer of such great American standards as "I Fall to Pieces," "Busted," and "Heartaches by the Number." Harlan was a good friend and mentor to me when I first started out.

As I look through the legal pad today, on one page I can see my old house-hunting notes, where I'd jotted down new terminology—new to me anyway—like "earnest money" and "fixed mortgage." On a list of things to do, I'd written "check for termites and radon." In the midst of all this, there's a phrase in quotation marks: "Girl in a bubble, stayin' out of trouble . . . that's all."

I doubt the idea of a "girl in a bubble" would ever have come to mind had it not been for the much-publicized plight of a boy in Houston, Texas, named David Vetter. David spent his entire twelve-year lifespan in a plastic, germ-free environment where no one could touch him, not even his parents. He became known the world over as "the bubble boy" or "the boy in the bubble." He was born in 1971 with SCID (severe combined immune deficiency) and died in 1984 after an unsuccessful bone marrow transplant.

In a metaphorical sense, I identified with "the boy in the bubble." And on that gray October morning, as I stood alone at my window watching the rain come down, I, too, felt like one of the untouchables: "A girl in a bubble / staying out of trouble / that's all."

On the next page of my legal pad, I started writing stuff down. Sometimes a song doesn't materialize right away, and I'll write anything just to get something started. Jumper-cable lines like:

> *Let's try being human*
> *Living from day to day*
> *Let's put the monsters to rest*
> *That used to save the day*

Sounds good, but what does it mean? Still grasping for straws I continued:

> *The lamp's out in the yard*
> *Broken pieces everywhere*
> *It's not on the table by the couch*
> *There's broken glass everywhere*
> *And every time I look in the mirror*
> *The only word I hear . . . is Ouch!*

Where is this *shit coming from?* I wondered. Then I remembered the very first night I spent in my fifty-dollar-a-month apartment at 3008 Dudley Avenue. I was awakened in the wee hours by something thumping against the wall and the muffled sounds of a man yelling and a woman screaming. Moments later, there was a crash somewhere out in the front yard. It sounded like glass breaking on pavement. The next morning, as I walked out to get the paper, I had to be real careful not to step on the broken pieces of a shattered lamp that lay scattered all over the sidewalk.

About then, another memory began firing in my subconscious. On New Year's Eve 1984, there had been a murder/suicide involving a prominent man from back home who owned a chain of newspapers in the Carolinas. He and his wife had a summer home on Lake Summit a few houses down from my family. There was an article about this event in *The Tennessean*. I had cut it out and pasted it in a journal I was keeping at the time.

So whenever I write something and wonder *Where did* that *come from?* I often later realize *exactly* where it came from. And the place is usually a very real place. Such was the case with "Looking for a Kiss," a song that just squirted out while I was writing "Girl in a Bubble." The shattered lamp from Dudley Avenue may have been the spark, but the Carolina murder/suicide was the fuel that propelled me to write:

> *There's broken glass*
> *Mixed with blood*
> *On the floor in the hall and the den*
> *Now there're strangers in the house*
> *Tracking in mud*
> *Wonderin' how it all began*
>
> *A wheelbarrow track*
> *Cutting through the backyard*
> *Leading to the garbage can*
> *Don't look now*
> *Oh god, how'd he get her . . .*
> *Get her in the shape she's in*
>
> *Down at the morgue*
> *They tried to lay her on the table*
> *But rigor mortis had set in*
> *With bruises on her face*
> *And underneath her fingernails*
> *Were traces of his flesh and skin*
>
> *How did it happen?*
> *How did it ever come to this?*
> *Two people fall in love*
> *Then they kill each other*
> *Looking for a kiss*
>
> *They went out looking for him*
> *But they didn't go far*

They got a call from the Holiday Inn
We've got a man in a bathtub
A mess here to clean up
It happens when you do yourself in

But . . . how did it happen?
How did it ever come to this?
Two people fall in love
Then they kill each other
Looking for a kiss
Two people fall in love
Then they kill each other
Looking for a kiss

The original working title of this song was "Partners in Crimes of Passion." It was an idea I'd had for years. But as often happens, it got "written out" of the song. "Looking for a Kiss" ended up the obvious title. It was too perfect to resist. The hard "k's" gave it an ominous sound, and just saying the words out loud . . . felt like a violent act.

Around this time, the powers-that-be from the Nashville recording industry announced to a large gathering of songwriters: "We are only interested in 'positive, up-tempo love songs' for radio!!" I wasn't at the gathering, but as soon as I heard about it, I decided "Looking for a Kiss" would be on my next album.

Before the ink had dried on "Looking for a Kiss," I went back and finished up "Girl in a Bubble." The words were coming out so fast I felt like I was going to spontaneously combust. So I took a short break to do some psychic housecleaning. By then, I think I was having an out-of-body experience. I saw myself go gather up all the love letters I'd ever received from the Texas songwriter—letters, which, by the way, would have made for *strong* supporting evidence in a big fat palimony suit—and throw them down the garbage chute.

Then I wrote another song. This time there was no fumbling around. The words came out perfect from beginning to end:

I don't want to hurt anymore
I don't want to cry
I don't want to love anymore
If it makes me cry
I want to sing and dance like I used to
Before I fell for you
And if I ever take a chance like I used to
And find somebody new

He won't be like you
He will know how to show his love
(Not like you)
He will know how to grow with love
(Not like you)
He will know
A thing or two about love . . .
He won't be like you

I've known a lot of men in my lifetime
Yes there've been a few
But I've never known a man who could stand there
And lie the way you do
So go away and leave me alone
And take your stuff with you
I hope I never fall in love again
But if I ever do

He won't be like you
He will know how to show his love
(Not like you)
He will know how to grow with love
(Not like you)
He will know
A thing or two about love . . .
He won't be like you

I don't want to hurt anymore

After that, probably for comic relief, I started writing a blues lyric with the working title "Somebody's Gonna Spank You Some Day":

> *You got bad bones in your body*
> *Bad blood in your veins*
> *You write bad checks in the morning*
> *You're in a bad mood when it rains*
> *Yes, baby, you are evil . . . uh-huh*
> *And you better change your wicked ways*
> *'Cause if you don't get with the program now, baby*
> *Somebody's gonna spank you some day*

And that was the last thing I wrote on the last page of that legal pad. By then I'd been up for over sixty hours, so I crashed.

The next day, Sunday, I called my friend Diana Haig, and she had an idea going for a song called "X-Ray Eyes." I was immediately into it, so I drove over to her apartment on Natchez Trace, and we finished the song in no time. It ended up with a snaky blues riff running all the way through it.

> *I've got X-ray eyes*
> *And nobody knows*
> *I've got X-ray eyes*
> *And nobody knows*
> *I can see your disguise*
> *Baby I can see through your clothes*
>
> *Like a peeping Tom*
> *I can see in the dark*
> *Like a peeping Tom*
> *I can see in the dark*
> *I got twenty-twenty vision baby*
> *I can see in your heart*
>
> *I can read your mind*
> *Like a magazine*

I can read your mind
Just like a magazine
I can turn you on my TV
Turn you on my TV screen

I got X-ray eyes
I can see in your head
I got X-ray eyes
I can see in your head
What you do in your car
Baby what you do in your bed

X-ray eyes (X-ray eyes)
X-ray eyes (X-ray eyes)
Don't tell me lies
'Cause baby you know I've got those
X-ray eyes

It's interesting to go back and read through these old legal pads of furiously scribbled lyrics and actually see the creative process at work. Sometimes I will hit a wall in a verse and I'll write *anything* just to keep moving. When songs are being born, it's good not to get too bogged down in details.

In the second verse of "Bubble" I originally wrote:

I had a lover last year
I thought the coast was clear
Then he blew up in my face
I went out lookin' for him
But there weren't any clues
He'd disappeared without a trace

I knew that wasn't quite it, so I changed the last three lines:

I had a lover last year
I thought the coast was clear

> *Then he blew up in my face*
> *I went a-rockin' and a-reelin'*
> *Out a-lookin' for the feeling*
> *Wasn't nothing there to take his place*

Now we're cookin'!
To start the third verse I scribbled:

> *There's people on airplanes*
> *People on trains*
> *People flying up in space*
> *There's people out jogging in the pouring rain*
> *Keeping up the human race*

That obviously wasn't it. Then I remembered the words of Motown founder Berry Gordy, Jr., instructing his stable of songwriters to always write in the first-person singular. "Keep it immediate!" he said. "That's rock and roll!" So I changed it to:

> *I've flown in a Lear jet*
> *Ridden on a train*
> *I even tried to go up in space*
> *I've been out jogging*
> *In the pouring rain*
> *Trying to join the human race*

Nah, that's not it either. Then:

> *I've danced in the moonlight*
> *The moon lasted all night*
> *On a love boat named* Desire

Hold on. Now that might be something. Then out of nowhere I wrote:

> *I've put things in my mouth*
> *I can't talk about . . .*

Come on now, Marshall, Get serious! Why would you even write something as silly as that? (Maybe I was referring to that pill I'd ingested two days earlier.)

Then over to the side, you can see where I scribbled:

> *Marooned in the Keys*
> *Higher than the seas*
> *Doing as we pleased*

Finally, it all came together:

> *Flying on a Lear jet*
> *With Jimmy and the jet set*
> *Settin' ourselves on fire*
> *We hit the high seas*
> *Off the Florida keys*
> *On a love boat named* Desire
> *The fast lane's a nice place*
> *To visit for a while*
> *But I wouldn't want to live there*
> *I got to get back*
> *To where I once belonged*
> *Now I'm so happy just to be right here*
> *A girl in a bubble*
> *Staying out of trouble*
> *That's all*

I could just as well have written:

> *Now I'm so happy to be through with this song!*

I guess the hardest thing about any writing is to not let words get in the way of the truth. You just keep scraping them away until the truth shines. Sometimes I want to scrape them *all* away. These days, whenever I listen to music at home, I put on Charlie Christian or Thelonius Monk or Miles Davis or Chet Baker. Cool-with-an-attitude instrumental-type stuff. As a songwriter, I find it easier to relax listening to that kind of music. Lyrics often activate the analytical side of my brain: "Someone left the cake out in the rain?" *What? I mean, what could Jimmy Webb have possibly been thinking about when he wrote* that *line? Was he on acid or what?* Seems like the older I get, the less I want to *think* while listening to music. I don't need some kid wailing on about who's gonna save my soul.

Recently, I was having a massage, and the masseuse had a cassette of music playing at low volume in the background. It was some far-out songstress singing far-out lyrics.

"Would you mind playing something that doesn't have any words?" I asked.

"No problem," she replied. "I had another client request the same thing. She's a songwriter, too."

I like to "get lost" when I'm listening to music. And sometimes it's easier to get lost when there're no words. Not "lost" in the sense of being lost in my own head but lost in the sense of being "out there" . . . *out* of my head. The Chet Baker kind of lost.

It's like words are something that evolved here on earth and therefore keep us earthbound, whereas instrumental music seems to come from somewhere else. I imagine that when I leave this world and hear the music of the spheres, it will be music without words. But as long as I'm here, I'll always love that BeeGees' line about words being "all I have to take your heart away."

.   .   .

In 1990, I recorded "Girl in a Bubble" (along with "Looking for a Kiss" and "X-Ray Eyes") for *Inside Job* (Tallgirl, 1991). "Bubble" was also included on *It's About Time . . .* (Margaritaville/Island, 1995).

I used to introduce "Girl in a Bubble" saying "I wrote this next song after spending two years crawling around in the self-help section at Mills Bookstore in Hillsboro Village. I'd slink in there and start reading the titles of some of those books—books like *Women Who Love Too Much*—and think, *How can anybody* love *too much? Sounds to me like somebody out there's not loving enough!* Then there's the one that always stopped me dead in my tracks: *Men Who Hate Women and the Women Who Love Them. Jeez! I thought I was depressed when I walked in here. Now I'm really depressed!*"

11

A Mystery to Me

It was bound to happen sooner or later. I mean you can step up to the plate and strike out only so many times. The thing about love is, you have to keep swinging. You can't just stand there and watch the ball whiz by and pop into the catcher's mitt. Keep swinging and eventually you *will* make contact. And, hell, you might even hit a home run. As Tammy Wynette once sang, "I'm gonna keep on a-lovin' 'til I get it right."

I'm talking about true love here. For me, it happened on December 6, 1991. That's the day I found it. Or, I should say, it found me, seeing as it happened in the off-season while I was considering retirement. I was just standing there in the batter's box minding my own business when . . . Bam! . . . I got hit on my blind side by a wild pitch out of nowhere. Next thing I know, the ump is motioning for me to take a base.

"Honey, why don't you just take *all* the bases," he said.

So I did. I sashayed to first, then second, then third, and on around to home plate easy as you please. It was the first inside-the-park, hit-by-a-pitch, walk-all-the-bases home run in baseball love history.

I believe there is a connection between not looking for love and finding it. It's that "power of least desire" thing. So, yes, I finally found it because I had quit looking. But first, I had to give up my career of dating criminals.

Jeanie C. Reilly ("Harper Valley PTA") once said, "I kept falling in love like it was a ditch." And that's exactly what I did from early on until the mid-'80s. I kept falling in love like it was a ditch. And to extricate myself from that last ditch, I had to check myself into a treatment center out in the middle of an Arizona desert. The date was December 14, 1988. I was thirty-nine years old, standing at a crossroads. I knew I couldn't go back to doing the things I'd done before and expect different results, but I was clueless as to how to proceed. Nothing in my life seemed to be working. I'd been in therapy and celibate for over a year, and I *still* wanted the Texas songwriter. I was not free and I was pissed off about it.

So they kept me in the desert for, believe it or not, forty days and forty nights. Just like in the Bible. I recently asked Robert Early, a friend and ordained Presbyterian minister, to shed some light on this "forty days and forty nights" business.

"Hasn't it got something to do with Jesus being out in the desert? Or was it Moses in the wilderness?" I asked.

"Well," he began, "It is written that Jesus was in the desert for forty days and forty nights, and it was there he was tempted three times by the Devil. And Moses . . . that was forty *years* that he wandered in the wilderness with the people of Israel. Then there's Noah and the ark and the Great Flood, which lasted forty days and forty nights. So the word *forty* appears in the Bible a lot, but it's not necessarily to be taken literally because it comes down through many translations from a word meaning 'a very long time.' So whenever you see the word *forty* in the Bible, it is usually associated with a time of great trial, a time of testing, a time of cleansing . . . followed by some sort of transformation. For Jesus, it propelled him into his Messiahship. For Moses, it was a time to prepare the people of Israel for the Promised Land. And as for Noah . . . well, the Flood represented the washing away or cleansing, if you will, of the old, unrighteous, wicked world to make way for a fresh new start."

Okay, so nobody knows the exact timetable for Jesus, Moses, and Noah, but as for little Maah-shul, I'm here to tell you that it was *literally* forty days and nights that I stayed in the desert, and it was the most profound, life-changing experience of my life.

In treatment, I heard people say things like this:

"Happiness is not having what you want, but wanting what you have." And this:

"Happiness is not something that you find like a hidden treasure; it is something that happens within . . . an inside job."

"Happiness is a by-product of rightful living, and that's all we ever have to do—the next right thing."

And this:

"Waiting is sometimes the most profound activity of all."

I didn't particularly like that last one. Patience was never one of my virtues. It was something I had to pray about, as in "Oh Lord, grant me patience . . . and grant it to me *now!*"

After a few weeks in treatment, my whole way of thinking got reprogrammed, and I began to notice some changes. Like what it means to be a human being rather than a human "doing." As I began to unwind, I let go of some of the survival skills I'd developed in my thirty-nine odd years on the planet. Those skills had served me well, but I no longer needed them. Life was not something to overcome, conquer, or survive. It was something to be lived. Period. It was more about surrender and acceptance than winning and struggling.

When I was in my early twenties, I remember one time Mrs. Chrisman said to me, "Hon', you go at life like you're fighting snakes!" In treatment, I learned I could keep an eye on the snakes without getting all worked up. Or, better yet, stay away from the snakes.

At one point in treatment, one of the counselors had me write a detailed description of the type of *relationship* I wanted to be in. What a concept! I realized that most people, myself included, take more time and do more research in buying a new car or set of golf clubs than they do in choosing a life partner. My modus operandi had always been to go to bed with whoever I was attracted to, then try and figure out the rest. Of course, if the sex was good, it'd be hard to figure out anything because most people will say or do anything just to keep *that* going.

As for finding a significant other, I remember somebody saying "Marshall, you're not going to attract what you want, you're going to attract *who you are.*" That hit me like a ton of bricks. I had to take a long look in the mirror, and I didn't particularly like what I saw. I saw someone who was tired of hurting.

So I remained celibate for another three years. During that time I went to AA, NA, ACOA, CODA, SLAA . . . you name it. If it ended with a capital A, I was there.

It was at AA that I met an elderly woman named Margaret. The first time I saw her, she was sitting in an upstairs room at a popular Nashville meeting house, waiting for the meeting to begin. It was a cold January day. She was wearing old-fashioned galoshes with newspaper stuffed in them to keep her feet warm. Her bright red lipstick had been carefully applied, and when she spoke, her voice was like music. I could tell by her manner that she'd been raised Old South proper. She had gray-white hair that looked like it wanted to fly around even though she'd recently had it "set" at Fantastic Sam's. The lines in her angular face told of hardship and sorrow, but they were more than offset by her bright blue eyes so full of life . . . of love and humor with just a touch of mischief. I was intrigued.

Whenever Margaret talked—or "shared"—at meetings, I held on to her every word, which wasn't easy because she rarely completed a sentence. Listening to Margaret was like watching somebody squeeze a chunk of coal. If you didn't hang through all her digressions and detours down dead-end roads, chances are, you'd miss out on the diamond that popped out in the end.

And Margaret never *tried* to be funny or entertaining, which made her one of the funniest people I've ever known. She could talk about her most tragic circumstances in a way that had everybody in the room roaring with laughter. Of course, in laughing with her, we were laughing at ourselves because each of us, in our own way, had been there.

One time, Margaret was describing her state of mind during a particularly rough period in her life that had her contemplating suicide.

"I started thinking I might drive down to the Shelby Street bridge," she said, referring to the historic overpass that spans downtown and East Nashville. Occasionally somebody jumps off and disappears into the murky waters of the Cumberland River below, only to have their body discovered a few weeks later by some unsuspecting fisherman a mile or so downstream. So when Margaret mentioned driving down to the Shelby Street bridge, we all understood the implication.

"But *then*," she continued, "I started worrying about my *car*. I mean, *where* was I going to *park*?"

In AA, one of the first things newcomers are encouraged to do is to find a sponsor. A sponsor is usually someone with many years sobriety who is willing to take the newcomer under their wing and show them the ropes. I'd been in the program a couple of months when I realized I wanted Margaret to be my sponsor. So I asked her.

"Margaret," I said, "will you be my sponsor?"

"Oh, Marshall, honey, I can't . . . I'm too *old*!" she replied.

One of the many sayings in AA is "Act as if." In other words, if you act as if you are sober, then chances are you'll stay sober. So I decided to apply this principle to Margaret. I ignored her protests and began following her around like a puppy dog. I just acted as if she were my sponsor, and by golly, after a few months, she *was* my sponsor. And she remained my sponsor for the next seven years . . . right up until I quit going to AA the day my brother died in 1996. But I'm getting ahead of myself, so let me back up and say this about AA.

I went to AA for eight years on a regular basis. One of AA's traditions states that "the only requirement for membership is a desire to stop drinking" and that alone gave me the feeling I had a right to be there. I didn't want to drink and I wanted to be around others who weren't drinking. But in the beginning, I had a hard time accepting the word *alcoholic* as it applied to me, because deep down I didn't believe I was an alcoholic; I just had "a desire to stop drinking." What I really wanted was to go back and be who I was when I was eleven years old. I didn't drink then, and I was happy; maybe there was a connection. At one point, I even called up my mother and asked her to send me the twin bed I slept on as a child.

"Hey, Mama," I said. "Do you remember those twin beds Dorothy and I used to sleep on? Would you mind shipping one of them out here to me in Nashville? . . . Why? Because I want to sleep on it, that's why. . . . I was happy sleeping on that bed. . . . Yes, ma'am. . . . Yes, ma'am. . . . Yes, ma'am. . . . Well, go ahead and send both, if you like, but I only need . . . Oh, okay. . . . Yes, ma'am. . . . Thank you, Mama." *Click.*

AA worked. I can't tell you *why* it worked; I just know that it did. There was a group of us who became like family. It was me, Margaret, a divinity student from Vanderbilt named Jon, and two undergraduates named Tom and Tim. We regularly met for dinner after our five o'clock meeting, and sometimes we'd go to a movie or just drive around in the country. With this new family, I began to enjoy life again, and things started changing for the better. After a while, I no longer cringed when I said the word *alcoholic*. By then I would have said "My name is Marshall and I'm an orangutan" if it meant I could still receive the gifts that the program had to offer.

I once heard M. Scott Peck refer to Alcoholics Anonymous as "the most successful church in America," and there's probably a lot of truth to that. People don't go to AA to improve their social status; they go because their lives aren't working and they are hurting. Once, at a meeting, I heard a visitor from Knoxville say "Religion is for people afraid of going to hell. Spirituality is for people who have been there." And the same could be said for AA: It's for people who have been there. I have never once heard of anybody waking up in the morning having their first thought be "Wow, I think I'll go to an AA meeting today" like it was a good idea or something. AA is usually the last thing anybody wants to do.

I've also heard it said that the Big Book is the greatest blueprint on how to live ever written. All a matter of opinion, but for eight years, AA was my church and the Big Book was my Bible.

Today, I no longer attend AA. My "church" seems to be wherever I am when I am in a mindful state. But to achieve that mindfulness, I have to practice things that slow me down, like yoga and meditation. Otherwise, I'm back to fighting snakes.

One of my greatest fears, initially, about living a sober life was that I wouldn't be able to write songs anymore. I mean, if I'm not writing myself out of some bad relationship or some evening turned funky, then what's there to write about? I soon found out.

Back in Nashville, after treatment, I agreed to a co-writing session with a staff songwriter at Acuff-Rose named Terri Sharp. I didn't know Terri that well, but we had been in the same therapy group a year before, and I guess I figured that might give us some good common ground from which to draw inspiration.

Co-writing is something that happens quite frequently in the songwriting world. You don't find many co-written novels or poems, but I would venture to say that the vast majority of songs are co-written. I usually write alone, but whenever I hit a dry spell, I'll call on one of my songwriting buddies and book a session. Co-writing is a good way to jump-start those creative juices into flowing again. It's also a great way to learn new approaches and techniques. But the best thing about co-writing, for me, is that it's a good excuse to hang out with my songwriting buddies, a list that today includes Tim Krekel, Gary Nicholson, Matraca Berg, Danny Flowers, Beth Nielsen Chapman, Don Henry, and Annie Roboff. And earlier in my career: Jimmy Buffett, Will Jennings, Fred Koller, Diana Haig, Mike Utley, Dennis Walker, Dave Hickey, Joy Wahl, Joe South, and Jim Rushing.

I love some of my co-written songs even though the ones that give me the greatest satisfaction are generally the ones I write alone. But every now and then, a co-write will result in a jewel. Such was the case with "It's Never Too Late to Have a Happy Childhood."

"Happy Childhood" was a breakthrough song for me. It restored my faith and confidence because it made me realize that if you're a writer, it doesn't matter if you're happy or sad, drinking or sober, young or old, or if your life is quiet or crazed. A writer writes about *whatever* is going on in his or her life. For years, I had subscribed to the Hank Williams syndrome, which says a writer must live a life of turmoil in order to be creative. I was burning the candle at both ends, hoping both ends would meet and there would be an explosion. And if the explosion didn't kill me, I might end up with a new song.

My friend Virginia Team once said, "These days the world is moving so fast . . . hell, you don't even have to *die* anymore to be reincarnated." If what she says is true, then I am on my third go-around. In the first, I was the dutiful daughter. In the second, the female Mick Jagger. "Happy Childhood" signaled the beginning of simply being myself:

> *It doesn't matter*
> *Where you're coming from*
> *It doesn't matter*
> *What damage was done*
> *We're all on a journey*
> *Our goal is the same*
> *We're gonna be happy*
> *Like children again*
> *So be your own parent*
> *And treat yourself good*

It's never too late
To have a happy childhood

I used to think freedom
Meant running away
And love was a feeling
That never would stay
I searched this world over
But I never found
A big enough shoulder
To muffle the sound
So cry if you need to
It might do you good
It's never too late
To have a happy childhood

Some never make it
Some never try
Some try to fake it
Some barely get by
Survival is easy
It's living that's hard
And it takes lots of courage
Just to be who you are
So do what you love
Not what they say you should
It's never too late
To have a happy childhood

"Happy Childhood" was a love song in the deepest sense. Deeper than yin and yang. It was balm for my battered soul.

December 6, 1991

I went to my five-o'clock AA meeting as usual. I was in a very bad mood that day, and I didn't care who knew it. I was even mad at God. I had been clean and sober for three years—celibate for four, I was going to meetings, working the steps, I had a good sponsor named Margaret, I was trying to be a good friend, a good sister, a good daughter, a good *artist,* for chrissakes. I'd just released a new album called *Inside Job,* and it was getting rave reviews. I was performing again with a new band called The Love Slaves, and we were hot, hot, hot. So why was I still single? Sure I was forty-two years old, but unlike Elvis who keeled over on the crapper after *he* turned forty-two, I was coming into my own. I was blond, six feet tall, good-looking . . . prancing around in a miniskirt and high heels with my Love Slaves, I was sober, I was a homeowner, having lived for nearly five years in a sexy, high-rise condominium with breathtaking views of downtown Nashville and Vanderbilt University, I had money in the bank and was driving a black 740IL BMW with tan leather interior . . . and damn it to hell . . . I was a *good catch,* by god, so why wasn't anybody casting?

That was my frame of mind as I walked out of the meeting. It was just after six and already dark outside, when a tall man approached me with two tickets in his hand.

"Hi, Marshall," he said. "Would you like to go to the Boston Camarata with me tonight? It's at eight o'clock at Langford Auditorium on the Vanderbilt campus."

I'm thinking: *Who is this guy and where does he get off thinking he can even* approach *me when I'm in this bad a mood? I mean, I am in one of my room-clearing bad moods, and this guy seems* unfazed. *Is he blind . . . an idiot . . . or what?*

"The Boston Camarata . . . what's that?" I responded, all the while thinking, *It must be some boring highbrow bullshit thing. Too bad it's not Bobby Blue Bland or Wilson Pickett. I might rally for that.*

"It's a singing troupe out of Boston," the man went on to explain. "They sing old Christmas carols in Middle English, French, and Italian, you know, from the fourteenth and fifteenth century."

The man was wearing a nice suit and tie and had an intellectual air about him. I, on the other hand, was wearing gray sweatpants with holes in both knees, looking like a bag lady in training.

Now, I can still recite the first twelve lines of Chaucer's *Canterbury Tales* in perfect Middle English thanks to my high-school English teacher, Elizabeth Nowack. Miss Nowack taught junior English at Salem Academy, a girls' boarding school in Winston-Salem, North Carolina. Both Miss Nowack and Ruth Krouskup, who taught senior English, were notorious for having their students memorize long passages from classic literature. Besides Chaucer, there was Milton, Wordsworth, Shakespeare . . . you name it. The curriculum was the same every year. The same lessons in the same order, with the same tests, and the same damn lines to memorize.

One by one, we'd walk to the front of their classrooms and stand waiting for them to nod so we could begin.

> *When that Aprill with his shoures soote*
> *The droghte of March hath perced to the roote*
> *And bathed every veyne in swich licour*
> *Which vertu engendred is the flour . . .*

It was like going before a firing squad. Only there was nobody to shoot you and put you out of your misery. Chaucer was particularly brutal because we had to recite it in the original Middle English. To our mostly Southern ears, it sounded like a whole nother language. Even worse than hearing Yankees talk. There were rumors of girls being denied their diplomas because they had failed to properly deliver a recitation. One girl got so worked up she had to be sent home.

Twenty years later, I returned to Winston-Salem to perform a rap version of Chaucer's classic lines to the pulsating beat of a locally hired rock and roll band. The occasion was the one hundredth anniversary of the Salem Academy and College alumnae associations, which happened to coincide with my twentieth class reunion. My performance was part of an evening of entertainment called The Parade of Stars. I had been brought in, along with several other alumnae whose career paths had led them into the entertainment arts. Actor Celia Weston (College, '70) and talk-show host Rolanda Watts (Academy, '77) were flown in from New York; actor Kathryn Harrold (Academy, '68), from L.A.; and a couple of opera singers and a classical pianist were brought in from Europe. It was a big whoop-de-doo. Hanes Auditorium was packed to the gills.

When the time came for my segment, I walked out on stage wearing black high heels, a faded Levi's jacket, and a black stretch miniskirt, with my '56 Stratocaster slung over my shoulder looking like a machine gun ready for action. I was just getting ready to tear into "Betty's Bein' Bad," when I glanced down and noticed my old senior English teacher, Ruth Krouskup, sitting in the very front row. *Oh, my gosh!* I thought as I suddenly realized I was wearing not one but *three* dress-code violations from the 1967 Salem Academy rule book.

1. Girls may not wear denim.
2. Skirts and dresses must be no shorter than the middle of the knee.
3. Girls must wear a full slip when leaving their rooms.

They meant *leaving their rooms to go to the bathroom.* Salem Academy didn't want any naked or scantily clad girls parading about in the dorms. Of course, it went without saying full slips were required underneath dresses or skirt-and-blouse outfits *at all times.*

Needless to say, I was *not* wearing a full slip that night. Nor, in fact, was I wearing a bra. And it's probably safe to say there were no underpants underneath my black sheer Hanes pantyhose.

After spotting Miss Krouskup, I realized that the woman seated next to her was the dreaded Alice Litwinchuk, retired headmistress of Salem Academy, who once summoned me to her office for a private meeting behind closed doors. "Marshall," she said, fixing me with a stern look, "you have enormous leadership ability—perhaps more than any girl we've had here at the Academy. But it's always been in the *wrong direction!*"

Normally, I'd've been intimidated seeing those two formidable women seated together not fifteen feet away, but I was prepared. Besides, Jack Clement had once told me: "Remember, Marshall . . . you're the only one in the room with the microphone." I was also the only one in the room who knew what I was going to do next.

"It's great to be back in the land of cigarettes, panty hose, and higher education!" I shouted out. The crowd response was immediate. As their laughter subsided, I began: "Betty's out bein' bad tonight / Betty and her boyfriend, they had a big fight."

After the last chorus, the band dropped into a quiet pulsating rhythm so I could talk to the audience—or *signify,* as it's called when Millie Jackson does it.

"You know, it's been twenty years since Salem Academy sent me out into the world." By now my tongue was firmly planted in my cheek. "And a lot has happened during that time: some good, some bad. But whenever I find myself in a jam, I always remember these words I learned at Salem. And somehow, they give me the strength I need to carry on."

And with that, I began to rap to the pulsating beat of the band:

> *When that Aprill with his shoures soote*
> *The droghte of March hath perced to the roote*
> *And bathed every veyne in swich licour*
> *Which vertu engendred is the flour . . .*

Of course, I punctuated that with a . . .

> *Boom shaka laka laka*
> *Boom shaka laka laka*
> *Boom shaka laka laka*
> *Boom*

> *Whan Zephirus eek with his sweete breeth*
> *Inspired hath in every holt and heeth*
> *The tendre croppes, and the youge sonne*
> *Hath in the Ram his halfe cours yronne*

Then:

> *Boom shaka laka laka*
> *Boom shaka laka laka*
> *Boom shaka laka laka*
> *Boom*

Someone took a snapshot of some of my classmates while I was doing this. They are laughing so hard, tears can be seen on their faces.

You have to understand that back when we were students, Salem Academy was notorious for being *very* strict. It was basically a Moravian convent. The rule book was thicker than the yearbook. We weren't allowed to leave campus, which meant we couldn't date. The Moravians weren't big on men and women being together. Even in death. There's an old Moravian cemetery in a field next to the Academy where the men are buried on one side and the women on the other, with a white picket fence separating the two.

The only man I saw during my two years at Salem Academy was the religion instructor. His name was Mr. Hege. Mr. Hege had this routine he would do on the first day of class. (I think he did this to get our attention.) He'd throw the Bible down on the floor and *jump* on it. Then he'd pick it back up and dust it off while proclaiming "It's not the Bible that is sacred, but the *words* that are in it!" A girl once fainted during this demonstration. Mr. Hege would also say things like "People are no damned good, but there's hope anyway!" Of course, the only person we thought that applied to was Mr. Hege himself.

But back to junior English and the *Canterbury Tales*. Of the twelve lines we had to recite, the one that gave us the most difficulty was the tenth. It contained the Middle English word *night*—spelled "n-y-g-h-t." In order to pronounce it correctly, you had to make a weird kind of guttural sound. Sometimes spittle would fly from Miss Nowack's throat during a demonstration.

> *And smale foweles maken melodye*
> *That slepen al the* nyght *with open eye*

Miss Nowack was strict. But Miss Krouskup was intimidating. In fact, I was terrified of her. First of all, she was extremely obese. She'd come waddling down the hall, and you'd have to back up against the wall to get out of her way. Also, she was from Chicago. Her favorite person in the world was Illinois Senator Charles Percy. Only she called him Chuck. She kept a framed photograph of him on her desk, along with a statue of Buddha. Of course, rumors circulated she was an atheist. I mean if you weren't a Christian in the cigarette and panty hose manufacturing town of Winston-Salem, North Carolina, in the mid-'60s, the only thing left to be was an atheist or a Communist. Either way, you were going to hell.

Most of the teachers and administrators at the Academy were scary-looking spinsters with scary-sounding names. Besides the three-hundred-pound Ruth Krouskup and headmistress Alice Litwinchuk, there was history teacher Isabelle Quattlebaum, house counselor Paralee Fentriss, and the aforementioned Elizabeth Nowack, who was so pale she looked like she'd been embalmed. Miss Nowack reminded me of a little bird. Her eyes would dart around, and when she was being stern, they sometimes looked evil.

But let me tell you about Miss Litwinchuk's hair. It was *real* long. But you wouldn't know it because it was braided and pinned up into a bun that she wore on top of her head like a crown. Now this is where it gets weird. There was a secret "tradition" at Salem Academy that went like this: One night, toward the end of the school year, all of the senior boarders would be herded into the dark and empty dining room to witness the spectacle of Miss Litwinchuk letting her hair down. I mean, literally.

It was just before "lights-out," and we all had our pajamas and bathrobes on wondering what in the hell was going on. We thought someone was getting expelled or something. As we entered the dining area, Miss Litwinchuk was there waiting for us, sitting under a recessed light, looking like the Virgin Mary in a painting of the Annunciation. After we sat down, she reached up and began to unpin the bun on top of her head. A few girls gasped as the loosened braid fell to the floor. After it was all combed out, she arose and began to parade around the room, her long, gray-flecked auburn hair trailing behind her like a bridal veil.

"That was disgusting!" Mary Lee Meares muttered under her breath as we filed back to our rooms.

"Sicko!" whispered Jane Harrold.

One last comment about Salem Academy: Even though I was forced to memorize lines from Chaucer's *Canterbury Tales,* just like I was forced to read a lot of boring books by dead people and to conjugate verbs in a dead language that nobody speaks anymore, it is fair to say I got a good education. Salem Academy was a college preparatory school, and they did exactly what my father paid them to do: They prepared me for college. By the time I got to Vanderbilt, there was nothing Vanderbilt could throw at me that I hadn't already seen. For the first time in my life, I had a lot of unchaperoned free time on my hands, which I promptly filled by falling in love and hanging out with musicians. I was no longer interested in the academic world and spent the next twenty years trying to get as far away from it as I could. The only school I was interested in was the school of hard knocks. Of course, all that did was get me into treatment. But now it's December 6, 1991. Could the pendulum be starting to swing back the other way?

The man was still standing there, not three feet away, with his two tickets for the Boston Camarata. He was watching me, waiting for my reply. Finally . . .

"Nah, I think I'll pass," I answered. "It doesn't sound like my kind of thing."

As I turned and began walking away, I felt the man's hand on my shoulder. He gently turned me around, then took my right hand and placed a ticket in it.

"I want you to have this ticket," he said, "because you may change your mind. But if you don't, the ticket is yours to do with as you like. You can throw it away or give it away, it doesn't matter (he held his ticket up for me to see) . . . because *I'm* going." And with that, he turned and walked away.

I was stunned. I didn't know what to think. Time was standing still. I must've looked like I was in a trance. I certainly felt like I was in one. What happened next surprised even me. I went home, bathed, dressed, then drove to Langford Auditorium, arriving fifteen minutes early. This was all new behavior on my part.

When I got to my seat, he was there. I knew his name. It was Chris Fletcher. And I knew that he was a physician. I'd heard him share at meetings, and we had spoken once or twice. He seemed happy enough to see me, but not surprised. We began to converse. Turns out he grew up in Boston. I can't remember what all we talked about. But I remember asking about his family. And I remember him telling me his mother had died when he was fourteen. And of course I had to ask how she had died, and he told me: "A gunshot wound." "Really," I replied, not knowing what else to say, but not wanting the conversation to end. "How'd that happen?" "Well, my father was tried for murder."

He said all of this without a trace of self-pity. And, of course, I was intrigued.

I'd always hated dating because I was never very good at small talk. One thing was for sure: *this* was not small talk. I'd been through some trials and tribulations in my life, but this man obviously had experienced some things I couldn't even begin to imagine.

Soon the house lights dimmed and the stage lights went up for the Boston Camarata. And as I sat there in the darkness listening to the music, sitting next to this man I barely knew, this man who had witnessed the death of his mother at the hands of his father when only a boy of fourteen, I felt a strange shift going on inside my chest. And in that instant, only one thing mattered. I wanted to know this man whose elbow was now brushing against mine.

June 20, 1994

It is evening and Chris is across the hall with his administrative assistant, Cherry Snider. They are unpacking a new computer system that had arrived that afternoon in big cardboard boxes. They are both real excited about what they are doing and I don't understand why. I mean, Chris already *had* a computer. But this computer, he assures me, is better. The monitor is much bigger and it does everything faster. Of course, he tells me this using words I can't remember because I don't know what they mean.

All day long, I had envisioned a romantic evening at home with just the two of us. My plans did *not* include a computer and an administrative assistant. I was thinking more along the lines of candlelight, gumbo, a garden salad, and making out on the sofa.

Chris and I have been living together for the past two and a half years in a two-bedroom high-rise condominium called the Sky Palace. This was the place I bought in 1987 with royalties earned from "Betty's Bein' Bad." It was my first go-around with home ownership and I was so excited that I wrote a song called "Come Up and See Me":

> *I had a little run two years ago*
> *So I moved out of my jail cell*
> *Bought me a palace up in the sky*
> *Now I'm living so very well*
> *I can see all the way to Memphis*
> *From my balcony on high*
> *When those storms roll in from way out west*
> *The lightning lights up my sky*
> *Well there's magic in the weather*
> *There's magic in the air*

There's magic when you look up
You can see it everywhere
Why don't you . . .
Come up and see me

I got a big screen color TV set
So bright I wear my shades
I got a tape of every movie
Robert Mitchum ever made
I got a brand new set of World Book
Encyclopedias
If there's anything I need to know
Well, I just look it up
I never knew I'd be so happy
Living up in the sky
Until I moved up here
Where all the angels love to fly
Why don't you . . .
Come up and see me

I've been living
Real close to my heart
But I can make some small talk
If that's what it takes to start

I got a Maytag washer and dryer
With a lifetime guarantee
No ring around the collar
And no grass stains on my jeans
My therapist makes house calls
When my head gets off the track
I love this life I'm livin'
I ain't never goin' back
You see I don't need nobody
To save me from myself
But I'd love to hear that song

By Billy Swan called "I Can Help"
Why don't you . . .
Come up and see me
Come up and see me
Sometime

When I was first shown the Sky Palace, I fell in love with it on the spot. It had great light, and when I opened the glass sliding doors to the two balconies on either end, the breeze that blew down the central hallway made me feel like I was at the beach. Then I noticed the number on the door—803—and that pretty much sealed the deal. 803 was South Carolina's area code at the time. This was just before the explosion of computers and fax machines, back when many states only had one area code. So I took it as a good omen.

I lived in the Sky Palace alone from 1987 until 1992, when Chris moved in. After a year, he decided we needed more space, so he leased a one-bedroom unit across the hall—804. And that's where he and his administrative assistant were on the evening of June 20, 1994, as they began unpacking and setting up the new computer.

I'd gone over there at first to see what they were doing. But they paid me absolutely no attention, so I went back across the hall and started writing a song.

Chris claims I will do anything to get attention. He loves to tell people that I have attention deficit disorder—not because I can't *pay* attention, but because I can't get enough.

After I wrote the first verse, I was so pleased with the results that I went back across the hall with my Takamine guitar and sang it for Chris and Cherry.

He likes things
That he can do with his brain
He's put together that way
She falls apart
When something touches her heart

Her feelings give her away
He loves his computer
She loves her guitars
And while he sits and stares
At his screen saver
She stares at the stars

I'd like to think that Chris was trying to hide the fact that he was charmed. His only comment concerned the line about the guy staring at his screen saver. "Anybody who'd do that would be looked upon as being dumb," he said. *Exactly,* I thought to myself. *And anybody who would ignore me when I feel this cute . . . is dumb!* Meanwhile, they went back to ignoring me and I went back to the Sky Palace.

Regardless of their reaction, I felt like I was on to something, so I wrote another verse. I was "feeling it." And when you're feeling it, you gotta go with it.

A year earlier, Chris and I had been in Washington, D.C., staying at one of my favorite hotels, the Hay Adams. That first morning, as we ordered up a pot of coffee with croissants, I noticed the headline on the front page of the *Washington Post.*

"Oh, no, Pat Nixon died," I exclaimed, holding the paper up so Chris could see. "Umm," Chris barely acknowledged from behind the sports section. Soon I was reading about our former first lady and was touched when I came to the part about the secret service and how much they adored her. Their code name for her was "Starlight."

"Chris?"

"Uh, huh."

"Will you call me Starlight while we're here in Washington, just while we're here?"

"Uh, huh . . . but then what will you call me?"

"Air Force One," I replied without batting an eye.

"Starlight" didn't stick beyond Washington, but "Air Force One" did. Besides, Chris already had a pet name for me: "Little Mademoiselle." Lately, he's been calling me "Mello" or "Mello-icious." I call him "Crisco." I think this is something that all couples do.

After a while, I finished the second verse and, undaunted by my previous cold reception, went back across the hall to sing it for Chris and Cherry.

> *He calls her*
> *"My Little Mademoiselle"*
> *'Cause she can parler Français*
> *And just for fun*
> *She calls him "Air Force One"*
> *He's first class all the way*
> *He loves his espresso*
> *She prefers herbal tea*
> *How these two lovers ever*
> *Got together*
> *Remains a mystery to me*

This time, Chris was visibly charmed but still would not stop what he was doing. Chris can be very single-minded at times, especially when it comes to computers. One time I called him at work to confirm the facts of this story and he said, "Yep, my memory gels with yours. It was a new Dell computer and I didn't even know what a *modem* was back then, but we were going to by-god-figure-it-out!" So while they continued to by-god-figure-it-out, I retreated to the Sky Palace once again.

By now, I knew the title of the song was either going to be "Remains a Mystery to Me" or simply "A Mystery to Me." I began writing a third verse and continued on with a fourth, until at last the song was finished. Then I went *back* across the hall and sang the completed version for the man who had inspired it all . . . and, of course, for his administrative assistant, Cherry Snider.

> *He likes things*
> *That he can do with his brain*
> *He's put together that way*

She falls apart
When something touches her heart
Her feelings give her away
He loves his computer
She loves her guitars
And while he sits and stares
At his screen saver
She stares at the stars

He calls her
"My Little Mademoiselle"
'Cause she can parler Français
And just for fun
She calls him "Air Force One"
He's first class all the way
He loves his espresso
She prefers herbal tea
How these two lovers ever
Got together
Remains a mystery to me

He loves his hotels
Hermetically sealed
A chocolate mint on his pillow
She prefers motels
Her car parked by her room
Where she can open a window
He frequently travels
She prefers staying home
She is happy
Just to hear her own breathing
While he CD roams

She writes letters
That are ten pages long
He sends memos by email

She shops for bargains
At outlet store malls
He goes for that retail
She loves the desert
He loves the sea
How these two lovers ever
Got together
Remains a mystery to me

Quelles differences!
Impossible . . . oui?
How these two lovers ever
Got together
Remains a mystery to me

Cherry said, "Oh, that's great!" but then the look on both their faces said, "Now run along!" *Screw them and the modem they rode in on!* I thought, as I walked triumphantly back across the hall. By now I realized there wasn't going to be a romantic evening at home with just the two of us. But I no longer cared, because I had a new song to sing. And if I have to choose between a new song and a romantic evening at home, I'm taking the song.

. . .

I recorded "A Mystery to Me" on my eighth album, *Love Slave* (Margaritaville/Island, 1996). Dave Marsh called it "the year's most misnamed record" in a review for *Playboy.* He must not have read the quote in the CD artwork that says "We're all slaves to something—might as well be love." In the Nashville industry publication *Music Row,* Robert Oermann wrote: "Incidentally, there is no *Music Row* weekly award for songwriting excellence. But if there was, it would surely go to Ms. Chapman for her clever and downright delightful 'A Mystery to Me.' Lend this your ears."

Ten days before *Love Slave* was released, my brother died. Two months later, Margaritaville Records closed their doors.

In the weeks preceding my brother's death, all I knew to do was write songs. They just seemed to pour out. I wrote enough to record yet another new album, but that would have to wait. I needed to take some time off. There were some big shifts going on. Maybe it was time to get down close to the ground. So Chris and I bought a house together, and I reluctantly moved out of the Sky Palace. I even planted a vegetable garden.

12

Call the Lamas!

Dream: July 26, 1996

I am in a large room full of people—some I recognize, and some I don't. Linda Ronstadt, another woman, and I are rehearsing a song—working up the harmonies while nearby, some musicians are laying down an energetic "Lay Down Sally" sort of groove. Across the room, there are women cooking. One young woman is wearing a long apron over her jeans. The apron is held up by a belt worn on the outside. Her long brunette hair is worn folded at the nape of her neck. Next thing I know, I am sitting at a table in the middle of the room next to a large black woman. Linda Ronstadt is sitting on the other side of her and the three of us are swaying back and forth in unison, leaning on each other, as we listen to music only heard by us. At one point, I look up and notice an elderly black man sitting directly across from me at the table. I have never seen him before, but he nods at me like he knows me. I nod back, acknowledging him. About that time, Pallas Pidgeon walks up and asks, "Have you seen my children?" She says this not because she is looking for them, but because she wants me to acknowledge them.

"I don't think I have," I say as I move to an open window where I look out and see a willowy young girl of eight or nine with long blond hair, and her younger brother who has a stocky build and brunette hair. The children are laughing and playing together underneath a large tree. The sun shines down through the tree, casting a dappled light on their fresh faces and hair. The minute I see them, I realize that indeed I have seen them before—only they were frozen in the snow.

Next thing, I am walking around the room. As I do this, I become acutely aware of my legs so strong and sturdy beneath me. I look down at them (I have on shorts) and notice how tan and powerful they are, firm and long. There is a man walking around who loves me. He is bringing in a case of imported bottled beer to put in the refrigerator. He has come to help the women prepare a feast for us all. He is adorable. (I've never seen him before, but in the dream, he is my boyfriend.) He has bright eyes and curly, brown hair.

There is nothing for me to do in preparation for the feast, so I walk outside alone, away from this happy house full of happy people. I walk toward the nearby sea. As I crest the nearest dune, I notice it is high tide and the wind is blowing hard. I am carrying a large, soft linen shirt in my right hand. With my left, I clutch a small sheet of clear plastic bubble wrap—the kind used for packing— against my chest to keep it warm against the wind. Only I know I won't need it. As I step into the ocean, it suddenly rises up and spills over the dune. There are colorful live fish everywhere. A beautiful pink sea salmon washes over the dune and is flopping around in the shallow water. "I will pick it up and take it back to the house. That would be delicious for dinner."

I wake up feeling wonderful and immediately began writing the dream down in a spiral notebook. Otherwise, I might forget it. That's what happens when you become too conscious. You forget your dreams. It's tricky business, too . . . being conscious enough to grab a notebook and pen and start writing, all the while staying with your dream. That's why I don't like alarm clocks. An alarm clock will blow a good dream into smithereens if you let it. Then it's lost forever.

I love being in that semiconscious state when you're not sure if you're asleep or awake. *Is this real or am I dreaming?* "Twilight consciousness" I call it. It's a place all dreamers and poets love. And sometimes you'll be having such a good dream that you don't want to wake up. And when you do, you think, *Oh, no! I don't want this to end!* And so you *will* yourself back into dreamland, and voilà! There it is! Your dream! It was there waiting for you all along. And so you recapture it like a butterfly collector with a net. And if you are right on the edge of consciousness, sometimes you can even *control* it, you know, steer your dream like a car. It's better than a good ride at the fair because it can last a lot longer. I have spent entire mornings doing this.

And I love my dreams. Even the ones that scare me. I love them like I love my songs. Maybe it's because dreams and songs both come from the same part of the brain. The part that deals with the subconscious. That's where all the good stuff is. Did you know that only 7 percent of our brain deals with the conscious, while 93 percent the subconscious? I heard that at a lecture on Post Traumatic Stress Disorder a few years ago.

. . .

This particular spiral notebook is full of good stuff. Dreams, song ideas, lyrics, drawings, inspirational quotes, funny things people said, you name it. Anything that caught my fancy or blew my mind in the summer of 1996 got recorded in this notebook. That's how I kept my sanity that summer.

Some of the lyrics are fragments. Others became songs. Whenever I complete a song, I always record the date in the top right-hand margin of the page. With a #2 pencil, of course. I always use a #2 pencil when I'm writing songs.

On the other hand, I use a ballpoint pen to record my dreams. Maybe I use the pen because dreams can't be revised. Who knows?

I also just noticed that I date my dreams in the *left*-hand margin. I have no earthly idea why I do this—left-hand margin for dreams, right-hand margin for songs—but I imagine a psychologist might have a field day with this information. If a dream is particularly disturbing I record the actual *time* that it awakened me. It's been my experience that scary dreams—the ones that have you wake up screaming—occur in the middle of the night, whereas the ones that leave you feeling good—as in "Oh, wow!"—happen in the morning just before you wake up.

"My songs are like my children." I've heard a lot of songwriters say that. Hell, I've probably said it. A mother always loves her children, even if they're bad. And a mother always thinks her baby is the most beautiful baby in the world, even if that baby is as ugly as homemade sin. So in that context, I will confess: I think all my songs are great. Of course, if I'm writing one that's El Stinko, I make sure I don't finish it. I cut bait and move on.

My songs can be shocking, sad, sentimental, moving, disturbing, goofy, ironic, irreverent, political, or unabashedly romantic. It doesn't matter as long as they are not boring. "Boring" is my definition of El Stinko. One of my favorite songwriting axioms has always been "Don't bore us. Get to the chorus!"

The cover artwork on my 1996 notebook is dramatic. A unicorn is rearing up on its hind legs amidst thunder and lightning, while standing on a reflective, futuristic, gridiron surface. Dark, ominous clouds produce white bolts of lightning that cast an eerie, purplish glow on the unicorn's white coat, mane, and tail. The lightning also highlights a wispy little beard growing underneath its muzzle. Regular horses don't have this little beard. Neither do they have a long, spirally twisted horn growing out of the middle of their forehead. The one on this unicorn looks like a lightning rod. Everything about the cover looks exciting and dangerous. That's why I picked it out of the school supplies section at Eckerd's drugstore.

In my early songwriting career, I would write lyrics on plain yellow legal pads. But lately, I've taken to writing in spiral notebooks with crazy, goofy artwork on the covers. I've come to realize that writing is a crazy, goofy business.

The summer of '96 was an intense time for me, both professionally and personally. The release date for my second CD on Margaritaville/Island had been set for September 10 and already the phone was ringing. Chris had hired an administrative assistant named Tina Krah to deal with the phones for me so I could concentrate on other things.

Promoting a record is a lot like a political campaign in that there is no limit as to what can be done in terms of energy and expenditure. But there *is* a limit to the amount of time you have to do it in. Eventually the voters have to go to the polls. And with a record, if it isn't "happening" after six months, most labels will back off and go roll the dice with somebody else. But it's always an exciting time, just before and just after a record gets released. That little shrink-wrapped jewel case containing a piece of your soul is going out all over the world and anything can happen. Even the sky might not be the limit.

By the first week of August, a West Coast publicity firm had joined our team, and suddenly there were photo shoots, bios, press kits, VPKs (video press kits), interviews, phoners, TV tapings, and on and on. Also, I had a new manager, and plans were underway for a record-release party at The Boundary in Nashville, and a showcase at The Bottom Line in New York to be followed by a "meet and greet" at a club nearby called Rio Dizio. Then there was Farm Aid '96 with Willie Nelson at William Brice Stadium back in my home state of South Carolina, and a date opening for Jimmy Buffett in Austin, Texas. Chris and Tina were busy setting up my website (www.tall-girl.com) and having 5,000 postcards printed and sent out to everybody on my mailing list. Also, preparations were underway for a seventeen-city West Coast Borders tour, and on, and on, and on.

There were cheers all around when Bob Mercer, president of Margaritaville, announced that Polygram (PGD) would be distributing my record. But in a way, that only added to the pressure. I was forty-six years old. I'd been making records for twenty years, but this was the first time in fifteen I'd had major distribution. I'm thinking this could be my last shot.

All the while, I was scrambling to keep the band—the one I'd assembled to play on the record—together. This latest incarnation of The Love Slaves included Tim Krekel and Kenny Vaughan on guitars, Jackie Street (original Love Slave) on bass, and Andy Peake on drums. We were in rehearsal and all the while, I'm breaking to interview booking agents, etc., and on and on, just an endless vortex of activity.

All this activity was just the tip of the iceberg. Because back in South Carolina, my brother was dying from an HIV-related illness. This is my baby brother, my only brother, Jamie. He is forty years old. And I am wild with grief.

Without Chris, Tina Krah, my therapist, Kenneth Robinson, and my spiral notebook with the unicorn on the cover . . . I'm not sure I would have made it through that summer.

Toward the end of July, I flew home for a brief visit with my brother at the Spartanburg Regional Medical Center. I was somewhat apprehensive, having heard things and not knowing what to expect. But as soon as I walked into his room, any apprehension I may have had was quickly dispelled. Jamie was sitting up, alert and bright that day, cracking jokes as usual. Joey Barnes and Ben Collins, two friends of his from Georgia, had arrived only moments before with a gift, something they had purchased at a yard sale. It was a pink portable hair dryer, one of those mid-'60s models with the tube and bonnet, and, of course, it was a big hit. Jamie immediately put the bonnet on over his head and had me plug in the hair dryer. Then he turned it on "high" and just sat up in that hospital bed—all six foot seven of him—with that portable pink hair dryer going and that bonnet full of hot air, looking like the cat that just ate the canary. At one point, a nurse came in to draw his blood. She never said a word about the hair dryer, which, of course, remained running during the entire procedure. If I had come to that hospital thinking Jamie and I were going to have a meaningful conversation about the human condition or anything remotely heavy, well, I had another thought coming. Anyway, that was the last time I saw my brother in a conscious state—wearing a pink portable hair dryer. Sometimes life is perfect.

When I returned to Nashville, I knew I was in a state of high anxiety. I was worried about Jamie, worried about my record, worried about everything. *Oh, my god, what if it doesn't sell? Then again, what if it does? What if something happens and it never gets released? What if Jamie dies? What if I die? What if we all die?* I was et up with fear and I knew it. I'd been in that spiral before, and I'd learned that the only way to get through fear is to ride it out. Trying to avoid it or deny it would only prolong it and make things worse. Finally it broke on the morning of July 26, the morning of the dream about the ocean rising up with all the colorful fish. There had been a shift in my psyche during the night, and when I awakened that morning, I felt that peace that passeth all understanding and thus entered into a period of grace unlike any I had ever known. It lasted over a month, and during that time, I wrote song after song after song.

But back to the dream: After writing it down, I immediately phoned Brenda in Pensacola, Florida. Brenda is the most far-out person I have ever known. Everybody needs a friend like Brenda—someone who's more far-out than they are. Anyway, I read her the dream, and she laughed and said, "Why, honey, your life is overflowing with love and abundance." Then she told me to write that down, so after we hung up, I wrote "My life overflows with love and abundance!" right there in the margin above my dream, just like she told me. Then I picked up my guitar and started writing a kind of goofy love song.

For the past four years, Chris had been working for Corrections Corporation of America, a private company that managed over seventy prisons worldwide. So he was constantly traveling, and I'd become used to getting up and driving him to the airport, sometimes before the crack of dawn. But I never got used to seeing him disappear behind those big automatic glass doors at the terminal. Every time one of those doors closed behind him, I'd get a lump in my throat. I figured one day, I'd get used to it and no longer get the lump, but it happened every time, and it still does. To keep from crying, I'd say things to myself like *Those pilots better damn well fly that plane good!*

And they damn well better know how precious their cargo is! Damn it to hell! But then I'd invariably burst into tears.

The song is called "I'm Just Pitiful That Way."

I cry
Every time you leave me
I can't
Stand it when you leave me
I'm like
A little bitty baby
Crying for its mama
I'm just pitiful that way

Tears
They squirt out of my eyes
'Til I can't see to drive
I pull over
To the side of the road
Ah, it's great to be alive!

We've been
Lovers for a long time
Still I'm
Uneasy when you leave me
Your job
Involves a lot of travel
I always come unraveled
I'm just pitiful that way

Pride
It seems like I'd have more pride
And pull myself together
But inside . . .
There's just too much inside
Oh, it's great to be alive!

(instrumental interlude)

Once
I took an uplifting pill
I thought I'd died inside
Now I'm glad
I'm sentimentally ill
Ah, it's great to be alive

I cry
Every time you leave me
I cry
I'm just pitiful that way
I'm just pitiful that way
I'm just pitiful . . .
Don't talk to me about abandonment issues
While I'm reaching for my Kleenex tissues
Ah . . .
I'm just pitiful that way

Later that day, I went by Sunshine Grocery to pick up some produce for supper. While standing in the crowded checkout line, I suddenly noticed myself becoming impatient. *Marshall, you don't have to stop living just because you're waiting in this long line. Take a deep breath, girl, and relax! Come on now. You can do it!* So I did. I closed my eyes and took in a long, deep breath.

When I opened them, the first thing I noticed was this baby. He looked to be about eight months old and was sitting in the back of a grocery cart directly in front of mine. And he was looking right at me, like only babies can do, and I swear, he was laughing at me like he was in on the joke about my impatience.

In the line next to us, an exasperated mother was trying to check out while her three daughters, who looked to be about two, four, and six, were all running around out of control. Then an amazing thing happened. The three little girls suddenly stopped running around and just froze. They were all looking at the baby in front of me, who by now had affixed his hypnotic gaze on them. The six-year-old girl then walked over to the baby, stood on her tiptoes, and I swear, the baby leaned down and they kissed each other right on the lips! I couldn't believe it. Her two sisters then followed suit. Each one stepped forward to take her turn kissing the baby, with the baby leaning down to receive each kiss, all the while cooing and making those cute little sounds that only babies make.

A few days later, I recounted this experience in detail to my therapist. His response was: "Call the lamas!" Sounded like a good title to me. So that night after supper, I started writing the song.

At about three o'clock in the morning, I was so close to finishing it, I could taste it. I only needed one more word in the last line. But I was struggling, trying to find just the right word. I don't know if I was getting lonely or lazy or what, but suddenly I decided I needed to wake up Chris. So I slunk down the hallway to the master bedroom.

"Chris?" I said sheepishly.

"What!?" he yelled out. "Dammit, Marshall, this better be good."

After five years living with Chris, I had learned to differentiate between Chris *really* being mad and him being kind of annoyed but *acting* like he was mad.

"Well, you know that song I've been working on about the little baby in the grocery cart?" There was silence. Had he gone back to sleep? I kept on talking like he could hear me.

"Well, he's kissing these little girls in the checkout line at the grocery store, see, and I need an adjective to describe the kiss. It's a sweet, playful kiss, not a passionate or lascivious kiss. Something like a "cosmic" kiss, but I need four syllables. It's the very last line of the song and . . ."

"Transcendental."

"What?"

"Transcendental," Chris repeated as he rolled over and fell back asleep.

I couldn't believe it. I went back down the hall, grabbed my guitar and sang the song all the way through with the new word. It was perfect.

Call the lamas!
I saw little Buddha in the checkout line
At the grocery store
Today

Call the lamas!
He was sitting like a prince in his grocery cart
With a perfect smile
On his face

His mom and dad
Preoccupied
With paying for their food
They could not see him
Smile at me
With calm beatitude

Call the lamas!
I saw little Buddha in the checkout line
At the grocery store
Today

Call the lamas!
He was sitting like a prince in his grocery cart
With a perfect smile
On his face

Ommm . . .
Ommm . . .

Then suddenly
In front of me
I saw three little girls
Their mother bagging groceries
While around her feet
They swirled
Their peals of laughter
Silenced when
They all looked up to see
Little Buddha
Smiling at them
Beatifically

He leaned down towards them
Holding all them
In a state of bliss

Then one by one
They each received
His transcendental kiss

Call the lamas!
Ommm . . .
Call the lamas!
Ommm . . .
Call the lamas!
Ommm . . .
I saw little Buddha in the checkout line
At the grocery store

In the process of writing "Call the Lamas!" I kept wondering, *Why am I writing this? And who is going to give a rat's ass about a little baby kissing girls in the checkout line at the grocery store?* More than any song I ever wrote, this one truly felt like it was coming from somewhere else. My only job was to get it down on paper as fast as I could.

It wasn't until a couple of weeks later that the true meaning of the song hit me. I was driving my car down Belmont Boulevard, and I damned near had a wreck. *Oh shit!* I said. *Little Buddha is Jamie! And the three little girls are me and Mary and Dorothy. And we're telling him "goodbye" because he's getting ready to check out. And* that's *why he's in the checkout line. Oh, my god. This is too much. I can't stand it!*

So I pulled my 740IL over to the side of the road, leaned my head on the steering wheel, and just sat there and wept until I could weep no more.

A few days later, I got the phone call. It was my sister Dorothy. She was crying. "Oh god, Marshall, it's awful. He's thrashing about like you wouldn't believe." I could hear moaning in the background.

"I'm on the next plane," I said.

I called Chris at work and told him what was going on. A couple of hours later, Dorothy called back. She sounded calm. "You probably don't need to come right away. We've got him stabilized now. I mean, he's comatose, but it could be weeks . . . we just don't know."

Then Chris came home from work and handed me a plane ticket. I told him what Dorothy had said, but there was no doubt in Chris's mind that I needed to be on that next plane.

My brother was born James Alfred Chapman IV in 1955, but everybody always called him Jamie. Everybody except Cora Jeter, that is. Cora was our black maid and she called him "King James."

Next to Richard Pryor, Jamie was probably the funniest human who ever walked the earth. Funny and *bad*. He had a police record by the time he was old enough to walk. When he was two and a half years old, he wandered down to old Mrs. Littlejohn's yard and stole all the handles off her spigots. When she looked out her window and saw him doing this, she called the police. I'll never forget standing in the front yard with Mother and some of the neighborhood kids, when the police drove up with Jamie in a squad car. You never saw a child so happy. He was standing up in the policeman's lap, his little two-and-a-half-year-old hands on the steering wheel like he was driving, all the while turning off and on the headlights, the windshield wipers, the siren . . . you name it. If there was a switch or a lever turning anything on or off, you can bet Jamie had his hands on it.

As soon as he got out of the car, Mother gave him a spanking like you wouldn't believe. I hated to see it, I really did, because Jamie was having the time of his life and the spanking just ruined everything.

Jamie had the highest IQ in our family. I think it was 154. One time when he was five, Mother took him to the Children's Clinic to get vaccinated. This was in the summer and it was sweltering hot outside. To make matters worse, the window air conditioner in the waiting room had quit working. So while Mother sat there fanning herself with a magazine, Jamie proceeded to take the front off the air conditioner and fix it. Word about this soon spread, and the legend of Jamie Chapman began.

Early on, Mother knew she was in for a long haul as far as Jamie's education went. After his first day of school in Mrs. Turner's first-grade classroom at the Spartanburg Day School, Mother asked, "Son, how'd it go?"

"Mama!" he replied breathlessly, "you're not gonna believe it! Mrs. Turner's girdle is *so* thick that when I stuck her in the fanny with a pencil, she didn't even *feel* it!!"

. . .

There has always been a lot of diversity in my family when it came to politics. Daddy always voted for whoever he thought would win because that's who he'd be dealing with whenever he went to Washington to lobby for restrictions on textile imports. So he always voted for Fritz Hollings, a Democrat, and Strom Thurmond, the Republican. This would sometimes drive my mother nuts because she was a staunch Republican.

Daddy once said "The only person who can remove a South Carolinian from the U.S. Senate is the Lord!" He said this while reading an obituary for Olin D. Johnston, who served South Carolina as a U.S. senator for twenty-two years—from 1943 until his death in 1965. Daddy didn't know how prophetic his words were. More than three decades later, South Carolina's two senators had *both* been in the Senate longer than Olin D. ever was: Ernest "Fritz" Hollings since 1966 and Strom Thurmond since 1954. Strom probably grew tired of waiting for the Lord to remove him, so at age one hundred, he removed himself. Thurmond's record of forty-eight years in the Senate will probably never be broken; and Hollings's record of thirty-six years as a junior senator will probably never be broken either. Toward the end of Thurmond's tenure, Hollings was probably thinking, *Lord, isn't it about time you got Strom outta there? I mean, the man's been in for nearly forty-eight years! Surely he needs a rest.*

Daddy also once proclaimed the U.S. Senate to be "the most exclusive men's club in the world." He said this in 1972 while the two of us were sitting at the breakfast table.

"No, it's not," I replied.

"Well, then what?" he said.

"The most exclusive men's club in the world is The Rolling Stones. There's only five of them and there's *fifty* senators." (Actually it's a hundred but who's counting.)

Daddy always said Mother's politics ran "to the right of Strom Thurmond and just this side of Attila the Hun." After Daddy died in 1983, Mother remarried in 1985, and for a while moved back to North Carolina. When Jesse Helms was making his fourth bid for the U.S. Senate in 1990, Mother sent him a thousand dollars. But she didn't stop there. She tried to get all four of us children to sign some form so she could send him four thousand more. I don't think any of us signed it. At least, I know I didn't.

And Jamie sure as hell didn't. His reaction was classic: "Mama!" he said, "how you can purport to love your *three* daughters who are women, and your only son who is an avowed homosexual, and *still* vote for that misogynistic homophobe is beyond me!" Jamie could always say things to Mother the rest of us wouldn't dare.

And Jamie never stopped being funny. Right up until he slipped into the coma. During one of his last times at the hospital, Mother was there with him when, all of a sudden, she could no longer hold back her tears.

"Mama!" Jamie snapped good-naturedly, "if you think for *one minute* that I plan to predecease *my* three sisters and leave them *my* fourth of *your* estate, then you have got another thought coming!!"

When Jamie died late in the morning of August 29, he was lying in a big four-poster bed in the upstairs guest bedroom at Mother's. Dorothy, Mother, and I were there on the bed with him as he took his last breath. (Mary was racing in from the airport with Aunt Liz.) We'd been holding him and loving on him all morning, just being with him as best we could. Every now and then, somebody would cry. But when it got real close, we all knew it, and one by one, we thanked him for his life. Mr. Pete—Jamie's beloved Boston terrier—was there, too. Ever since Jamie had slipped into a coma, Mr. Pete had not left his side. Not even to eat or go to the bathroom. And you never saw such a helpless expression on a dog's face. It would just break your heart to look at him.

Also in the room, or just outside in the hall, was Dorothy's husband, Julian Josey, who was wearing a neck brace due to recent surgery. And Joey Barnes and Ben Collins and, I think, my aunt Susan. And while all this was going on, Lula Mae Moore and Stephanie Durham were downstairs singing "Blessed Assurance."

Lula, as you may remember, was our maid when we were growing up. I always liked to think she loved me the best because I did my Elvis imitations for her in the basement while she was ironing clothes and because I always cleaned my plate. But much as I hate to admit it—it was Jamie she loved most. He was her favorite, no doubt about it. "I can't tell you how many switchings I saved that child from," she once confessed. "Oh, how I would lie to your mama . . ." Then she'd laugh and shake her head. "Anything to save that boy from another whupping!"

I had only met Stephanie Durham the day before. She was a big white woman from rural Georgia, a folk artist, who loved Jamie more than anything. She once told me, "Your brother's not easy to forget. He was a rare bird." Anyway, Stephanie had just dropped everything in Georgia to come be with Mother during Jamie's final days.

After Jamie took his last breath, a strange thing happened. Mr. Pete suddenly got up, jumped off the four-poster bed, and ran downstairs to the front door, where he started barking like crazy. I swear, it was like he was trying to follow Jamie's spirit out of the house. I remember getting up off the bed and falling into Joey and Ben's arms. The three of us just stood there holding on to each other while we all wailed. I tell you, there was a lot of wailing going on in that room.

When things quieted down, Todd Jones, the minister at our old First Presbyterian Church arrived. Mother was crazy about Todd, and, for a preacher, I thought he was pretty hip myself. His jogging buddies called him "Todd Almighty." Anyway, the Reverend Doctor Todd Jones walked up to Jamie's body and proceeded to offer up a beautiful prayer as we all stood around, some with our heads bowed.

About thirty minutes later, some men from Floyd's Mortuary arrived wearing these garish blue rubber gloves. As they filed up the stairs, Joey and Ben started chanting under their breath, "Gloves don't match your shoes, gloves don't match your shoes, gloves don't match your shoes . . ." which cracked us all up.

The man in charge of "the removal of the remains," as they liked to say, was named Glenn Miller. Of course, every time he walked by, Joey and Ben would start humming "In the Mood" by the world-famous orchestra leader of the same name. And that cracked us up even more.

At one point, Glenn Miller announced, "Would the family please retire into the den," as he motioned toward the door of the upstairs library where Mother liked to read and watch TV.

"Why?" Mother's voice cut through the air like a knife. She was facing Glenn Miller and I was standing right behind her. My chin was resting on her shoulder so that my head was next to hers, and I swear, in that moment, Jamie's "devilment" spirit must have entered my body because, before Glenn Miller could answer, I said, "We don't mind anybody but our mother in this house." I was laughing on the inside, but hell, I might as well have said, *Who are you to think you can come in here and start ordering us around?*

Glenn Miller cleared his throat, then patiently began to explain: "Well, it has been our experience that family members become upset during the removal of the remains." I hated that word—*remains*. It sounded like Jamie's body was in a bunch of little pieces instead of all in one piece like it was.

Julian Josey was standing between Mother and Glenn Miller during this entire exchange. Whenever Julian feels the least bit uncomfortable, his eyebrows start to move up and down. Just like they were doing now as he turned to Glenn Miller and said, "This is a very spiritual family. They have been to treatment twice. They are not afraid of their emotions." I couldn't believe I was hearing this from my brother-in-law, who often refers to family therapists as "referees."

Needless to say, nobody "retired into the den."

I called Floyd's Mortuary recently to confirm some of the facts of this story. Glenn Miller was with some customers, so I left word for him to call. Thirty minutes later, my phone rang. It was Glenn Miller.

"Mr. Miller," I began, "were you the man in charge of picking up my brother Jamie's body after he died?"

"Yes, I was."

"And was it you that was upstairs trying to get us to go into the den while his body was being removed?" I was starting to feel like Perry Mason.

"Yes, that was me." Then he voluntarily began describing some of the things that can happen when a body is being removed. Something about muscles relaxing causing discharges of unwanted matter and something else about twitching and flailing of limbs. "You know, that can be upsetting to most families," he said.

"Well, Mr. Miller," I went on. "Let me ask you this. On a scale of one to ten, 'ten' being cooperative and easy to deal with, and 'one' being a pain in the ass, how would you rate our family?"

"Now, Ms. Chapman, you know I'm too professional to answer that."

"Well, then, let me ask you one more thing. Is there anything in particular that you remember?"

"Well," Glenn Miller replied slowly, "I just remember thinking 'Whew, I wish they'd of had him on the first floor.'"

. . .

Jamie's body—all six feet seven inches of it—was zipped into a blue plastic bag that matched those damn gloves. And I'm telling you, of all the shades of blue I've ever seen, this shade was the worst. It should have come with batteries.

It took four men, huffing and puffing like you wouldn't believe, to get Jamie's body out of Mother's upstairs guest bedroom and down the stairs. Todd Jones and I were standing at the top of the stairs as they began their descent. They did okay down the first flight, but they ran into trouble when they got to the landing. They were having a hard time negotiating the turn. They couldn't decide whether to stand Jamie up or pass him over the rail. While the debate was going on, I suddenly felt possessed again by Jamie's "devilment." Because, in that moment, I heard myself say to the four struggling men below, "Ah, it's okay if you drop the body. But if you knock those sconces off the wall, there's gonna be hell to pay." With that, Todd Jones and I had to rest our foreheads on the railing as we shook from laughter. And I'll never forget the looks on the faces of those men from Floyd's. It was like *Damn! These people are crazy. Let's get the hell out of here!*

There never has been and there never will be another funeral like Jamie's. The First Presbyterian Church was packed to the gills. Friends flew in and drove in from all over. A cousin arrived with a hundred purple bandanas—just like the one Jamie wore tied around his head during his last days—which the men wore folded in their suit breast pockets and the women carried as handkerchiefs. Seeing my conservative uncles with those purple bandanas in their breast pockets just pierced my heart.

I found out later that Mary used one of the purple bandanas to line the French walnut humidor that held Jamie's ashes. Mary, among other things, is a talented seamstress. She once made me a jacket out of an Elvis wall hanging that is one of my most treasured possessions. You can rest assured that the bandana seams in the lining of that humidor all matched and lined up.

Our family alone can fill most churches—without getting into second cousins. Jamie's funeral procession was led by Mother, who was escorted by her brother, Jeff. Then came Mary and her husband, Joe Webster, and their daughters, Catie and Frances. Chris and I were next, followed by Dorothy and Julian and their oldest daughter, Martha Cloud. But the best thing about the whole funeral, and my most vivid memory, was the sight of Lula Mae

Moore and Stephanie Durham, who walked behind Dorothy and Julian. Lula was decked out all in black—black stockings, black dress, and a big black hat with a black veil that only partially concealed her beautiful black face. But the pièce de résistance was her shoes. All that black perfectly showcased a pair of gold lamé spike heels. Oh, how Jamie would have *loved* that outfit.

Next to Lula was Stephanie Durham with her henna-red dyed hair, wearing a loose-fitting long black dress and cradling in her arms Mr. Pete, who wore a purple bandana tied around his neck. After Lula and Stephanie, came our aunts and uncles and cousins. It was one hell of a procession.

There were many firsts at First Presbyterian that day. Some debatable. Some not. Most everybody agreed it was the first time homosexuality had been openly and lovingly addressed from the pulpit. But there was no disputing the fact that Mr. Pete, in his purple bandana, was the first Boston terrier to ever sit in the front pew during a service.

The night before Jamie died, I couldn't sleep. So I sat on Dorothy and Julian's front porch all night listening to the crickets out in the trees. The noise they made was deafening and somehow comforting.

The day after the funeral, Chris and I flew back to Nashville. The next day was Labor Day and it rained all day long. It was a steady, soothing, white-noise kind of rain. I sat up on the guest bed in the Sky Palace—the same bed I'd slept on as a child—and wrote the following song on my Martin D-28 guitar, using a dropped D-string tuning:

> *Now the rain is falling*
> *And my tears are falling too*
> *It's been four days*
> *Since I said goodbye to you*
> *The sun can't shine*
> *'Cause there's too much to shine through*
> *While this rain is falling*
> *And my tears are falling too*
>
> *How the crickets screamed*
> *On the last night you were here*
> *Like you they knew*

Their departure time was near
When summer is over
The frost is what they fear
How the crickets screamed
On the last night you were here

When they carried your body outside
I did not care
The thing I loved had died
And was not there
It had vanished like the wind
Into thin air
When they carried your body outside
I did not care

I don't think I can live
And feel this way
I have to think you've gone
To a better place
I have to believe
I'll join you there one day
Otherwise I cannot live
And feel this way

And now the rain is falling
And my tears are falling too
It's been four days
Since I said goodbye to you
The sun can't shine
'Cause there's too much to shine through
While this rain is falling
And my tears are falling too
And this rain is as real
As the love that I feel for you

Epilogue

Last night I dreamed
Dreamed I was a particle
Not a human being
But a particle . . . in space
Moving at the speed of light
Towards a bright red sunset
And I dreamed in my dream
Of that bright red sunset

Then I heard a voice of doubt
Say You'll never make it there
It's too far away
For you to ever make it there
Even at the speed of light . . .
You'll never make it there
Still I dreamed in my dream
Of that bright red sunset

Then suddenly
I began to see
Other particles . . . all around
Some were light like me
But now and then I'd see
One that was red . . . bright red
Then more and more were red
'Til all of them were red
That's when I knew

Bright red sunset
Bright red sunset (fade)

I was as happy as could be
With other particles like me
What a dream!

"Bright Red Sunset" was written in the late afternoon of July 13, 1998. Earlier that day, Chris and I had attended a funeral service for Bobby Herbert, and now Chris was back at work and I was at home, leaning back in my office chair, staring out the window. I was barefooted, wearing a pair of men's boxer shorts underneath a big white T-shirt. It felt good to be out of my funeral togs.

As I stared out the window, I was thinking about Bobby and wondering where he was. Was his spirit still floating around Nashville somewhere? Could he see me? Then I started thinking about a dream I'd had a year or so before. It was different from any dream I've ever had. In all my other dreams, I've always been my *self* in the dream. But in this dream, I was a particle in space. I mean, I was still me, but without a body or anything. And in the other dreams, I'd always been on Earth, or at least close to Earth, as in the ones where I'm flying over houses and the tops of trees. I've always loved those flying dreams. So much better than falling. But this particular dream went beyond flying to being a particle in space moving at the speed of light. Only I didn't *feel* like I was moving. It was like I was floating but with full awareness that I was traveling at 186,000 miles per second.

When I awakened from the dream, it was like *Wow!* I had never felt so happy and free in all my life. It was ecstasy. Like a sneak preview of heaven.

I started writing this book in August 1998 and finished the first draft on Valentine's Day, 2001. I would have finished sooner, but a lot happened during that time. First of all, Chris and I moved twice. Once, out of our house, then—sixteen months later—back in. During that period, we lived in a walk-up apartment with a fire-escape entrance while our house was being completely renovated. Also during that time, *four* thefts occurred on our property. In the first, all of my musical equipment was stolen, plus Chris's computer, which contained not only our financial records and my Tall Girl mailing list, but the first hundred and thirty-five pages of this book! Of course, I had saved most of it on a disk, but when we opened it, it came out in a crazy format that was unreadable.

I was beside myself with despair. A friend tried to cheer me up. "Remember, Marshall," she said, "Hemingway's wife left one of his manuscripts on a train one time, and he ended up rewriting the entire book from memory. Said the second version was even better than the one that was lost."

"I'm not Hemingway!" I said. "And besides, he ended up divorcing that wife and I don't blame him!"

Anyway, I soon went on a mission to recover the stolen computer, but that's a whole nother story.

ACKNOWLEDGMENTS

Above and beyond: Lee Smith, Joëlle Delbourgo, Elizabeth Beier, Jill McCorkle, Chris Fletcher, Dave Hickey, and my mother, Martha Cloud Chapman.

St. Martin's: Elizabeth Beier (again), Sarah Delson, Kathryn Parise, Mark A. Fowler, Michael Connor, and John Karle.

Home front: John and Beth Stein, Alice Randall, The Grammar Doctor (aka Phil Sparks), Detectives Tommy Jarrell and Billy Cothren of the Nashville Metropolitan Police Department, Ronnie Pugh, John Organ, Matraca Berg, Jamie and Lola, Tori Taff, Carol Caldwell, Elaine Wood, Constance and Gordon Gee, Gaile Owens, Jim and Donna Foster (even though you moved, dammit!), John Beasley II, Mack and the Vandyland gang, John Ingram, Betty Herbert, Mike and Elizabeth Schoenfeld, Virginia Team, Luellyn Latocki, Don Light, Eileen Hosking, Margaret G., Helen and the twins, Barbara South, Jack Clement, Ron Watson at Ingram, and Roger Bishop at Davis-Kidd.

Carolinas (South): Mike Bucknell, Dorothy Chapman Josey, Rob Chapman, Robert F. Chapman, Gene Crocker, Betsy Teter, Gary Henderson, Lula Moore, Daryl Black at Sparta Bus Services, Sunshine Smith, Lucy DuPre, Monte Parsons, Kim Harrelson, and Charles Swenson of the *Coastal Observer*. (North): Hal Crowther, Carolyn Sakowski, Copey Hanes, Maria Jenkins Mills, and Julianne Still-Thrift.

. . . and beyond: Mary Chapman Webster, Diana Haig, Larry Brown, Jimmy Buffett, Peter Guralnick, Terry Allen, Roy Blount, Jr., Carlyne Majewski, Joy Wahl, Libby Lumpkin, Tom Beard, Phil Walden, Mike Ramos, Jane Harrold Sorensen, Mike Poller of Poller & Jordan Advertising Agency, Miami, Florida.

Trails of gratitude (song permissions): Christy Ikner at Sony/ATV, Bobby Braddock, Terri Sharp, Karyn Kristy-Dworkin at Leiber & Stoller, Corky Hale, Mike Stoller, Arminda Trevino at Carlin America, Jennifer Chartier at Hal Leonard, Frank Callari, David Anderson, Mark Rothbaum, Willie Nelson, Mike Utley, Donnie Fritts, Tracy Tyson, Lisa and Kris Kristofferson, Regina Washington at Bug, Wendy Leshner at Universal, Jim Rushing, Will Jennings, Pat Higdon, Steven Price at Careers-BMG, Ken Levitan, John Hiatt, Carol King at Chrysalis, Thomas Levy, Esq., and Gary Hovey at Elvis Presley Enterprises.

"The Hero" trail: Leighton Grantham, Dave Marsh, Bob Oermann, Nancy and Ima at BMI, Steve Propes in Long Beach, Joe Peck, Lloyd Davis (World's Foremost Authority on Teen Records), Lloyd's brother Ron (World's Foremost Authority on Teen Tragedy Records), and Ron's wife, Brenda, in Ashland, Oregon.

Posthumous appreciation: Generalissimo Snowflake (aka Leon Brettler), Big Joe Turner, Doc Pomus, Harlan Howard, Waylon, Jamie Chapman, James A. Chapman, Jr., Roger Miller, Lynn Shults, Cora Jeter, Barbara Tole, and, of course, Elvis.

CREDITS

LYRICS
(in order of appearance)

1. **Goodbye, Little Rock and Roller**—Title
   by Marshall Chapman © 1986 Tall Girl Music (BMI). Administered by Bug. All rights reserved.

2. **When Two Worlds Collide**—Epigraph
   by Roger Miller © 1961 (renewed) Sony/ATV Tree Publishing (BMI). All rights administered by Sony/ATV Music Publishing, 8 Music Square West, Nashville, Tennessee, 37203. All rights reserved. Used by permission.

3. **Somewhere South of Macon**—Chapter 1
   by Marshall Chapman and Jim Rushing © 1975 Universal—Songs of Polygram Int., Inc. (BMI) on behalf of Vogue Music and Bibo Music Publishing, Inc. All rights reserved. Used by permission.

4. **So Fine**
   by Johnny Otis © 1955 (renewed 1983) Eldorado Music (BMI). Administered by Bug. All rights reserved. Used by permission.

5. **Old Habits**
   by John Hiatt and Marshall Chapman © 1991 Careers-BMG Music Publishing, Inc./Tall Girl Music (BMI). Administered by Bug. All rights reserved. Used by permission.

6. **Leaving Loachapoka**
   by Marshall Chapman © 1996 Tall Girl Music (BMI). Administered by Bug. All rights reserved.

17. **Texas Is Everywhere**—Chapter 6

by Marshall Chapman © 1980 Tall Girl Music (BMI). Administered by Bug. All rights reserved.

18. **Shotgun Willie**

by Willie Nelson © 1973 (renewed 2001) Full Nelson Music, Inc. (BMI). All rights controlled and administered by EMI Longitude Music. All rights reserved. International copyright secured. Used by permission.

19. **Hillbillies Ain't Hillbillies Anymore**

by Marshall Chapman and Bobby Braddock © 1985 Tall Girl Music (BMI). Administered by Bug. Sony/ATV Tree Publishing (BMI). Administered by Sony/ATV Music Publishing, 8 Music Square West, Nashville, Tennessee, 37203. All rights reserved. Used by permission.

20. **The Perfect Partner**—Chapter 7

by Marshall Chapman © 1981 Tall Girl Music (BMI). Administered by Bug. All rights reserved.

21. **Don't Let It Go to Your Nose**

by Marshall Chapman, Dave Hickey, and Joy Wahl © 1977 Enoree Music (BMI). Administered by Bug. All rights reserved.

22. **Go On 'bout Your Bidness**

by Marshall Chapman © 1982 Tall Girl Music (BMI). Administered by Bug. All rights reserved.

23. **Suspicious Minds**

by Mark James © 1968 (renewed) Sony/ATV Songs LLC. All rights administered by Sony/ATV Music Publishing, 8 Music Square West, Nashville, Tennessee, 37203. All rights reserved. Used by permission.

24. **Betty's Bein' Bad**—Chapter 8

by Marshall Chapman © 1984 Tall Girl Music (BMI). Administered by Bug. All rights reserved.

25. **Rockabilly Sweethearts**

by Marshall Chapman and Will Jennings © 1985 Tall Girl Music (BMI). Administered by Bug. Blue Sky Rider Songs, administered by Irving Music (BMI). All rights reserved. Used by permission.

26. **I'm a Dreamer**

by Marshall Chapman and Sharon Leger © 1995 Tall Girl Music (BMI). Administered by Bug. All rights reserved.

27. Do You Love Too Much?

by Marshall Chapman © 1986 Tall Girl Music (BMI). Administered by Bug. All rights reserved.

28. Little Egypt

by Jerry Leiber and Mike Stoller © 1961 (renewed) Jerry Leiber Music and Mike Stoller Music. All rights reserved. Used by Permission.

29. Last Kiss

by Wayne Cochran © 1961 (renewed) Trio Music Co., Inc. (BMI)/Fort Knox Music, Inc. (BMI). All rights reserved. Used by permission.

30. Teen Angel

by Jean Surrey © 1959 Sony/ATV Acuff Rose Music. All rights administered by Sony/ATV Music Publishing, 8 Music Square West, Nashville, Tennessee, 37203. All rights reserved. Used by permission.

31. The Hero

by Bill Nosal and Pierre Maheu/Nan-Li Publishing (terminated in 1970) (BMI). No further information.

32. Bad Debt

by Marshall Chapman © 1984 Tall Girl Music (BMI). Administered by Bug. All rights reserved.

33. Girl in a Bubble—Chapter 10

by Marshall Chapman © 1987 Tall Girl Music (BMI). Administered by Bug. All rights reserved.

34. Looking for a Kiss

by Marshall Chapman © 1987 Tall Girl Music (BMI). Administered by Bug. All rights reserved.

35. I Don't Want to Hurt Anymore

by Marshall Chapman © 1987 Tall Girl Music (BMI). Administered by Bug. All rights reserved.

36. X-Ray Eyes

by Marshall Chapman and Diana Haig © 1987 Tall Girl Music (BMI) Administered by Bug. Queen of Sheba Music (ASCAP). All rights reserved. Used by permission.

37. A Mystery to Me—Chapter 11

by Marshall Chapman © 1995 Tall Girl Music (BMI). Administered by Bug. All rights reserved.

38. **Happy Childhood (aka It's Never Too Late to Have a Happy Childhood)**
    by Marshall Chapman and Terri Sharp © 1990 Tall Girl Music (BMI). Administered by Bug. Sony/ATV Acuff Rose Music (BMI). Administered by Sony/ATV Music Publishing. All rights reserved. Used by permission.

39. **Come Up and See Me**
    by Marshall Chapman © 1990 Tall Girl Music (BMI). Administered by Bug. All rights reserved.

40. **I'm Just Pitiful That Way**
    by Marshall Chapman © 1996 Tall Girl Music (BMI). Administered by Bug. All rights reserved.

41. **Call the Lamas!**—Chapter 12
    by Marshall Chapman © 1996 Tall Girl Music (BMI). Administered by Bug. All rights reserved.

42. **Now the Rain Is Falling**
    by Marshall Chapman © 1996 Tall Girl Music (BMI). Administered by Bug. All rights reserved.

43. **Bright Red Sunset**—Epilogue
    by Marshall Chapman © 1998 Tall Girl Music (BMI). Administered by Bug. All rights reserved.

PHOTOGRAPHS

Title page photograph © 1973 by Slick Lawson c/o Clearance Quest

Chapter Five photograph courtesy of Dorothy Chapman Josey

Chapter Six photograph courtesy of Winfield Potter Crigler

Chapter Eight photograph © 1977 by Gene Spatz

Chapter Ten photograph courtesy of George Estrada

Chapter Twelve photograph courtesy of Mary Chapman Webster

Epilogue photograph © 1977 by Tom Dunn

All other photographs appear courtesy of the author.